Rw

Fire in the Iceman

Autobiography of Tom Flores

Tom Flores
with
Frank Cooney

Bonus Books, Inc., Chicago

96 95 94 93 92   5 4 3 2 1

Library of Congress Catalog Card Number: 92-73249

International Standard Book Number: 0-929387-80-5

Bonus Books, Inc.
160 East Illinois Street
Chicago, Illinois 60611

First Edition

Composition by Point West Inc., Carol Stream, IL

Printed in the United States of America

Contents

1. Back to Coaching   1

2. La Bamba, Deja Vu   13

3. Sanger   25

4. Pacific, Playing for the Love of It   37

5. Early Raiders—This Is Pro Football?   57

6. 1962   75

7. Raiders Revisited—This IS Pro Football   85

8. Coach Flores   111

9. Bedlam in Raiderville   127

10. Super Bowl XV   143

11. Moving South—The Vagabond Raiders   167

12. People and Peeves   191

13. All Raiders Team   213

14. Gone North, The Seattle Seahawks   237

Index   251

one

Back to Coaching

I'm glad my wife Barbara isn't a defensive coordinator. She knows what I'm going to do before I figure it out. So by the time I decided to get back into coaching, I was the second one to know. I went through the formality of telling Barbara anyway.

She smiled, shook her head and gave me that here-we-go-again look.

"Tom," she said. "You are a masochist. But I understand."

Understand? How could anybody understand why a person would want to be a head coach in the National Football League? It's a carnivorous job that nibbles away at your guts. It can consume your whole life if you let it.

Barbara knows that better than anybody. That's why we left the Raiders four years earlier. I was almost consumed. I was on the brink of burnout.

But during those four years I realized I missed being on the field. I missed being in the huddle with the players at practice. I missed the locker room before the game. Except for one horrible year, I spent every season from 1960 to 1987 on the field, in the huddles and in those tension-filled locker rooms. I was there as a player, assistant coach and head coach.

As president of the Seattle Seahawks I at least got back into football for the last three years. But it wasn't the same. Maybe it just teased me. I felt detached, especially on game days. I sat up in the booth, a million miles away from the game.

Now Chuck Knox was gone as head coach of the Seattle Seahawks and it was up to me to find a replacement. I could pick anyone, including me. Coaching the Seahawks isn't going to be easy because we had a tough 1991 season. Our 7-9 record was good enough for fourth place in the AFC West, which isn't good enough at all.

Four years away from all that gave me plenty of time to recharge my batteries; to relight the fire that was so close to burnout in 1987. In fact, the idea of coaching again excites me. I'm not concerned about being consumed by the never-ending little worries that nibble at your guts. They are part of the challenge. And confronting challenges is what sports is all about, right?

Ha! Who am I kidding? Certainly not Barbara. She hit the nail on the head. If I really want to coach again, then I must be a certified masochist. And I really want to coach.

Maybe it shouldn't be too surprising that I feel more comfortable on the field than in a cushy luxury suite. It's not just that I have spent so much time as a player and a coach on the field. I was literally raised on fields.

Not football fields. Lettuce fields, fruit orchards, berry patches. My family traveled from crop to crop in California's hot, lush, central valley. We picked whatever needed to be picked. We were like thousands of Mexican-American families then and now.

Don't expect me to complain. I had a great childhood. We always had food, clothes and a place to sleep. My father, Tomas Cervantes Flores, never complained about his childhood and he had reason to. He and his parents had to escape Mexico because the infamous bandit, Pancho Villa, kept raiding his town. Villa and his gang stole anything, shot anybody and raped the women.

I'm proud of my Mexican heritage, but I've never made a big deal about my ethnicity. It bothers me to hear people constantly tell you how they single-handedly pulled themselves up from a tough childhood. That's a bunch of bull. First, nobody makes it all by themselves. Second, a lot of people have had it tough. Just look around and I'll guarantee you can find somebody worse off than you ever were.

I never had prime rib until I was 17, but there was always a pot of beans on the stove. My first home was on a farm near Del Rey. One bedroom, one kitchen and two grape boxes (one for my crib and one for my brother Bob). A bent nail on the screen door was our lock. But we always had a home and that's more than you can say for thousands of unfortunate people even today.

When I was five, we settled in Sanger, another little town near Fresno. My parents eventually opened their own corner store and built the house they still live in today.

There have been many stories written about how this skinny kid made it from the farmlands of Sanger to the top of pro football. Stories of how I overcame things like rejection by the Canadian Football League and even tuberculosis in 1962 when my playing career was just beginning. Of course, I'm proud of what I have accomplished.

I had plenty of help along the way, starting with my parents. Where would I be if they didn't work so hard and instill in me the values that have served me so well? They, too, are proud of their Mexican heritage. Still, they are just as proud of this country, the United States. I will always clearly remember the day in 1949 when my father was sworn in as a U.S. citizen. He was so happy he damn near cried.

If I want to think of somebody who came a long way, I think about my parents.

Some people want to think that there is always a hidden agenda, a secret plot, behind everything that happens.

When I first took the job as president of the Seahawks there were stories going around that said I was really hired to replace Chuck Knox as head coach. When Chuck left and I stepped back into coaching, some said "Ah-Ha!"

Many of these people are convinced that our majority owner, Ken Behring, pressured me to take the head coaching job. They believe it was all part of a master plan he had when he hired me in 1989.

I learned long ago that you can't do anything about what people think. I don't even try. They are going to create their own fantasies and then find facts to make them sound believable.

All the time I was head coach of the Raiders, there were never-ending stories that Al Davis was really calling all the plays. When I had to step away from coaching in 1987, the media refused to believe it was my decision. They insinuated that Al Davis fired me and then orchestrated a retirement ceremony.

Why can't anybody believe what they are told? I guess it just doesn't make a good story that way.

If you listen to enough of that crap you just have to laugh. First they said I retired from coaching because the owner of the Raiders pressured me to leave. Then they said that I only took the job as head coach of the Seahawks because, again, the owner pressured me.

Even when they gave me credit for making a decision on my own they still had to make it sound like part of an intriguing plot. So, they claimed I wanted this job all along so I could get out from under the shadow of Al Davis. They claimed I need to validate my ability to coach without Al pulling the strings.

I don't feel the need to validate anything. I'm proud of my record as head coach of the Raiders. In nine years, most of them chaotic because of the move from Oakland to Los Angeles, we had a 91-56 won-lost record. We were in the playoffs five times, won three AFC West championships and two Super Bowls.

Certainly Al Davis had a lot to do with that success. After all, he is one of the most knowledgeable and respected men in football. He is the one who established a winning tradition with the Raiders when he became head coach in 1963.

In 1960 I began my pro football career as the Raiders' first quarterback in the new American Football League. By 1963 we had won a total of nine games. In Al's first year as head coach we were 10-4. So nobody needs to tell me how good a coach Al Davis is.

Fact is, as long as Al is around he will overshadow every Raiders coach. John Madden was, I was and Art Shell is. It would be unrealistic to deny that. The press and media prefer to make it that way. But Al's main function with the Raiders is to get players. That doesn't mean I always agreed with his moves. Far from it. I certainly did not want to trade away quarterback Ken Stabler in 1980. And there were times Al became fixated on a player, sometimes a draft prospect and sometimes a veteran available in a trade, that I didn't really want.

But isn't that the same in many businesses, where executives in middle management do not have total control over personnel? Input yes, but not total control. That's how it works if you are a head coach with the Raiders.

So Al got the players and I coached them. I ran the practices. I made up the game plans. I called the shots in the game. I accepted the blame for our failures. So I'll be damned if I won't take my full share of credit for the success the Raiders had when I was the coach.

With the Seahawks I face an even bigger challenge. Now not only will I coach the team, but as president I oversee building the team. At this time the only other NFL coach with that much authority, that much responsibility, is Jimmy Johnson of the Dallas Cowboys.

Even before the end of the 1991 season it was obvious that Ken Behring and minority owner Ken Hoffman were not happy with the direction the team was heading on the field.

After the season they told me it was time to sit down with Chuck and discuss a change. That was on December 23, the Monday after our last game. I wanted to do it after Christmas, so I scheduled a meeting with Chuck for Friday in Palm Springs. That's where we both planned to spend Christmas with our families.

I knew that Chuck would not have trouble staying in coaching if that's what he wanted. John Shaw, general manager of the Los Angeles Rams, already had called to ask permission to talk to Chuck about their coaching job. I knew of at least two other teams that were interested, the Green Bay Packers and Pittsburgh Steelers. In all, eight other head coaching jobs were open.

Still, I admit I felt a little uncomfortable flying down to Palm Springs on Tuesday. I happened to be on the same plane with Chuck and his wife, Shirley. We made small talk about nothing. Not a word was mentioned about our Friday meeting.

On Thursday morning I got together with our owners, Ken Behring and Ken Hoffman, at the Vintage, a beautiful restaurant in one of my favorite settings, a Palm Springs golf course.

First I made sure that Chuck could go out with dignity because basically I favor coaches. He had a contract that was extended the year before and it had a buyout clause that had to be executed within 15 days of the final game. I made sure that Chuck received everything he had coming, like country club membership, insurance, compensation and the buyout money.

On Friday morning, Ken Behring, Chuck Knox and I met back at the Vintage in a private room. Chuck knew what he was there for. It didn't take long to decide on announcing a mutual agreement between Mr. Behring and Chuck. We called Gary Wright, the Seahawks' vice president in charge of public relations. Each of us made a statement for him to forward to the local media.

Within a few days Chuck was to meet with the Rams. Within two weeks he was named head coach of the Rams.

After Chuck left the Vintage that Friday morning, Ken Behring gave me something to think about.

"Tom, you are my first choice to take over the coaching job," he said. "But if you don't want it, do not take it. Hire somebody you feel good about and then just continue on doing what you are doing right now. I just want you to know that you are my first choice and we'll go from there."

That didn't surprise me. Ken Behring and I have had a good relationship since we met in 1972 when I was an assistant coach with the Raiders. When he hired me as president it was because he wanted somebody he knew and trusted to run the team. Still, we never discussed the possibility of me becoming coach until that day in Palm Springs.

I needed time to think about whether I wanted to take the coaching job. I also had some people I wanted to consider. Rusty Tillman, our special teams and linebackers coach, called me shortly after the announcement and wanted an interview. I wanted to talk to Dennis Erickson, head coach of the University of Miami Hurricanes.

Barbara and I went to Lake Tahoe for New Year's and stayed at the Horizon Hotel. The place seems to change its name every couple of years, but it's where I go to get away and think. Four years earlier, when it was called the High Sierra, I went there to ponder the heavy subject of retiring as the Raiders coach. I didn't realize how short-lived the retirement would be, of course.

On New Year's Day, 1988, the thought of retirement seemed so final. A little more than 27 years earlier I was the starting quarterback in the Raiders' first game ever. We had gone so far and been through so much together.

The thought of cutting the cord was difficult to handle. But we had slumped to only a 5-10 record in the 1987 season and I knew we had a major rebuilding job ahead. I didn't think I had the energy to see it through. I didn't have enough spark left. Al Davis knew that and told me to think about what I wanted to do.

Now I was back at Lake Tahoe after Ken Behring told me to think about what I wanted to do. But this time I had plenty of spark. And by this time I had learned how much I missed coaching.

When I became the Seahawks' president, Chuck Knox told me to speak up if I had any input. But I didn't want to do that. Sometimes he would share a game plan with me when we were flying to a game. However, he never really consulted me. On game days I felt kind of empty just sitting up in the press box eating popcorn.

Chuck Knox has been a very successful coach for a long time in the NFL. In 19 years as head coach he has gone to the playoffs 11 times with three different teams, the Los Angeles Rams, Buffalo Bills and Seattle Seahawks. He obviously has found his own formula for success.

However, there is more than one way to be successful in pro football. Chuck has his way and I have mine. He is basically a conservative coach. I am not. Ever since I first picked up a raggedy, old football when I was ten years old and threw a perfect spiral, I have been fascinated with the passing game.

Ken Behring, who lives near Oakland and was a Raiders fan, also likes a more wide open brand of football. He calls it "playing to win rather than playing not to lose." There was a lot of criticism all over the league in 1991 that too many coaches were "playing not to lose." I don't think I've ever been accused of that. And I don't expect to be.

Dennis Erickson likes to put the ball in the air, too. However, he would prefer to do it for the Miami Hurricanes, thank you. That's what he told me when we finally talked on January 3.

That put the ball in my court, although even if Erickson accepted an interview it didn't mean I was going to hire him. He is an outstanding coach who likes to throw the ball and he is from Everett, which is just outside Seattle. He would have been a popular choice for the Seahawks fans. And he would be a good coach in the NFL.

More and more it looked like I was supposed to be the Seahawks' coach. Despite what Behring said to me, I didn't feel pressured. Hell, I felt great. On Saturday, January 4, I made up my mind to get back into coaching. The following Monday we made the announcement at a press conference.

Just before the press conference, Ken Behring pulled me aside.

"Are you doing this just because I want you to do it?" he asked.

"Nah," I said. "I'm doing it because I'm a masochist. I might as well hurt on the field as up in the press box eating popcorn and doing nothing."

The time has come for the team to change quarterbacks. It's time for Dave Krieg to step aside. He was the Seahawks' starting quarterback since 1984. We have Kelly Stouffer and Dan McGwire in the wings.

Going through a transition at quarterback can be pure hell. I know that all too well. I went through it my second year as head coach of the Raiders. Ken Stabler was traded for Dan Pastorini. Then Pastorini broke his leg and Jim Plunkett had to step in.

Five weeks into that 1980 season I thought I might lose my job as head coach. Talk about a challenge. Talk about something eating away at your guts. Yes, we did go on to win the Super Bowl Championship that year and then another one in the 1983 season.

Still, I'll always remember how close I came to missing all that, how close I came to getting fired before we accomplished anything. I was almost little more than a footnote in coaching history.

Then I think how great it feels to be in a Super Bowl. I was fortunate enough to be a part of four Super Bowls. Mike Ditka and I are the only two people who have won Super Bowls as a player, assistant coach and head coach. But that may be about the only thing we have in common.

I went to the Super Bowl as a reserve quarterback for the Kansas City Chiefs in the 1970 season, then as an assistant coach under John Madden with the Raiders in the

1976 season, and finally those two as head coach of the Raiders.

The Seahawks have never been in a Super Bowl. The fans in Seattle, who are as loyal as they are loud, deserve to have a Super Bowl championship. God, what a feeling it would be to bring them one.

But do I really want to dive back into all that endless work? Do I want to be staring at video tapes before dawn, sparring with the media at noon and rarely have time to get home for dinner with Barbara? As president of the team my hours were flexible. As a coach you seldom have time to do anything but be a coach. Do I miss the players, the field, the huddle and the locker room that much?

Yes.

two

La Bamba, Deja vu

When I saw the beginning of the movie *La Bamba* I almost fell out of my chair.

The very first moments in *La Bamba* are deja vu for me. Anybody who remembers those scenes of young Richie Valens in the fields of an itinerant farm camp has a picture of my earliest memories.

Those times were really a lot of fun for me and my brother Bob, who is a year and a half older than me. Sometimes we helped pick whatever it was—lettuce, grapes, berries. But we probably weren't much help. We looked at everything as fun, like most kids that age. What we probably did best was get filthy dirty playing in the fields.

My parents and grandparents weren't playing. I

didn't realize it until many years later, but we were on some kind of welfare and they were working their tails off just to make ends meet. We traveled from farm to farm, camp to camp. Places like Suisun and Brentwood in the San Joaquin Valley. Some camps were better than others. Some had little shacks with dirt floors. Sometimes we slept in tents or outside.

I remember the camp in Brentwood was nicer than the one in Suisun because it had wooden floors. It was really just a wooden platform with a canvas tent over it, but it was nicer than sleeping on the ground.

When we moved from camp to camp we took everything we owned and piled it on this old Chevy truck. One time a trunk fell out and we didn't know it. My mother was very sad because that trunk had all our family pictures, going all the way back to Mexico.

In *La Bamba* you see a typical picture of a woman working over a campfire or a stove making fresh tortillas. That really hit home. My mother and grandmother always cooked up a pot of beans and made those fresh tortillas, which we used just like bread.

Like most good Catholics then, we never ate meat on Fridays. I know most people ate fish, but we had these great meatless enchiladas. Cheese enchiladas. To this day the family recipe for meatless, cheese enchiladas is one of my favorites. I didn't know it at the time, but the main reason we ate cheese enchiladas on Fridays was they were not expensive to make.

In Del Rey we worked the grape fields much of the year and in exchange part of our pay was that little one bedroom house. It had a wood stove and outdoor plumbing. I slept in a wooden grape box that my mother made into a crib. What the hell was the difference between a regular crib and a grape box to a two or three-year-old kid? It was better than a dirt floor or a cot in those camps.

People have described me as being stoical. I remember one newspaper article likened my sideline demeanor in the final seconds of a close game to that of "somebody casually waiting for a bus." I guess that's true because I've heard it all my life. On the outside I know I appear calm. Inside I know my thoughts and feelings are as snarled as Los Angeles commute traffic at 5 p.m.

What good does it do to let your emotions take over? You waste energy that you need for thinking and you waste time. If you get emotional when you are supposed to be thinking, then you may make a decision based on emotion rather than logic. So I'm glad that I stay calm. If that's being stoical, then I'm guilty. I think it's a family trait that was born of necessity back in the hills of Mexico and handed down to me.

My grandfather was very private and quiet. When I was young, my father wasn't the kind of person you would sit around and BS with. Only after I married Barbara did I learn the fascinating history behind my father's trek to the United States. Like my father, I guess I just wasn't the type who would either ask many questions or volunteer much information.

Barbara has one of those inquiring minds that want to know. She sat and talked to my father for hours until he opened up and told her his life story. As quiet as he was, I never dreamed he had such a wild childhood. Yet therein lies the story of why both my father and grandfather were so private. That was the only way they could survive back in Mexico.

My father was born in the state of Durango, Mexico, in 1907. He had seven brothers and sisters and they lived in a town called Dynamite. Ostensibly it had that name because they mined dynamite. But the name was apt because of the way the area often exploded into violence.

Pancho Villa and his gang of bandits raided the town whenever they felt like it. There were no police or sheriffs or anything like that to protect anybody. The family dug hiding places for the women under the house and down the hill. The bandits would ride up and shoot right into the house through the windows. They killed people who got in the way and they stole what they wanted. They raped women and even little girls.

One night when my father was 12, the family gathered up all its belongings and sneaked away. They loaded everything and everybody onto one of those flat-bedded things that you pump, a handcar. They rode that to the nearest railroad station, then hopped a train for the United States.

California was paying Mexicans to come into the valleys and work the crops. After the hell they endured in Dynamite, my father's family thought picking crops in California sounded like a vacation. Eventually all my dad's relatives moved from Mexico to California and settled in or around Del Rey.

Each household worked just about the same. All the children who lived at home gave their paychecks to the parents. That was the traditional or typical setup for most Mexican families back then. It was the only way they could survive.

That's how my dad lived until he was 27, when he moved out and got married. My mother, Nellie, was born in Sanger, but her family was from the state of Jalisco in Mexico. I was born March 21, 1937, technically in Fresno, where my mother went to a hospital. My first home was that little one bedroom place in Del Rey. But my most vivid memories from my first four years are of traveling to those farms and staying in those camps like you see in *La Bamba*.

December 7 is a big date in our family history.

First, my parents married on December 7, 1934.

Then, shortly after December 7, 1941, we moved from Del Rey to a big country home on Dockery Road, outside Sanger. It's no coincidence that the move was right after the Japanese attacked Pearl Harbor and drew the United States into World War II, but I didn't learn about the connection until years later.

All I knew at the time was that this was a great house. It had indoor plumbing and the whole bit. My father and grandfather became sharecroppers with the owner, Mr. Giovacini. Sharecropping is a big step up from being an itinerant farmer.

We were going to split the profits from the ranch 50-50 with Mr. Giovacini. That was 25 percent for my grandfather and 25 percent for my father.

However, the only reason we were able to make that big step was thanks to one of the most embarrassing chapters in U.S. history. After Pearl Harbor was bombed, the U.S. rounded up Japanese-Americans and put them in camps.

Mr. Giovacini had worked his ranch with Japanese sharecroppers. When they had to leave, he was without help. It's difficult to understand now how people felt then, but Mr. Giovacini was one of the few who believed the country was committing a crime against humanity by virtually imprisoning innocent Japanese-Americans.

He promised the Japanese who worked with him that they could return to their jobs and their homes when the country came to its senses. In the meantime, my parents took advantage of a chance to get a financial foothold.

I loved that ranch. We had cotton, peaches, plums, horses, dogs and all kinds of animals. We were able to stay in the same place all year. We were through following the crops.

My world expanded in 1942 the same way it does for every kid when he first goes to school. Granville Elementary School was straight out of a Currier and Ives painting. A little red schoolhouse with white trim. This one had three rooms, eight grades, and three teachers. One room had grades one and two, one room three through five, and the other six through eight.

Almost all the kids in this school were farm kids, but not all of them were Mexican-Americans. Any farm kid who wasn't Hispanic, we called an Okie. Most of them were from Oklahoma anyway. But even if they were from Arizona we called them an Okie. We were Spicks, of course.

We got along fine calling each other Okies and Spicks because we didn't mean anything derogatory. If somebody from the outside had called us such names, he would have had hell to pay.

The most important thing I learned at Granville was that I loved sports. We played softball and kickball on fields that were nothing more than layers of dust on rock-hard dirt. Talk about getting filthy. By the time I was in the fourth grade I was already getting attention for doing well in sports. I think that positive reinforcement way back then sealed my fate.

Just before Christmas in 1945, we suddenly packed up and moved. I was shattered at first. I loved the ranch, the animals, the big house and playing sports at Granville. I didn't understand why we had to move.

Again, I didn't learn the reason until years later. I probably wouldn't have fully understood at the time, anyway. Mr. Giovacini was keeping his promise to the Japanese-Americans who sharecropped the ranch before we got there. The U.S. had finally came to its senses and set them free.

It was time for us to move on. My world was about to become a little bigger.

Our share of the sharecropping must have been pretty good. My father saved enough money to buy a piece of property at 424 L Street in Sanger. Soon he began building a house there that would become the family home where my parents still live.

About the same time, my cousin and her husband wanted to give up their little store and move north, to Marysville. My dad made a deal to buy them out. So in little more than five years we had gone from being itinerant farmers to sharecroppers to home owners with our own corner store.

It was one of those all-purpose, mom and pop, corner stores with a meat counter where we made sandwiches. My friends thought we were rich, but we really worked hard to run that little store.

And we never lost touch with the fields. Even when my parents ran the store, my brother and I still worked mornings in the fields. We would jump in a truck at five in the morning to go out and pick berries, or whatever. My parents arranged it so the truck made its morning pickup right in front of the store so workers could buy sandwiches or lunch meats to take with them.

At Wilson Grammar School I knew I hit the big time. One classroom and one teacher for each grade. This was a much bigger school than Granville. For the first time in my life I met a lot of people who didn't work in the field.

The playgrounds were still layers of dust on hard packed dirt and I still loved playing sports. It was at Wilson that I was introduced to the sport that would dominate my life. Introduced is a bit of an overstatement.

After school one day I was walking along with a friend, Manuel Martinez. We saw this weird looking ragged ball. It was different from most because it wasn't round. It was oblong and pointed at both ends. I knew what a football was, but I had never picked one up.

It was made of rubber and was worn so thin that it probably had several holes. When I grabbed it I was able to squeeze some of the air out of the holes in it. As I held up this weird ball, Manuel became intrigued.

"Throw it," he said.

"How?" I responded.

"I don't know, just do it," he said.

I did.

It spiraled perfectly as it arched through the air, then nosed into the ground about twenty-five yards away. Not bad for a ten-year-old who had never even picked up a football before.

"Wow, what a throw," said Manuel. "How did you do that?"

"I don't know, I just grabbed it and threw it," I answered, sparing the technicalities.

Some people like to shoot guns. Some people like to shoot basketballs. Some like to shoot pool. At some point in their life they realized they were fascinated or challenged by such things.

When I threw a football for the first time, that's how I felt—fascinated and challenged. If it had fluttered end over end and flopped on the ground a couple of yards away, maybe my whole life would have been changed. But from that moment on, I knew I loved to throw a football. It just felt natural.

Little did I know that my love for throwing a football would keep me working in fields for most of my life.

Taft Junior High introduced me to the outside world. It was literally on the other side of the tracks in Sanger. Welcome to gringos, bologna sandwiches and flag football.

Most of the rich (at least we thought they were rich), anglo kids in Sanger lived on the west side of the tracks and went to Harding Elementary School. It was as if they were in a different town or a different world although their school was only about twenty blocks from ours. Unlike the Okies, who lived a lot like we did, these kids had different customs. When we played them in sports it was a big deal.

We called them gringos, which sounds kind of immature and funny to me now but was a big deal at the time. We were supposed to be the renegades from the bad part of town. I guess it was my childhood training for the Raiders.

I thought everything was a little overstated because I didn't think people on our side of the tracks were so rough. We did have some gangs back then and there were fights, but I thought that was normal.

Once there was a fight right across the street from our store and when I saw the commotion I ran over to see what was going on. What I saw was blood gushing from a kid that I knew. He was about 17 and I was only about 11, but I knew him a little. He was stabbed in the fight. The blood scared the hell out of me and I ran away as fast as I could, to the back of the store where I sat down on the floor. I was shaking and scared. My mother couldn't get me to move and she couldn't figure out what was wrong.

Then somebody ran into the store and said the kid died. That was my first encounter with human mortality. A kid I knew was stabbed to death. I still didn't think our neighborhood was that rough, but from that day on I didn't hang around with anybody who fooled around with knives or guns.

Taft Junior High took the kids from Harding and Wilson Elementary Schools. It was a culture shock for some of them. I loved it because I traded my bean burritos for bologna sandwiches. I didn't know what the hell bologna was, but I had served it at the store. My mother still packed traditional Mexican lunches for me. Some of the gringos loved burritos, so I traded for their bologna.

I guess that's when I first began to have a feeling of ethnic pride. Despite the hell he went through in Mexico, my father was obviously proud of his heritage. He liked baseball and boxing and he was partial to Hispanic players, especially if they were from the San Joaquin Valley.

Mike Garcia was from the valley and became one of the Cleveland Indians' Big Four pitchers in the late 1940s and early 1950s. The Indians had another pitcher named Jesse Flores for a brief while. I remember one day my dad was showing everybody the headlines in the paper. Garcia and Flores had won both ends of a doubleheader. He was really proud.

My dad listened to baseball games and boxing matches on a little, old radio that had one big dial in the middle. Usually I didn't pay much attention, but one hot evening in the fall of 1948 I noticed he was pretty excited about a boxing match on the radio. I didn't know anything about boxing, but he was so enthusiastic for a change that I sat down and listened to see what this was all about.

World lightweight champion Ike Williams was fighting a title bout against a guy named Jesse Flores. I should have guessed. As we sat there and listened to the fight, my dad began talking to me about it. It was great to see him so animated for a change. He was really into it. We talked between rounds. It became a special event because, as I said, we rarely talked at length about anything.

It would have been great if Flores had won that fight, but he was knocked out in the tenth round and Williams retained his championship. My dad was disappointed, but I wasn't. Hell, that may have been the most time we spent—my father and I—talking about something.

As proud as he is of his Mexican heritage, my dad is even more proud of being a U.S. citizen. I remember when he went to night school so he could pass a test on the U.S. Constitution. Then there was the night he was sworn in as a citizen. He got all dressed up for the occasion. He was nervous, happy, excited...the most emotional I've ever seen him. After he was sworn in I could see tears in his eyes.

Without saying a word to me, he taught me a lesson about respecting the United States. Many years later I finally understood how much it meant to him. It was a long, difficult journey from the fears he faced in Dynamite, Mexico, to the nice life we had in Sanger, California.

Many of us never tell our parents how much we appreciate what they did for us. With our track record for conversations, I suppose I never will tell my father exactly how much I appreciate what he went through for us. It would be hard for me to put into words. Anyway, like most parents I think deep down he already knows.

three

Sanger

Sanger Union High was a comfortable, everybody-knows-everybody school of about 700 students tops. There should have been more, but too many kids dropped out to go to work as soon as they turned 16.

Many of my friends weren't expected to go to school because their parents would rather have them work and bring home money. Some needed to help their families run small spreads or little businesses. It was a matter of survival, not choice.

I always felt a little sad when one of my friends dropped out of school to work because they were missing out on a great opportunity they would never have again. But staying in school wasn't a way to get out of work. Everybody on the east side of the tracks in Sanger worked. But going to school just made your schedule a lot busier.

Manny Martinez: *I was Tom's best friend through grammar school and junior high. But I was one of the many kids who dropped out of high school. I had to get married and, of course, make money. I left school after my sophomore year. I know Tom was disappointed. Many of us from Sanger look up to Tom for all that he has accomplished. He did it not by fighting the system, but by working with it. Through it all he has not forgotten Sanger or his old friends. He gives time and money to children and the underprivilged in Sanger. I live in Hawaii now and when Tom was there for an NFL function in 1991 he and Barbara visited me. It's amazing, but he really hasn't changed. He is a role model for kids who think they have it tough.*

Three things gave me a great advantage in high school. First, I loved damn near everything about school, from the girls to classes to sports and even the choir. Second, I was more than six-feet tall, which in those days was up there, especially compared to most Hispanics. And third, my parents encouraged me to go to school.

So I never thought for a second about dropping out of school because I was having too much fun. I got involved in everything. You name it, I was in it.

I played football, baseball and basketball and would have gone out for track if they had let us take part in two sports during one season. I was fortunate because my parents understood that going to school was more important in the long run than going to work at the age of 16.

Parents may not realize how much influence they have on young children. When we first moved to Sanger my father gave Bob and I baseball gloves for Christmas. From a practical person like my father, a recreational thing like a baseball glove was a big statement. And when he came out to watch us play softball, I'm sure that deep down that further reinforced our attraction to sports.

Music was my second love and my mother gave that a major boost by surprising the hell out of me one time.

In junior high I played the drums and remember four of us marching in a downtown Sanger parade. No instruments, just four drums going rat-a-tat-tat, rat-a-tat-tat. The drums were a lot of fun, but I really wanted to play the slide trombone. There was only one trombone at Taft Junior High and it didn't become available until my last week in the seventh grade. I had only enough time to learn one song, "Pomp and Circumstance." I learned it just in time for the graduation ceremony. After that I was a bona fide trombonist.

When I started Sanger Union High School I wasn't going to be in the band because all the trombones were being used. Then one day I was watching the band practice and the teacher asked me to come in. He handed me a brand new trombone and said I could sit in and try it. I joined the trombone section as the seventh seat, puckered up and gave that new horn a blow.

God, was it beautiful. It wasn't like those tin ones back in junior high where the slide would stick all the time and make you sound terrible. With a horn like this I could play first chair. Then the teacher said that the trombone cost ninety-nine dollars.

"Thanks, it was fun," I heard myself say as I put the trombone away, knowing that ninety-nine bucks was way out of my reach. As soon as I got home I told my mom about playing that new trombone with the band. I thought that would be the end of it.

Next thing I know my mother gets this job at the packing shed. We had just sold the store so she wasn't working there any more. I didn't put two and two together until she came to me about two weeks later and gave me the money to buy that trombone. Darned if she didn't go get that job just so I could have the trombone.

She continued working at the packing shed for many years and I continued playing the trombone in the jazz band all the way through high school. My brother Bob, a pretty good sax player, and I even had our own band for a short while.

Along with sports and music I also was involved in student government as commissioner of student athletics. I lost an election for school president, but was voted in as senior class president.

This was in the pre rock-and-roll and cruising era, but music and cars were still a big part of our high school scene. In fact, I'm sure we were part of the generation that opened the way for cruising, which supposedly began in the late fifties in Modesto or San Jose, both a little north of Sanger.

The hot summer and autumn nights in the valley were an invitation to stay outside and do something, anything but go inside. We used to cruise neighboring towns, which was like taunting because everybody was very territorial. Usually we'd go to towns where there were high schools that we played against, like Reedley, Selma, Clovis and sometimes Fresno.

We'd be driving along in a car packed with guys and suddenly another car would come up real close behind and somebody would throw something at us. We'd do some smart aleck thing to bug them a little and then take off. I remember some wild rides all the way back to Sanger on those winding, two-lane roads with some car chasing us and guys screaming and horns honking. I guess we were minor lea-guers on the mischievous scale, but we had our fun.

The rivalry among those little valley towns did reach the warfare stage sometimes, although nothing along the lines of the gang wars they have nowadays. One place you could count on seeing a fight was at those little carni-vals that traveled from town to town in the summers. Gangs, and I use that word loosely, from one town would visit a carnival in another town and sometimes the fights were so bad they wrecked a concession or two.

Sometimes there were knives, chains and maybe even guns, but when the heavy artillery came out I disap-peared. Watching one kid die was enough for me. By the time I was a junior in high school, Sanger banned carnivals because they caused too much trouble.

It was no big loss. Those carny crooks had taken ad-vantage of my curiosity ever since I was a little kid. "Hey kid, win something for your mother if you just hammer this nail all the way in three whacks." I was still thinking about it and he already had my fifty cents and three whacks later the nail didn't budge and I was broke. Every year they'd come up with another scam that robbed me somehow. I could live without the carnival just fine, thank you.

I played quarterback, defensive back and punter for the Sanger Union High Apaches. Until my senior football season in 1953, I played backup quarterback to Nick Papac, who was a year ahead of me. In 1961 I returned the favor when he was a backup to me for the Oakland Raiders. Not bad for a couple of grape pickers who both began in little Del Rey.

We had a decent little team my senior season. San Joaquin Memorial, a Catholic school in Fresno, was the big power in our league but we had a chance to take the champi-onship from them in the next to last game. Coach Clair

Slaughter—isn't that a perfect name for a football coach?—had us convinced we could win. And we almost did.

The key play in that game was a fake punt on fourth and 15. I completed the pass but we came up about one foot short and lost the ball and the game. That was the closest we ever came to winning a championship at little Sanger High, but the school did honor me in 1981 by naming the football field after me.

After my sophomore year in high school I got a job that, in one way or another, has stuck with me my whole life. I became an ice man.

The Sanger Ice House was run by Led Blue, who was an avid booster of young people in our area. He not only gave me a chance to earn money, he gave me a job that helped build my strength. The first year I went to work for 75 cents an hour lugging these huge blocks of ice. The key was to get 40 hours in three days and then work four days at time and a half.

Ice was a big commodity back then because there weren't a lot of refrigerated railroad cars. So my job was to take a gig and drag ice over to a boxcar and dump it in the cooler. Those boxcars would then take food all the way across the country.

I was a scrawny kid when I first went to work there, but lifting and dragging those ice blocks put some beef on me. Not that I ever qualified as being bulked up, mind you, but that job at least made me more than skin and bone. It was such a good combination of making money and working out that I worked there every summer and some Christmas holidays from 1952 to 1958, when I tried out for pro football.

Summer days were like a zoo at our house. My mother would get up at 4:30 in the morning and make all the lunches and get dinner ready for that night. Then she and my father would go to work. I would leave to work in the fields about six and my brother would go out about seven. If I had another job, like working at the Ice House, I would leave the fields early and go to the other job. We usually managed to meet at the house long enough to eat and then go out and play in a baseball game or whatever else was happening.

During the school year, we had seasonal jobs. During Christmas break we could pick oranges because a friend owned an orange grove. Another friend owned a dairy, so we would go bale hay.

During baseball season we would get up at four in the morning and bale hay. I remember that because I once hurt my back baling hay and could barely swing a bat. The coach was furious. Anyway, after baseball practice we'd bale hay until it got dark, then go do our homework, get a little sleep and start all over again at four in the morning.

As hectic as it sounds, I still remember those years as being good times. I don't remember complaining because I didn't know there was any reason to complain. Everybody around us was working pretty much the same if they could. I'm just glad I was able to get a job in the Sanger Ice House. The Ice Man isn't a bad nickname when you consider it easily could have been the Hay Baler or the Grape Picker.

During my senior year I decided I really wanted to go to Stanford, where they threw the hell out of the ball. They had a string of All-American quarterbacks, like Gary Kerkorian in 1951 and Bob Garrett in 1953. And Stanford coach Chuck Taylor spoke at our sports banquet in 1953.

When he took a look at my high school transcript when I was ready to graduate in 1954, Taylor had to tell me there was no way I could get into Stanford. Although my grades were good, I had not taken the proper college prep courses for a university like Stanford.

Maybe it's just as well I didn't go to there. Another former high school hot shot from Oakland was already there, John Brodie. He later went on to have a sensational NFL career with the 49ers from 1956 until 1972.

It's interesting how our paths constantly crossed but we never met on the field. When I played for the Raiders, we didn't played against NFL teams yet. However, when I was a junior at College of Pacific and he was a senior at Stanford, we ranked 1-2 in the nation near the end of the season. I got hurt and missed most of the last game and Brodie won the NCAA passing championship.

So, all things considered, the best place for me to go was Fresno City College. It was close to home, cheap and gave me a chance to play three sports, football, basketball and baseball.

Wayne Hardin, the coach at Porterville Junior College, recruited me hard, but I decided on Fresno anyway. Hardin became an assistant coach at Navy the next year and sent me an application to the Naval Academy along with the sample tests and the name of a congressman who could give me a recommendation.

This was pretty heavy stuff for a skinny little kid from Sanger. I knew about Navy only because I saw the team on newsreels at the movies. In those days after the Korean War the newsreels were all about Navy and Army, of course. I took a look at the map to see where Annapolis was and said "wow." Then I took a look at the sample tests and said "Wow!" I would have had to go to another school just to get ready for those tests.

The night before my first football game for Fresno, the whole team went to the Los Angeles Coliseum to watch

Pittsburgh play USC. On the first play of the game, Pitt quarterback Rudy Mattioli surprised everybody with a great fake handoff and then threw a perfect, 59-yard pass to receiver Nick Passodelis for a touchdown.

This brought a strange silence over the Coliseum because here was heavily favored USC giving up a touchdown on Pittsburgh's first offensive play. It turned out to be Pitt's only score and Mattioli's only completed pass as USC roared back to take the game by 27-7.

For some reason that play impressed the hell out of me. I thought about it over and over later that night as I sat down to my first prime rib dinner at the motel. When I walked to the men's room I stopped in the hall and pretended to go through the play, faking a handoff and then dropping back casually like I didn't have the ball and then turning around to throw and. . . .

"Hi, coach," I said sheepishly when I found myself staring right at an assistant coach who was amused by my hallway practice.

The next day we opened our season in Van Nuys against Los Angeles Valley Junior College. On the first play from scrimmage, their defense put all 11 men right on the line of scrimmage, hoping to either smother whatever run we tried or smother me if we passed. We had a run called, but I thought I had a better idea.

I audibled to a play-action pass to the tight end. This was a surprise play not only for the defense, but for our own team because our tight end was a big guy who could block but was real slow and not known as a receiver. But he opened that 1954 season with one hell of a catch.

It worked as well as it had the night earlier for Mattioli and even better than my imaginary play in the hall, which was going for a touchdown until the coach got in the way.

I faked the handoff, kept my back to the line for a

split second and even allowed my left hand to dangle visibly as if I had just handed off the ball. Then I turned around and our big, slow tight end was all alone down the field. I hit him in stride about 20 yards deep. The defense was so surprised that they had nobody within screaming distance of him. He made it all the more agonizing for them by taking forever to get into the end zone for the touchdown, about 45 yards as I recall.

"Not bad for starters, Flores," I told myself.

When I looked at the sidelines even our coaches looked shocked. Unlike Pitt, we didn't stop there. Once you get a defense guessing whether you will run or pass, then you can toy with them. We kept them off balance and built up a 27-7 lead by halftime.

But by the fourth quarter I was exhausted. That's when they sent their fastest wide receiver toward me at right cornerback. I slipped for a second and that's all he needed to get open by two or three steps to catch a pass for a touchdown. They eventually wore down our whole team and managed to escape with a 27-27 tie.

After such a great start it was a major disappointment to settle for a tie. Our exhaustion and disappointment were obvious on the quiet bus ride all the way back to Fresno that night. I curled up my wracked body and tried to sleep but I had too many things on my mind, like the taste of prime rib and the great feeling of getting control of a game on the first play with a touchdown pass.

Our next game was against the No. 1 junior college team in the nation, Bakersfield. One reason they were No. 1 was that the team was loaded with guys who just returned from the Korean War and were there on the GI bill. They averaged about 24 years old. Hell, we didn't have one player that old.

Their coach was Homer Beatty, who ran the same great option-T offense that Bud Wilkinson used at Oklahoma. And the star runner was Carl Gordon, a guy many old-timers still say is one of the top three athletes ever to come out of the San Francisco East Bay Area. They rank him up there with Norm Van Brocklin and Dick Bass.

After feeling as if we blew a big win at L. A. Valley, our Fresno team wasn't going to be intimidated by the Bakersfield GIs, Marines or the whole U.S. Armed Services. We gave Bakersfield its toughest game that year, but still lost, 14-13.

I was happy with my decision to go to Fresno CC because it gave me time to become acclimated to college academics while still being able to play football, baseball and basketball. After two years at Fresno CC, it was time to make a choice of whether to go to San Jose State or College of Pacific (COP).

At the end of the semester I made up my mind to go to San Jose State, where coach Bob Bronzan had established a tradition of passing the ball. I called Bronzan and told him I was coming. Then I called Pacific Coach Jack "Moose" Meyers and told him I had decided on San Jose.

Minutes after I hung up from talking to Meyers, I got a call from Sid Hall, the former COP player who was the Porterville JC head coach. I found out years later that when he hung up after talking to me, Meyers called Hall and said, "do your best to get that Flores to come to COP. I don't want to have to play against him at San Jose."

Well, Hall talked and talked and talked until I was so confused I didn't know what I wanted to do. I was trying to stick to my decision to go to San Jose, but every time I gave him a reason he countered with another reason why COP was better. Finally it got down to a matter of dollars and sense.

"Sid, if you can help me get a job at COP so I have spending money, then I'll go there," I said to him.

"No problem, Tom," he said, and my fate was sealed.

I was due to go to COP the next morning. In the meantime, I didn't want to talk to Bronzan. I went out with some friends and told my mother that if anybody calls to say I would be out late and that she didn't know where I was.

Early the next morning my parents drove me to Stockton, to the COP campus. They dropped me off and said good-bye. I wasn't ready for that because I thought they were going to stay and have lunch or something. Next thing you know, this skinny kid from Sanger is standing alone on the sidewalk watching wistfully as his parents drove away.

Hello college. This is Tom Flores reporting for duty. Me and my one suitcase, one sport coat, two pairs of slacks, one pair of Levis and a few T-shirts. Man did I feel like a little guy in a big world.

That night my mother got a phone call from Bronzan.

"He's not here, he's at College of Pacific," she said.

"Well, thank you anyway," Bronzan said.

In the next two years I would fall in love with the COP campus and have the best games of my college career against San Jose State. But to this day I still feel bad about the fact that I changed my mind and didn't call Bronzan to tell him.

four

Pacific, Playing for the Love of It

If success is the product of being in the right place at the right time, then for me College of Pacific was the right place and 1956 was the time.

Pacific could have been the setting for any of those cornball movies about good times in the fifties. I sure had a lot of good times there. It was a beautiful, friendly campus that was just big enough for you to stay anonymous and small enough to know damn near everybody if you really tried.

For a quiet kid like me, Pacific provided just enough room for growth without being so big that it stole my identity in the process. If I had my wish out of high school and went to Stanford, I might have been chewed up and spit out by the faster social life, rigorous academics and maybe even the big-time athletic competition. And maybe not.

I can understand why Americans still look back on the 1950s with such fondness. By the middle of the decade we were a nation that was healing well from World War II and the Korean conflict. I was part of a generation that cut its teeth during the cruelties of that big war then matured into adulthood during the innocence of peace.

We struck a wonderful middle ground between the harsh practicalities of the 1940s and the loose self-indulgence of the 1960s. Everywhere you could see a nation beginning to exercise its energy and imagination while still showing respect and appreciation for traditional values.

On those popular new little transistor radios you could still hear benign hits like "Whatever Will Be Will Be" and, appropriately here, "Memories Are Made of This." Yet those radio speakers also blasted new ground, to say nothing of ears, when a brash Mississippi kid named Elvis sang "Hound Dog." It was a hit for teenagers and a pet peeve for adults. It was the dawn of Rock and Roll and music never would be the same.

On the streets young men were flexing self expression with new, American-made sports cars. In 1953 Chevrolet came out with its first Corvette. In 1955 Ford responded with the two-seater Thunderbird which, sadly, became a four-seater only three years later.

By 1956 there were televisions in most homes and my friends liked to watch pro football on those little black and white screens. The age of experimentation and progress was even evident in pro football. Cleveland Browns coach Paul Brown wired his quarterbacks with radio receivers so he didn't have to shuttle players in to call the plays. Soon other teams learned how to tune in and steal the signals.

The league banned such electronics later in the season. In the championship game the New York Giants beat the Chicago Bears on an icy field with the help of something that showed we still had our feet on the ground in the fifties. The Giants used tennis shoes, normal everyday sneakers, to get traction on the slippery field.

And where did I stand as all these historic changes were swirling around me? I was still a skinny kid from Sanger with no radio to play the new music, no car to drive, no television of my own and not even a clue that I would someday play and coach pro football against Paul Brown, the New York Giants and Chicago Bears. But I did have a pair of sneakers, just in case.

As I said, the COP campus was a perfect setting for those Happy Days type corny movies that reflected all the good times from the 1950s. We had tree-lined streets, ivy-covered brick buildings, dances, pep rallies, and even the ever-present soda shop, called the End Zone. We had some traditions, too, like Freshman Week, when all the new students had to wear beanies and name tags and were supposed to do whatever they were told by upperclassmen.

Most of the hazings on Freshman Week were carried out either inside or in front of Anderson Hall, the campus dining room. Football players were usually the biggest instigators. During meals they would recruit freshmen to fetch their food. Usually, they would pick the cutest coeds they could find, of course. Evenings everybody would hang around in front of Anderson Hall, where freshmen were really put through their paces.

We were insulated from criticism by the naivety of the time, so we got away with acts of chauvanism that never would be tolerated today. Betty Friedan would have had a fit. But we thought it was all in good humor and a way to bring students closer together. It was a tradition that made it easy for one shy, varsity football player to meet the cutest little brunette freshman coed that ever wore a beanie at College of Pacific.

Barbara Ann Fridell grabbed my attention the first time I saw her in front of Anderson Hall on that wonderful autumn day of 1956. Of course, she had a lot of people looking at her that time. After all, she was standing there with a can of dog food on her head singing "How Much is that Doggie in the Window?" That was a favorite Freshman Week request by one of our whacked out football players.

I was standing there with three of my roommates, Jack Larschied, a running back with the build and temperment of a bulldog; Bob Denton, a big tight end who was always pulling practical jokes; and Roland Rutter, a center who was always ready for a little mischief.

These guys became my closest friends at Pacific despite the fact we had very little in common. Or maybe because of it. They were all outgoing, crazy ex-Marines who made life totally crazy in the eight-man Quonset Hut we called home. Years later when I saw the movie *One Flew Over the Cuckoo's Nest,* it reminded my of my days in that Quonset Hut.

"Hey Flores, snap out of it," barked Larschied, who caught me staring at the brunette coed. "Judging by the look on your face, she could be singing about you. Hell, you look like a lost puppy. If you're that interested, then we should meet her."

He was still laughing at me as he moved closer to the coed and hollered for her to come on over. But another freshman was singing now and the brunette could not hear Larschied clearly.

"What?" she said.

"Watt, Watt," mocked Larschied. "Look, she's a light bulb."

This time she did hear him. Obviously embarrassed, she scrambled off the stairs and ran into the dining room.

"Nice going, Jack," I said. "Next time you want to

help me do something, warn me first and I'll do it without you."

We went in the dining hall to get something to eat and Larschied noticed that the brunette was standing on the other side of the room with her girl friend.

"OK, wise guy, your turn," said Larschied. "I'll bet you a buck you can't get her to talk to us. Two bucks if they sit with us."

Some people don't believe that stuff about football building courage and character. Well, I believe that by playing sports, especially football, you learn how to do things that you might otherwise be afraid to do. I mean, do you really think a person in his right mind would stand still to throw a ball while some 250-pound maniac was about to rearrange his anatomy? Nah. But football teaches you to be that dumb. You figure that you're already out there and you are going to get hit anyway, so you might as well try to complete a pass.

Eventually you learn that the same psychology sometimes works off the field. So before Larschied made things any worse, I decided to throw the best pass I could.

"Hi, Barbara," I said, showing that I was perceptive enough at least to read the name on her tag. "My name is Tom Flores and this is Jack Larschied, my loud-mouthed friend who means no harm. We were wondering if you and your girl friend would sit over here and have lunch with us."

Barbara Flores: *When I first saw Tom with all those football players I thought he was a music major who was just hanging around with them. He didn't look at all like a football player to me. He was wearing these big, thick glasses at the time. He was tall, skinny, had short hair and his ears stuck out.*

I was so concerned about not fumbling my own words, that I didn't realize she was even more self-conscious about all the attention she was getting. It's funny how a guy who can stand up to those 250-pound maniacs can be intimidated by a pretty little coed. I tried to look calm while seconds seemed like an eternity before she responded in a way that made her surprisingly like most other 18-year-old coeds.

She giggled.

"Sure, Tom," she said. "I'd love to sit with you.

Larschied elbowed me in the ribs so hard that I lost my breath. Or maybe it was Barbara that took my breath away. Anyway, I was speechless for a few seconds, so I tried to look cool while I silently ushered her and her girl friend to our table. By the time I regained my breath and my speech, Barbara and her friend managed to make me feel very relaxed by the way they were acting.

They looked at each other and giggled.

"Geez," I told myself. "She's cuter than hell, but she isn't going to bite or anything so calm down and be yourself."

"Well," I said aloud, trying to sound like I was in control. "You know it's a tradition around here for freshmen to do things for the varsity football players, like get the food. So, ah,. . . ."

I felt my face flush a little as I began to stammer because I was uneasy telling somebody I didn't even know to do something for me.

"So, ah, what would you like us to get you?" said Barbara, speaking up right on cue and saving me from extended embarrassment.

"Oh, just some milk," I said after realizing my tongue really wasn't tied in a double knot even if my stomach was.

The girls bounced to their feet and I could hear them

giggle all the way to the counter...and back. I casually mentioned to Barbara that we both had the same biology class at 8 a.m. the next day. She said she would look for me and with that the two girls got up and giggled their way out the door.

Later she told me they ran back to their rooms and pulled out a football program to see who they were talking to. She knew so little about football that when she did find my name in the program she had to ask her girlfriend what a quarterback was. Neither one of them knew.

Back at the dining room, it was my turn to elbow Larschied in the stomach. I caught him by surprise and knocked the breath out of him.

"Keep the two bucks," I said as he stood there unable to speak. "The pleasure was all mine."

The next day I walked into this huge, two-tiered biology class and sat upstairs. Just my luck. Although we sat alphabetically, the row split between the last names of Flores and Fridell. So while I was at the back of the class upstairs, Barbara was at the front of the class downstairs. As I strained to see her, she turned around and gave me a little wave. I waved back and just then the teacher came in and saw me. So the teacher waved back at me and I slumped down in my chair.

After class I gathered my books and hurried down the stairs.

"Hi, good to see you again," I said to Barbara.

She smiled, picked up her books and stood next to me.

"Tom, what's a quarterback?" she asked, showing that she had done her homework in more than biology.

"Oh, just the guy who hands the ball off or passes it," I answered. "Why do you ask?"

"Because you don't look like a football player, like

your friends," she said. "So I just wondered what a quarterback does. I bet you pass the ball real pretty."

Pretty? I had never heard a pass described like that before.

"Yeah," I said. "Real pretty."

I don't think we were talking about the same thing, however.

As we walked down the corridor I realized I had only five minutes to get to my next class. Football also teaches you how to manage the clock.

"Well, I have to get to class so how would you like to go to the the End Zone tonight for a Coca Cola or something," I said.

"Great," she answered.

And that's how Barbara and I arranged our very first date in a relationship that has lasted through four years of courtship and 31 years of marriage. During that time Barbara learned more about quarterbacking than some quarterbacks know. But that didn't stop her from saying the same thing whenever I left for practice or a game.

"Don't forget, Tom," she would say. "Pass pretty."

College football in 1956 was still climbing out of the stone ages. Whenever a quarterback says something like that you know he's talking about teams that preferred to run rather than pass. College of Pacific was one of those teams, but with good reason. We had one of college football's greatest runners in Dick Bass.

In our season opener, Bass, already known as one of the best in the country, carried the ball 12 times for 122 yards, caught 4 passes for 52 yards, returned 2 punts for 32 yards and 2 kickoffs for 47 yards and scored 2 touchdowns. We beat Colorado A&M, 39-14.

I wasn't even the starting quarterback yet. I split

time with Jim Reynosa. In that first game he threw 12 passes and I threw 13. We each completed 8, me for 105 yards and him for 101. So that hardly was enough of a difference to win the starting job.

The second week we played the University of Kansas at Lawrence, Kansas. That meant my first ride in a big airplane and my first in-flight meal. We stayed two nights in big Kansas City, which in no way reminded me of home. But it wasn't until after practice on the day before the game that I learned the real meaning of the word big.

We were sitting in our bus waiting for all the players to load up and Dick Bass was talking out his window to some guy that looked real familiar.

"Psst, Jack, who is that guy talking to Dick?" I asked Larschied.

"Wilt," he answered.

Of course. It was Wilt Chamberlain, the great Kansas basketball player I had heard so much about. As I looked again it suddenly dawned on me that Dick Bass, who was pretty far from the ground in our bus seat, was eyeball-to-eyeball with Chamberlain. Now that's big.

Larschied and I watched in awe as Chamberlain walked away from the bus and got into this 1955 Chevrolet that had only one seat, a back seat. He somehow got his long, seven-foot-three body in there and drove the car away from the back seat. I was impressed. This was the big time.

The next day my efforts to make an impression in the big time weren't exactly appreciated. Again, Reynosa started and I followed. On my first drive we were moving the ball smoothly with Bass doing most of the work. But he came up a little short on a third down run, leaving us with a fourth and one at their ten yard line.

So here we are in the opponent's stadium, leading 13-7 with a fourth and one on their ten yard line and the fans are screaming their heads off. We call a run in the huddle and I come up and stand behind the center and watch Kansas put all 11 defenders within an inch of the line of scrimmage.

For one fraction of a second my mind flashed to another time and another game. Instead of hearing that Kansas crowd and seeing that Kansas defense, I was remembering Vun Nuys, California. I thought of how I practiced that play-action pass in the hallway of a motel. I remembered how I called that on my first play at Fresno Junior College for a touchdown against Los Angeles Valley.

So I audibled. Bob Denton, the tight end, looked over at me like I'd just lost my mind. I took the snap, faked a handoff to Bass and the entire Kansas team tried to tackle him. Denton slipped behind everybody and I turned around and threw. Touchdown!

As I ran into the end zone and jumped on Denton, he shook his head and laughed.

"Man, I don't believe it," he said. "That was pretty cool, Ice Man."

That touchdown made the stadium so quiet I could hear only two people. One was a guy selling popcorn in the stands. The other was our offensive line coach, John Nicksovich. As we lined up for the PAT I could hear Nicksovich screaming my name.

"Flores, that was the stupidest play I've ever seen in my entire life," he hollered. "I don't care if we got seven points. I don't care if we got ten. We were running the hell out of the ball and you decide to throw a pass that could blow the whole thing. Stupid, stupid, stupid."

The poor guy was frothing at the mouth he was so mad. I was just glad that I was on special teams so I had to stay on the field for the PAT, then the kickoff. And after that I stayed in to play defensive back. I wanted Nicksovich to have a lot of time to cool down.

Anyway, my junior college play scored a major college touchdown whether he liked it or not. We led by 20-7 at halftime. But, just like that junior college game in Van Nuys, we folded in the second half. Kansas came back and managed to get a 27-27 tie.

Nicksovich may not have liked my play-calling, but by the fifth game of the season I was the starting quarterback and by my sixth game I was in a hot streak. In those days if you totalled 100 yards passing you had a pretty good day. I threw for 176 and 2 touchdowns against Washington State and for 177 yards and 2 touchowns against Tulsa.

Then it was time to face up to San Jose State, the school I originally agreed to attend. I remember before the game looking at the sidelines and seeing San Jose coach Bob Broznan and feeling like I should go over and apologize. Well, if I wanted to do it, I should have done it then. After that game it was too late.

I had the best game of my college career that November 10, 1956. I completed 12 of 14 passes for 195 yards and 3 touchdowns and ran for another touchdown and even had an interception on defense. We won, 34-7. If I had apologized after that, Broznan would have thought I was a smart-ass.

In all I was happy with my junior season. Despite splitting time at quarterback in most of the games, I finished first in the nation with a 147.5 quarterback rating and in touchdowns responsible for (18). I was fourth in completion percentage (57.5) and yards passing per game (111.9). Considering I broke my collarbone that spring it turned out to be a very productive year.

However, that injury would come back to haunt me in my senior year. The problem began when we were issued our equipment before preseason drills. During the 1956 season I wore shoulder pads that we built up with foam rubber to protect my injured collarbone. But when I showed up in the fall of 1957 we had new equipment. My customized pads were gone.

The special pads didn't help me as a quarterback as much as they did when I played defense. Despite all my hours of gigging ice in Sanger, I still wasn't what you would call a wide body. Skinny is what you would call me. So those big pads helped protect my bony shoulders when I had to make tackles.

"Look, is there some way I could get back the pads I had last year?" I asked the equipment manager.

"Listen kid, we got these brand new pads and they're better than that old stuff, so use them, OK?" he said.

"But I had this collarbone injury and . . . ."

He didn't even let me finish.

"Kid, the old stuff is gone, the new stuff is better," he bellowed. "Take 'em and like 'em."

I took 'em, but to this day I regret it. Looking back, that may have been the beginning of a lot of heartache I endured before finally getting a job in professional football.

It didn't take me long to realize how big a mistake it was to use the new pads. During that first day of practice we went through drills where you have to line up one-on-one and tackle ball carriers. I looked at the ball carriers' line and my line. I counted back to see who I would get to tackle. Damn. Just my luck. My guy was the biggest running back on the team, one of those guys who have only one move, straight through you.

You don't want to look like a wimp when you line up for these drills, so there was really no way out. I decided that in order to protect my throwing arm and my bad collarbone I would tackle this big bull with my left shoulder. Ready, set . . .

"Awwwwwww," I heard myself scream as a sharp pain went through my left shoulder. My hand went numb for a few seconds, then I finally got all my feeling back, which meant I was able to feel the throbbing pain in my shoulder.

I said I was all right, went to the back of the line and hoped I would get some little guy the next time. No way. Another big, slow, lug. I had no choice but to use my right shoulder this time because my left was already hurt. Ready, set . . .

"Yeowwwww," I screamed, knowing damn well I screwed up my right shoulder pretty good.

For the rest of my senior season I didn't throw the ball until Thursday before a Saturday game in order to allow my shoulder to rest. Dick Bass also broke his leg, so we had times when we really struggled on offense.

During one ugly three-game stretch, I punted for far more yards than I passed for. In a 7-7 tie with Kanas State I threw for only 16 yards and punted for 157. In a 7-7 tie with Idaho I threw for 90 yards and punted for 246. And, in our season low-light, we lost to Cincinnati, 7-2, as I completed only 5 of 24 passes for 59 yards and had to punt 10 times for 315 yards.

On days like that I would have loved to see Dick Bass in the backfield. Don't let quarterbacks fool you. They need a decent running game to keep the pressure off them. That's the reason I was so successful with my favorite play-action pass. The defense was geared up to stop the run. So it helps to have one.

That's exactly what my big-mouthed friend, Jack Larschied, finally gave us after those three consecutive lousy weeks. He carried 14 times for 179 yards and scored 2 touchdowns. Not coincidentally, I completed 10 of 18 passes for 137 yards and we finally beat a team that scored only one touchdown, 21-7, over Marquette.

After another decent game against San Jose State

(8 of 9 for 78 yards, 1 touchdown in a 21-6 win), we went against a UCLA outfit that was probably the best team I played against in college.

They had it all The legendary Red Sanders was their coach. He had spoken at Sanger High and showed us films of his team doing its famous serpentine from the huddle to the line of scrimmage and lining up their great single wing offense. Little did I know that this would be one of the last games Sanders' coached before he died in 1958.

I was really excited about this game, but I didn't like the fact that both Bass and Larschied were sidelined with injuries.

Despite the loss of our top rushers, we managed to gain more yards in total offense than the great Bruins, 374-365. Of the 21 passes I threw only one hit the ground. Sixteen were completed and four were intercepted. And we lost, 21-0.

One of the keys was that they really didn't respect our run. I should have remembered that when we drove to about the five yard line and our flanker, Chuck Chatfield, came back to the huddle screaming that he was getting open on every play. He convinced me to try a play-action pass. Without Bass or Larschied, that didn't make a lot of sense. But for some reason I went for it. This time the old play-action was no fun at all.

Just as I turned to throw I was blind-sided by a UCLA defensive end and the ball flew out of my hands kind of end over end. Instead of us getting a touchdown, they intercepted the ball in the end zone. Ever since that day I never allowed somebody to talk me into a play unless I felt good about it myself.

It's not often that you hear this ex-quarterback say that he should have run the ball instead of thrown it. But that was one of those times.

After my senior season I was selected to play in the East-West Shrine game. As it turned out I became more of a discarded pawn in a lousy game of politics.

Stanford football coach Chuck Taylor had just retired and everybody wanted the job. Jack Curtis was the head coach of Utah and the West team. His assistant was Oregon State's Tommy Prothro, who brought his single wing tailback, Joe Francis, to the game.

Curtis wanted the Stanford job and Prothro wanted to show the pro scouts that Francis could play quarterback, despite the fact he had never taken a snap from center in college. After a couple of days Stanford quarterback Jackie Douglas was suddenly added to the West roster.

Next thing you know, I'm standing on the sidelines most of the time watching these other guys practice. Prothro saw to it that Francis actually got more time than any of us in practice, which is where you have your best chance to impress the scouts.

While all this is going on, the National Football League conducts the first four or five rounds of its draft. Although I had received letters from teams saying I would be taken in the early rounds, my name wasn't called and I really wondered why. The Cleveland Browns sent me a telegram saying I would be taken as soon as the draft resumed after the game. OK, I could live with that. All I wanted was a chance.

Still, it was hard to be in a good mood when so many of the other guys on the team were celebrating that they were drafted. To make matters worse, I was getting tired of watching the other quarterbacks get in more practice time than me. Moose Meyers, my COP coach, didn't like it either and confronted Curtis during practice one day.

The next thing I know the word is that I was being held out of practice because my shoulder was sore.

Great. Just the kind of news you want the pro scouts to hear.

On game day I play the last three or four minutes to run the clock out, which surprises nobody because the big story about me know isn't how well I can play. It's about how bad my shoulder is. Damn those new shoulder pads at COP.

The bottom line was that Curtis got his head coaching job at Stanford and I never got drafted. And I do mean never, not by the NFL anyway. After the Shrine Game the NFL resumed its draft and, thanks to the widespread stories of my shoulder problem, no team took a chance on me in 30 rounds. Thirty rounds!

About the only scout I remember treating me halfway decent during the Shrine game was Don Klosterman, who was once a great quarterback himself before an unfortunate skiing accident ended his career. Years later I would call him when I was looking for a head coaching job in the NFL and he was working with the Rams. But this time he was nice enough to look me up when everybody else was ignoring me.

Don was working for the Calgary Stampeders, the team that had my rights in the Canadian Football League. He talked to me after practice one day and told me they were interested in getting me up in Canada.

When I was ignored for 30 rounds in the NFL draft— 30 rounds, hell, I still have a hard time believing it—Moose Meyers suggested that I go on up to Canada. He even got on the phone and negotiated a pretty good contract for me.

I signed for $10,000, which was only $2,000 less than John Brodie's first contract with the 49ers. But he got a new car as a bonus. All I got was a plane ticket to Canada. So in July of 1958 I was on my way to Calgary to have a shot at pro football.

Jim Finks was the general manager of the Calgary team that year and he acted like he was glad to see me and all that. But as soon as I got to practice I realized there were two American quarterbacks. We both knew one of us would have to go. But we were only half right.

After a few weeks, they called me into the office and told me it was obvious that my shoulder was bothering me and that they would have to let me go. When I walked outside I bumped into the other American quarterback. I congratulated him and told him they cut me. He said, "Well, I'll go with you to the airport because I've been cut, too."

The Stampeders had cut us both and signed Maury Duncan, a former San Francisco State star who was with the 49ers for two years before Brodie arrived.

Next thing you know I was back in Sanger answering a phone call from Moose Meyers.

"Get your ass back in school and work on your degree," he said.

That wasn't a half-bad idea. Not only did that give me a chance to work on my Masters, but there was a certain brunette I kind of wanted to see.

Moose Meyers gave me a job tutoring classes in exchange for a partial scholarship. I also tossed pizzas at Lugo's Pizzeria to earn spending money.

And I finally made it on a professional football team, of sorts. Moose knew somebody with a semi-pro team named the Bakersfield Spoilers. Four former Pacific players agreed to give this semipro team a try.

We got up at 4 a.m., on Saturday morning, drove to Bakersfield and flew to Tucson, Arizona for a night game. The flight was memorable because there was a big thunderstorm and this rickety, old plane we were in barely made it above the storm. But the plane was better than the field we played on. It was a rodeo field that was converted into a football field just for that one game.

Chuck Chatfield, a wide receiver from Pacific, was running a pattern when he slipped and fell in the middle of a big pile of manure. After that we told him to play lonesome end. He smelled so bad we didn't let him in the huddle. After the game we flew back to Bakersfield that night, then piled into the car and drove home by about 6 a.m., Sunday.

For that I was paid fifty bucks. I was the only one who went back for more games. I never practiced with the team, just showed up for games. I took the bus to Los Angeles for one game and to Bakersfield for the others. After each game the coach would take me behind a building and pay me in cash. He didn't want any of the other players to know I was getting paid. I guess that's what they mean by semi-pro.

In January 1959, Moose talked me into undergoing a new surgery procedure that would fix my shoulder. I knew that was the main reason I didn't make it in the pros in 1958 and I was only semi-effective in the semi-pro games. If I wanted to earn more than fifty dollars a game, then I would have to throw better.

After rehabilitating my shoulder and taking part in the spring game with Eddie LeBaron, he suggested that I try out for the Washington Redskins, the team he was playing for at the time. He went back and pitched my name to the Redskins and they sent me a free agent contract.

When I showed up at their summer training camp in Occidental, I knew my arm was far from 100 percent. But I was hoping that I could somehow make it through until I regained my strength. Another free agent at that camp was Bobby Beathard, a quarterback from Cal Poly-San Luis Obispo, where he said his roommate was a real character named John Madden. Beathard was trying out as a defensive back with the Redskins.

Years later, he would do much better as Washington's general manager. Now my former free agent buddy is running another AFC West team, the San Diego Chargers.

After two or three days with the Redskins it was

painfully obvious that this was not going to work out. For a guy who had always thrown so naturally this was just about the ultimate frustration. But I was kind of relieved when they let me go because I figured it was time to get on with the rest of my life. I left the Redskins believing I was finally leaving football forever.

OK, would you believe a couple of weeks?

As soon as I stepped into my parents' home in Sanger, my mother told me that Moose Meyers was on the phone.

"Get your ass back up here because there are things to be done," he said.

So the next week I was back at Pacific, tossing pizzas and wondering what I would eventually do for a living. Once again, Moose Meyers had the right answer, but neither of us really knew how right he was for many years.

"Tom," he said, "I think you would make a good coach. So I'm giving you a job helping Sid Hall coach the freshmen."

But when we opened practice in the fall, Moose moved Sid to a full-time job as varsity assistant and I became a full-time head coach of the freshmen.

Coach Flores. Kind of has a good ring to it.

My main problem was easy to see. We only had 17 players, including one who had never played football before in his life. Another broke his hand in the first week of practice, giving us 15 players going into a game against Cal-Berkeley.

Mike White was the freshmen coach at Cal, and they were out for blood because the only game they lost the previous year was to little COP. They had about 40 players and we had our full array of 15. It was about 100 degrees in Berkeley's Memorial Coliseum for that prelim to the varsity game.

But my guys surprised the hell out of me and everybody else by getting out to a 16-8 lead at halftime. After that it was all down hill. Like an avalanche is all down hill. Cal beat the hell out of us, 44-16, and was doing everything it could to run up the score.

Mike White wasn't so bad, but some of his assistants showed no class at all. With about two minutes to go the Cal assistants were yelling at this big tackle we had named Roy Williams.

"Hey big fella," they said. "Looks like you need another beer. You look like the kind of guy that enjoys a few beers. C'mon, have another beer."

These bunch of jerkos were saying every gross thing they could to demean our players. Then, with about four minutes left, they sent an official over who asked "do you want to call it now?"

That did it. I blew a fuse.

"Hell no," I screamed at him loud enough for everybody in the stadium to hear. "We're not calling this son of a bitch until it's done."

After the game two of my guys went to the hospital for heat prostration. Then we took all of them down to Jack London Square in Oakland for a big dinner. I was proud of them.

We played six games that year and won five. I always say that we had five and a half wins and a half a loss. My guys deserved that half a win.

I realized that coaching had the type of challenges and rewards that I liked. Hell, it might even make a good full-time job.

five

Early Raiders—This Is Pro Football?

By early 1960 I thought my dream of playing pro football would remain just that, a dream.

I was offered a job at Roosevelt High in Fresno with the understanding that when I received my Masters I could move to Fresno Community College. I might be working at Fresno CC right now, but somebody else who wanted to get into pro football was too stubborn to let his dream die.

While I was being turned down by the Canadian League and Washington Redskins, a Texas millionaire named Lamar Hunt was getting frustrated because the National Football League wouldn't give him an expansion team in Dallas and his efforts to buy an existing franchise were unsuccessful.

So he started the American Football League.

When you have $200 million you can do things like that. Hunt got the idea when he learned he was not the only one who was turned down in a bid to buy the Chicago Cardinals from the Woolfson family. In his final meeting with the Woolfsons, Hunt learned that they also rejected Bud Adams of Houston, Bob Howsam of Denver and Max Winter of Minnesota.

And that's how the Woolfsons accidentally supplied Hunt with the names of charter members for his new league. Barron Hilton, the hotel giant, agreed to finance an AFL franchise in Los Angeles. Harry Wismer, a former sportscaster, was eager to own one in New York. Ralph Wilson, a successful insurance man, took a franchise in Buffalo. And Billy Sullivan managed to gather $25,000 so he could have one in Boston.

If it had been left at that, then I might be coaching at Fresno CC today. But the NFL, which in 1958 had no desire to expand despite Hunt's pleas, suddenly wanted to place franchises in Minnesota and Dallas one year later.

The AFL's charter owners didn't learn about this NFL expansion until they met for the first time on November 22, 1959, in Minneapolis. That's when Winter thanked them for coming to his town and then said he was accepting an invitation to jump to the NFL. Hunt was also given a chance to join the NFL. But to his credit he turned it down.

Minnesota's rude departure opened the door for one more franchise. That's when Wayne Valley, a Northern California real estate developer, entered Oakland into the new league. Valley was actually the spokesman for a group formed by Oakland financier and real estate developer Y. C. "Chet' Soda. The group, which called itself "The Foolish Club," also included Ed W. McGah, Robert Osborne, Charley Harney, Don Blessing, Harvey Binns and Roger Lapham, Jr.

Their bid for an AFL franchise was almost turned

down in favor of Atlanta, but Barron Hilton pointed out that he needed another team on the West Coast for a "natural rival." That said, a new AFL team, as well as a tremendous rivalry, was born.

In February of 1960 the Oakland franchise hired Eddie Erdelatz as head coach. Erdelatz had coached at the Naval Academy. In March, Ernie George, an assistant coach who moved with Erdelatz from Navy to Oakland, invited me to their July training camp. Eddie LeBaron, another former College of Pacific quarterback, had recommended me to Erdelatz and George.

I owe my thanks to the NFL, the Woolfson family, Lamar Hunt, Max Winter, "The Foolish Club," LeBaron and Erdelatz. If any of them had made a different decision in that complicated series of events, then Ernie George never would have phoned me that day. And I wouldn't have had that one last chance to play pro football.

I told George that I would love to give it a try with the Oakland team, but that I wanted to see if my shoulder was ready this time. I had not thrown a football for almost a year. I wanted to have the doctors look at my shoulder. If I got their clearance I wanted to test it in Pacific's Spring Game between the Varsity and the Alumni.

But before I could see the doctors or play in the game, I had to face my mother. She wasn't happy about the idea of me making another run, or pass, at pro football. She had been thrilled when I told her I would teach in Fresno. When I told her I changed my mind she cried. She liked the idea of me staying near home and teaching better than going off again to try and play pro football.

Before the Spring Game I saw two doctors about my shoulder. One said he was sure I would never play again competitively. The second said I should go try throwing and see how I felt. His name was Dr. Lucky. I liked that.

The Spring Game was like being reborn. I drew plays

in the dirt and threw the hell out of the ball. It was a sensational feeling being back in the pocket again, throwing the ball. I was hot in that game, completing almost every pass.

After the game my shoulder was a little sore, but nothing out of the ordinary. I called Oakland and told them I was ready to sign. One thing did bother me, however. I heard that they named the team the Oakland Senors. As a Mexican-American I could already imagine people calling me Oakland quarterback Senor Flores. I didn't like the sound of that.

But when I received my contract to sign I learned they changed the name to the Raiders. That was something I could live with. And I did for many years.

On July 11, 1960, I was one of 11 quarterbacks to show up for the first day of training camp with the Oakland Raiders in Santa Cruz. This training camp was a cross between a zoo and a carnival. A bunch of animals acting like clowns.

But beneath all the bullshit these guys were all there because of one common bond. They loved to play football. And if they were in Santa Cruz, chances are they had been overlooked or turned down by every other professional team.

Because they were the last team to join the AFL, the Raiders didn't have much time to throw together a team. Anybody who was warm and could walk was given a uniform. Some of my teammates from College of Pacific shared this great experience with me, including halfback Jack Larschied and offensive lineman Wayne Hawkins. I later befriended guard Don Manoukian, who was only with the Raiders that one year but is one of those guys you just don't forget easily.

Of the 11 quarterbacks who were there the first day,

three were left after the first week, Babe Parilli, Paul Larson and me. Then Paul was let go, leaving only Babe and me.

Jim Otto, whose name was his number—"00"—was also there that first day. He's the center who started every game for 14 years and will forever be known as the original Raider. But many don't know that the original Raider wasn't originally a center. The first day of practice he was a 218-pound linebacker. However, he could snap for kicks and punts so he was moved to center.

I remember the first time I took snaps from Jim I thought "Wow this guy is lean," which was an interesting observation considering I was pretty thin myself. Jim eventually put on weight and got up to the 250-pound area. In the early years he got by on sheer determination. He kind of set the pace for what was to be the Raider attitude with a die-hard mentality on the field and a play-hard approach off it.

The first non-player I got to know was the trainer, George Anderson. He was the guy who somehow brought order to the chaos in that training camp and every Raiders training camp since then. If it weren't for his daily massages on my shoulder I never would have made it. That was the beginning of a close friendship that has lasted to this day.

George Anderson: *When I first met Tom I was a little skeptical because I didn't know if this skinny kid was tough enough. But I soon learned to respect him as maybe the toughest guy, pound-for-pound, that I ever met. In our first training camps in Santa Cruz his shoulder wasn't 100 percent and I know it hurt him a lot. He didn't complain, but he did ask for a massage. I was glad to massage him every day because it was obvious he would be able to help this raggedy-looking outfit on the football field.*

I signed for a whopping $9,000, but you didn't make any of that money until the regular season. In the meantime, you got three squares and a spot to flop plus $50 for each of the six preseason games, which I guess put our summer pay on par with that of the Bakersfield Spoilers.

We stayed at the Palomar Hotel, which looked like a retirement home. The food there was terrible on its best days and damn near inedible the others. We ate it anyway because we couldn't afford to eat elsewhere. The food wasn't the only bad thing about meal time.

After a couple of days there we were sitting at breakfast and an assistant coach comes up to our table and says, "The following guys report to coach Erdelatz's room." He started reading off names and by the time he was done, Hawkins and I were the only ones at the table. From then on if the players caught wind that somebody was going to be cut, then nobody went to breakfast. There were times the dining room was empty during meal times.

Erdelatz ran the quickest practices you ever saw, about an hour and a half at the most. In order to get all the drills done in that time period he demanded that you run all the time. We'd have to run going onto the field, from drill to drill, to the sideline, and off the field. Run, run, run. If you didn't run full speed all the time then he would make you go back and do it over at top speed. And there were no exceptions.

Anderson: *At Annapolis, Erdelatz had only 1½ hours to practice so they did everything in double time. That's how he ran our practices in Santa Cruz and God help the player who didn't run. Tom was one of the smart ones who figured Eddie out right away and moved fast. But I remember when Babe Parilli walked out to his first practice and Eddie made him go back four times. Each time Babe walked out again, not knowing what he was doing wrong. Eddie said 'If he walks out again he's going home.' I think somebody gave Babe a hint because he finally ran out. There were guys that Eddie sent packing because they didn't run in practice.*

Those short practices actually worked pretty well because we were all in good shape, anyway, and football wasn't that complicated then. Everybody used the 4-3 defense and tried to play mostly man-to-man pass coverage, with maybe one zone. Things were standardized. There were no three wide receivers, four wide receivers, shotgun, nickel, dime, three-four or five-man defensive line. Most teams did much the same things so it was easy to prepare for a game.

I guess Erdelatz felt at home during the regular season when our training facility was at the Alameda Naval base. His short practices made for unusual workdays because we would go to the base at 8 a.m., and after meetings, practice and a lunch we would be back in the apartment by 1 p.m.

Don Manoukian: *Wayne Hawkins and I roomed with Tom and played the two guard spots, trying to protect his ass. Practicing at that Naval base with Tom was torture. He's got one of these gentlemanly voices that you can barely hear when everything is quiet. But when those jet planes took off or landed while we were practicing, there was no way you could hear him call the plays. So Hawkins and I were forever running into each other behind the center, Jim Otto, because we didn't hear which way the play was going. Truth is, I think some of the biggest hits on Tom that first year were when he got caught between Hawkins and me pulling the wrong way.*

Our home games were really road games for the first two years because we went to San Francisco, playing at old Kezar Stadium in 1960 and Candlestick Park in 1961. And those who think Al Davis talked about moving a lot in later years should know that the Raiders were constantly trying new towns their first two seasons. In 1960 we played a pre-season game in Sacramento, and in 1961 we played one in Honolulu and another in Spokane, Washington.

The stability of the new league was constantly in question and we were always hearing rumors that the AFL was going to fold. I remember there was this big story about how much money the league was losing and a reporter went to the father of Houston Texans owner Lamar Hunt, who founded the AFL, and told him that his son might lose a $1 million in his first year.

"Well, at that rate he's only got 150 years to go and he'll be broke," the father said, as I recall. That was well and good for the Oilers, but we heard stories about checks bouncing all over the league, especially in New York, where Titans owner Harry Wismer was running the entire operation from an apartment that he couldn't afford to heat.

For fear of having our checks bounce, a group of us would go straight to the bank as soon as we got paid. Sometimes we had to wait for the funds to be transferred. We stayed right there in the bank until we got our money. Considering how we looked, a bunch of big, scraggly, loud guys, we must have scared the hell out of the bank security guards every payday. Luckily for those guards, the bank always came up with our money.

The road trips were really something to remember,

although there were some you wished you could forget. Like the first time we went to Dallas. We went to check into a hotel, but we were told they didn't let, as they said it, "colored people" stay there. Eddie Erdelatz told them what they could do with their rooms, then found another hotel where we could all stay.

To save on travel expenses the schedule would string together three or four road games at a time. In 1960, we made a 21-day swing through the East, playing at Buffalo, New York and Boston. Our most consistent problem on these trips was getting people to believe who we were.

Our first night in Buffalo a few players went out to this little place and started talking with the locals. It wasn't surprising that they never heard of the Raiders because, after all, we were a brand new team. But nobody knew where Oakland was, either.

That first night in Buffalo we tried to tell the locals we were football players, but they absolutely refused to believe us. This one gal was pretty adamant.

"C'mon, you think we're so stupid that you can con us with talk like that?" she said. "Tell us the truth. You're truck drivers, right?"

"No, we're really football players," I said as I began to explain the entire history of the new American Football League. But she didn't believe a word of it.

The next night we figured "why fight it?" When somebody asked who we were and what we were doing there, we said we were truck drivers in town for a truck drivers' convention. Darned if that didn't work. So that night the Oakland Raiders became a bunch of truck drivers and we didn't have one argument about who we were or why we were there. We had a great time.

In New York we played at the old Polo Grounds, which was where Willie Mays made his famous over-the-shoulder catch in deep left-center before the Giants moved to San Francisco. I found out that Willie Mays wasn't the only one who ran around in the Polo Fields. The place was full of cockroaches and rats. We practiced the night before our game and then had to leave the lights on all night and guard our equipment or rats would have gotten into everything.

When it was finally time to play the game, the Titans refused to come out of their locker room until Wismer, the owner, had his banker gaurantee the players that they would get paid on Monday. By the time they did come out, it was pouring rain. All we wanted to do was win the damn game and get the hell out of there. But nothing ever comes easily in New York.

The game had to be stopped because this drunk wandered onto the field. Usually that wouln't hold up a game too long, but the New York Police turned it into a three-act play. Act II was when they sent a paddy wagon onto the field to get the drunk and it got stuck in the mud right on the 20 yard line. In Act III the players from both teams were out on the field trying to push that damn paddy wagon out of the way so we could play our game.

It must have looked like an episode of the Keystone Kops. The fans in the stands were laughing so hard they probably didn't even mind that the Raiders won the game, 28-27.

I remember that first trip to New York as being a good one for my personal growth because we stayed at the Concourse Plaza for a whole week. Thanks to Erdelatz's short practices, that gave me plenty of time to see New York.

Except for the NYPD's Keystone Kop escapade, I had never seen a play and that year was a great time to start. Within a week I saw *My Fair Lady, West Side Story* and *Gypsy*. I remember coming out of a show, seeing all the people dressed up and looking at the tall buildings and saying to myself, "This is a long way from the fields of Sanger in more ways than one."

But it was also a long way from a first class operation. Earlier that year when we went to play the Boston Patriots in a final preseason game, our team's travel agent was partying in New York and we had no itinerary. Nobody knew where the hell we were supposed to stay or practice or anything. We only knew that we're supposed to play in Amherst, Massachusetts. So when we get off the plane the only thing we know is to get on the busses that are waiting for us. But not even the bus drivers knew where we were supposed to go.

We were driving through Holyoke, Massachusetts, when Eddie Erdelatz told the bus driver to stop at some old hotel. Erdelatz and a few players jumped off the bus and went into the lobby.

"Got enough rooms for about 50 people?" Erdelatz asked the guy behind the counter.

"Hell, yes," he answered. "Nobody stays here."

That was us. Nobody. Sounded like the perfect spot, so Erdelatz signed us in.

We soon learned why nobody stayed there. For air conditioning in this hot, muggy place we had ceiling fans. The food, well, it seems like terrible food followed AFL teams wherever they went. After the worst lunch anybody ever had, Erdelatz loaded everybody into the bus that night and took us to an Italian restaurant for dinner. He paid for the whole thing himself.

The next day we still didn't know where we were supposed to be staying or practicing, so we struck out to find a field. We piled off the bus at this baseball field and began using the public restrooms for our locker room. George Anderson lined up the players outside on the grass to tape their ankles. It must have been a weird sight, all these big guys sitting next to a baseball field wearing nothing but jocks in some cases.

After about 45 minutes, the Holyoke Police showed Erdelatz what a really short practice was. They kicked us off the baseball field, saying that it was reserved for a Little League game. The way we looked, we couldn't have fooled them into thinking we were one of the Little League teams. We weren't that organized.

Finally it was game day and we drove towards Amherst, where we were supposed to play. When we got there people asked where we had been because we were expected two days earlier. We were supposed to have stayed in nice, new dorm rooms. The cafeteria, which at least had edible food, was reserved for us. And they had a field all ready for our practices.

Did this mean we were better than a bunch of Nobodies? Did this mean somebody even knew who the Oakland Raiders were? Well, sort of. The good people of Amherst put up a big sign that said it all: "Welcome Oklahoma Raiders."

Oh well, at least I finally made it in pro football, such as it was. All things considered, we did pretty well that year with a 6-8 record.

On March 25, 1961, I married that pretty little brunette that I first saw at College of Pacific with dog food on her head singing "How Much Is that Doggy in the Window?" I guess first impressions aren't everything.

In one of my typically romantic moments I finally said something like, "Why don't we get married?" This smooth approach obviously swept her off her feet because she agreed. We both had jobs teaching that spring—she in Hayward and me in Cupertino—so we settled into a nice little midway apartment in Newark.

Soon it was time to get in shape for training camp so I began recruiting kids in the neighborhood to play catch. It wasn't too bad. Some of them even knew who the Raiders were. I did fairly well that first season, completing 136 of 252 passes for 1,738 yards, with 12 touchdowns and 12 interceptions. We thought we would be better in 1961.

We were wrong.

The Raiders reorganized their ownership in 1961, but they didn't open up the bank books enough to improve the team. Other teams in the AFL were more aggressive signing their draft picks and getting better players. I think we signed only one draft pick, George Fleming, a running back out of Washington.

And it didn't take long to find out how bad we were. We lost our season opener to the Oilers in Houston, 55-0. I was damn near in shock. It wasn't just because of the rough handling the Oilers gave me—and they gave me plenty—but I had never, ever lost a game by such a lopsided score.

To make matters worse, we had to stay in town all night and listen to the sportscasters gloat about the Oilers' win. We couldn't fly out because of a hurricane. We finally took a train the next morning.

Then we went to San Diego, where the Chargers had moved when they couldn't get enough attention in Los Angeles. On that day, September 17, 1961, we didn't give Barron Hilton the type of competition on which he could build a decent rivalry. The Chargers mauled us, 44-0.

So we lost our first two games of the season by a combined score of 99-0 and were scheduled to open our home schedule at Candlestick. I wondered if there would be anybody at the game besides the players, coaches and their families.

One guy who wasn't at the game was Eddie Erdelatz. He was fired after the second loss. That wasn't too surprising because when a team loses, even if it's because management didn't get good players, the coach is the first one to get the ax. I've never seen the owner or management take the blame, even when they were obviously at fault. I'm sure Eddie told them to stick their job where the sun don't shine, like in their wallets, which obviously were kept in a dark, secluded place.

Marty Feldman was elevated from assistant to head coach, but most of the players were rather emotional over Eddie's firing. Looking back, those run-everywhere practices he had beginning at our first workout in Santa Cruz helped set a pace that got us through that first season looking fairly good. But we couldn't use sheer hustle to outplay teams that improved much more than we did in 1961.

However, I think we did win one more game for Eddie. As I said, we were emotional when he was fired and I think that carried over into our game against the Dallas Texans at Candlestick Park.

It was the type of free-scoring affair that became legendary in the AFL. We also spiced the game up with one of the wildest free-for-alls ever seen at Candlestick Park. It began after I ran out of bounds by at least three steps and their rookie linebacker, E. J. Holub, walloped my head with his elbow and knocked me out cold.

This wasn't the smartest of moves on his part because he did it on our side of the field. Everybody on our bench went after him, knocked him down, and all hell broke loose. I didn't see any of this first hand because I was in lala land. The first thing I saw when I tried to focus my eyes was George Anderson standing over me like a mother hen protecting an egg.

Anderson: *Holub took a real cheap shot at Tom and all hell broke loose with Tom lying there on the ground, gone to the world. So I'm there with an ammonia capsule trying to re-*

> *vive him and bodies are flying everywhere. He*
> *looks up and says 'Is that you George?' and*
> *his frigging eyes are each looking in a different*
> *direction. Tom won't bitch about it, but he*
> *didn't get much protection that year. In our*
> *first preseason game we played Houston in*
> *Honolulu and he got the shit knocked out of*
> *him. He was lying on the field and I went out*
> *and asked him how he was. He said, 'Well, I*
> *got spots in my eyes, my head hurts and I can't*
> *see very well.' I said, 'Tough shit, you've got to*
> *stay in because we don't have anybody else.' I*
> *walked off the field and he got up and finished*
> *the game."*

I watched that fight many times on film and the best part of it was when our defensive end, Charlie Powell, punched a Dallas player with a short right cross. Powell never played college football. He had been a heavyweight boxer instead. This Dallas player was one of his best knockouts. He went down like a sack of potatoes and they had to drag him away.

Of course the Texans became the Kansas City Chiefs and when I joined that franchise in 1969, Holub was still with them. The Chiefs had a highlight reel of their great fights and I watched that one with him. Holub accused me of running into his elbow.

Right.

The good news was that I got back into the game and we almost pulled out a victory, 42-35. It wasn't a win, but after losing our first two games by 99-0, plus our head coach, being in striking distance of a win was great.

We got no satisfaction in our second meeting with Dallas later that year. Not only did they mangle us, 43-11, but we had to spend Thanksgiving in the Big D. And that obviously didn't stand for Big Dinner. Our Thanksgiving Day meal was canned turkey. I got food poisoning but played the game anyway.

We lost our last six games, including our final three appearances at Candlestick. Houston, which beat us 55-0 to open the season, closed it out by belting us again, 47-16. In the stands, I could hear some of the fans yelling "We want Nick, we want Nick." They were calling for the other kid from Sanger, Nick Papac, who was my backup now.

Nick Papac: *I told Tom that I instructed my wife to start that chant in the stands so the coach would hear my name. Tom's such a nice guy that he thought I was kidding. OK, I was kidding. But I'm not kidding when I tell you Tom took a terrible beating that year and kept coming back and coming back. He played extremely well under the circumstances.*

Nick went to Cal, then into the service, then to Fresno State. He began 1961 with the Dallas Cowboys of the NFL but was waived and the Raiders picked him up. That was the only year he played for us, but we have stayed in touch and our wives became very good friends.

In fact, he tells a story that his wife was the one who started the "We want Nick" chant. Of course he's kidding. I think. I've always been suspicious about stories that Barbara actually started that chant because she was tired of seeing me beat up and wanted me out of the game. Of course that's just another joke. I think.

I managed to keep my job anyway, but we lost just about everything else, like 12 games and the franchise's first head coach. But it was a good year for me personally. I married Barbara and then learned we were expecting our first child. We felt we had a lot to look forward to in 1962. It turned out to be more than we could imagine.

six

1962

Losing 12 games in 1961 was good preparation for what was to follow because 1962 was the toughest year of my life. On second thought, nothing could have prepared me for what happened that year.

Our problems began early in December 1961, when I got home from a 21-day, three-loss road trip. I didn't feel very good because we just had our tails whipped, 43-11, by the Dallas Texans, who later became the Kansas City Chiefs. I rushed home to see Barbara, who was about seven months pregnant.

She looked worse than I felt. She was pale, tired, weak and nauseous. Although this was our first pregnancy, we knew something was extremely wrong. We were also concerned that she was getting even bigger than we expected.

At the hospital the next day we found out why she looked and felt so bad. It was hepatitis. That's bad enough under normal circumstances but is extremely dangerous if you are pregnant. She stayed in the hospital for two weeks and by the time she came home, thank God the season was over.

She was restricted to bed and had to stay on a strict diet. That was a major hardship because you need so much nourishment when you are pregnant. Her appetite wasn't much to begin with and what she was allowed to eat wasn't that high on the nourishment scale.

She also had a problem with false labor, so doctors took X-rays to make sure the baby was OK. That's when we found out why she was so big. Twins. They didn't know they were both boys, but they did know she was carrying twins. If Barbara had been well, that might have been a shock. But with all that was going on, her getting ill and me trying to finish a horrible season, the news about the twins was one of the best things we had heard. At least we knew why she was so big.

Unbeknownst to us, she didn't have hospitalization because when we got married we didn't change her insurance policy. We finally realized she was not covered when the bills began to kick back to us. What great news. Here Barbara is pregnant with twins and fighting hepatitis and we don't have insurance.

"Don't worry, Barb," I said boldly. "We'll get through this. What the hell else can happen?"

I shouldn't have asked.

Barbara did not enjoy our first anniversary on March 25 because she was too uncomfortable. On March 28 the twins were born. Barb went through terrible labor and finally they were taken Cesarean, Mark at 2:59 p.m., and

Scott one minute later. Mark was 5 pounds, 9 ounces. Scott, who received only one-third of his nourishment because the umbilical cord was fouled up, weighed only 3 pounds, 15 ounces.

Barb and Mark were able to come home after 10 days. Scott had to wait until he was gaining at least an ounce a day. He came home after 17 days. The combination of hepatitis and childbirth left Barb so tired she could hardly do a thing.

Her mother, Harriet Fridell, moved into our little Castro Valley apartment to help us take care of the babies for a while. Scott was so small he needed to be fed about every three hours. Harriet took the day shift while I was out selling Red Star fireworks. I would come home and take the night shift.

It went on like that for a month. Harriet was so tired she went home and slept 24 hours straight. Barb was far from 100 percent, but she was gaining strength. We thought we were just about over the hump, except for the bills from 17 days in the hospital. Damn insurance didn't pay any of it.

We used all of our savings to pay off the hospital for the birth of the twins and the entire stay.

"Don't worry, Barb," I said with conviction. "We're going to be fine. The worst is over. I'll be back playing football soon and we'll have more money coming in."

Wrong again.

In May I began working out to get ready for the season. I ran, threw the football and played softball. I also worked like mad selling fireworks. My contract with the Raiders that year called for $15,000, which was decent money in those days. Too bad I never got it.

By mid-May a constant cough began to bother me. After a week of this my ribs were sore from hacking so I went to see Dr. McCrea, who gave me some pills. After another four days of constant coughing, I went back to the doctor and he said I might have walking pneumonia.

Great. I'm trying to work days to make money, work out in the evenings to get in shape for football, and take the night shift feeding the babies because Barb is still weak with hepatitis. The coughing bothered me around the kids because I didn't want them to catch anything. Now the doctor says I have walking pneumonia and I should rest until I'm well.

Rest? I had to work. I had to take care of the babies. How the hell could I rest? Pretty soon I didn't have much choice. I coughed so much I couldn't sleep and my stomach was in pain. Why in hell do they call it walking pneumonia if you are too sore and too tired to walk?

I suspected something worse than pneumonia, walking or otherwise. During the long, sleepless hours I began to read one of those home medical journals. I read that constant coughing and night sweats could be warning signs for tuberculosis.

TB? Me? That's serious stuff. I couldn't have slept the rest of the night even if I did stop coughing. Nice going, Flores. Things aren't bad enough but you have to scare the hell out of yourself. Let's not hit the panic button.

The next week I was back at Eden Valley hospital for more X-rays. I was coughing every waking minute and my insides hurt so much I wanted to scream, but I didn't have the energy. I was worried about the babies because I didn't want them to get this damn thing. After the X-rays I sat in the office, coughing all over the place, for about an hour. Please, won't somebody do something?

A couple of doctors came into the waiting room and I didn't like the way they looked at me.

"Mr. Flores, please come with us," said one of them as he put an oxygen mask over my face and put me in a wheel chair. "We don't know what you have, but we would like you to stay here for some further tests. We don't know if you are contagious or not."

Contagious? God, would the kids be OK? They don't know what I have! Would I be OK? All these questions were going through my head as they wheeled me into the isolation ward. On one hand I was scared as hell, but on the other I was glad they were keeping me because maybe now I finally could be cured.

I tried to keep my voice steady as I called Barb.

"They're going to check me in and keep me for a while to take some tests," I said. "They had to put me in isolation so I didn't keep anybody awake with all this coughing. Don't worry, everything's going to get better now."

I hung up quickly so she couldn't hear me cry. I was scared to death. Don't worry? Everything's going to be fine? Hell, they don't even know what I have.

For a week I went through a series of tests. I had seven doctors look me over. I had a bronchoscopy, where they stick a tube into your lungs and look around. They took a biopsy of a spot that was on my left lung. They were trying to decide if they should operate to take out a part of my lung.

Before doing that, they called in one more specialist, Dr. Jason Farber from Oakland. He studied all the records, charts and X-rays, then said he had it narrowed down to a couple of possibilities. That was the good news.

"You either have bronchiectasis or tuberculosis," he said.

TB? Had my worst fear come true? Why couldn't I be wrong this one time? Once he said tuberculosis I could feel my heart pump faster. I was really scared. People die from TB. I was only 25 years old with a new wife and twin babies. This was supposed to be the beginning of my life, not the end. My mind raced as I pretended to hear every word. The doctor said it would take a while for everything to sink in.

He put me on some medicine, little granules, and

said they would wait to see if the spot went away. I already had taken every form of antibiotic known to medicine. I had gone through night sweats so bad that the nurse had to change the whole bed twice a night. The coughing became so painful and tiring that a couple of times I wondered if I had the energy, or desire, to take another breath.

When Barb brought the kids to visit me, they had to stay outside. They'd look up at me from the parking lot. I would wave out the window. Was this going to be their last memory of their father? Did I have just some lousy infection or was it TB?

Wayne Valley, one of the Raiders' owners, was a bull of a man in appearance and personality. He barged into my room one day with one of his loud pep talks.

"Kid," he barked as a big unlit cigar dangled from his lip. "I came here to scare the hell out of whatever it is you have. This is a great hospital and these people are going to make sure you are just fine. Try to relax and get strong. Don't worry about a thing."

Easy for him to say. He meant well, but I still worried.

George Dixon, who was an assistant coach at College of Pacific and with the Raiders, was another who managed to make it into isolation to see me. He brought a six pack of beer.

"I sneaked it in so you could have something besides medicine," he said as he pulled the beer from beneath his jacket. "I know what it's like in these dumps. A few of these beers and you'll feel a lot better."

I sure as hell couldn't feel much worse, but I turned him down anyway.

"What are you worried about?" he said. "They aren't going to arrest you for sleeping under the influence of alcohol."

The way things were going, I wouldn't have been surprised if they did make such an arrest. Hell, nothing was going right. George, bless his heart, had to sneak the six pack back out of the hospital. I told him to save it so we could celebrate when I got out. At that moment I was hoping I left on my feet, rather than feet first.

After 10 days in isolation I was feeling just good enough to have a sponge bath. After 12 days I was up and around and feeling almost human. Finally they took me out of isolation, gave me a roommate and let me take a shower.

I've had many showers after hot, sweaty games or working in the field, but this was one shower I never would forget. What a treat. After almost two weeks of sweating in bed, that shower felt like a wonderful massage as the water ran all over my body. I stayed in the shower so long that I was too tired to stand. So I sat on the floor and let the water run over me.

Then I went out and enjoyed having a roommate, which may be more than my roommate did. I'm usually not into idle chatter, but I talked this poor guy's ear off. It was just wonderful to have another human being to talk to. I don't think I shut up long enough for him to get a word in.

Finally, they let me go home. In a little more than two weeks I had lost 15 pounds, but the coughing finally stopped and I was beginning to feel stronger. As my appetite increased I put on some weight and even began working out.

"Attaway, Flores," I thought to myself. "Have a positive attitude. Never mind all that TB stuff because you are obviously improving, so forget it."

I bugged some kids in the neighborhood to play catch with me. I was feeling pretty chipper. Hell, I was getting ready to go to training camp with the Raiders.

"Barb, I think we can finally relax now," I said with newfound confidence. "We're finally going to pull out of this damn tailspin."

You would think I would have learned to shut up by that time. Nope.

After two weeks out of the hospital, I went into Dr. McCrea's for a routine checkup.

"Tom, I'm afraid I have some bad news for you," he said.

I was dumbfounded. I felt super. What could be wrong?

"The cultures came back and you have a form of tuberculosis," he said.

It was as if somebody hit me square in the face with a two-by-four. I was stunned. I felt my energy drain right out of me as if somebody pulled a plug. My legs were weak and wobbly and I all but fell into a chair.

"Ah, I thought, well..." I stammered for a while, not knowing what to say.

"It's that spot on your lung," he said. "It's about the size of a quarter. But you will need to be under the care of Dr. Farber from now on."

It was only a five or six block walk from the doctor's office to our apartment, but I was in such a daze that even now I do not remember the walk home. I went in the living room and as soon as Barb saw my face she knew all was not well.

"TB," I said in a shaky voice. Then I broke down and cried like a baby.

After finally regaining my strength and confidence, I wasn't prepared for another setback. If they had told me while I was tired and weak in the hospital, I could have taken it better. I was ready for anything then. Anything.

Now I was scared, angry and confused. TB? All I knew about it then was if you had it, you couldn't breathe on people. What about my baby boys? They would send you to the desert or something and you couldn't do anything physical. What about my football career?

"This type of TB is not communicable," said Dr. Farber. "You can be out in public. But you can't overexert yourself. That means no football. Don't even think about it until
that spot is totally gone."

He gave me some of those granules and said I would
have to take them three times a day for three years. After
that I would take pills for two more years.

In the meantime, there we were with those two
little babies less than four months old and I had no job
and no money. What little money we did have coming
in didn't make a noticeable dent in our medical bills
alone.

I wrote a letter to everybody we owed money to and
explained the situation. I promised we would pay off every
penny. Some people, bless their souls, went out of their
way to be helpful. Dr. George Prlain, whom I didn't even
know that well at the time, saw both the boys for the price
of one.

However, I also remember writing a check to Standard Oil for $3.25 and had it bounce.

We moved in with Barb's parents, Harriet and
Squire, in Orinda. Barb's brother, Skeeter, was away at College of Pacific, so Mark stayed in his room with Barb's younger brother, Hank. Scott slept in the dining room and Barb
and I took over her old room.

Barb wasn't totally over the hepatitis, but she felt
strong enough to apply for a job. She was selected from 40
applicants and got a job teaching in Moraga.

I still managed to make headlines for the Raiders
in the sports section that season. George Ross, sports edi-
tor of the *Oakland Tribune*, gave me a job writing a pre-
game and a post-game story from a players' point of view
each week.

I was on disability and couldn't accept cash, so Ross
gave me a nice gift certificate at the end of the season.

That's how we bought Christmas presents for the boys on their first Christmas.

After that, I may have been the happiest person in the world on New Year's Day. I couldn't wait to bid good riddance to 1962.

seven

Raiders Revisited— This IS Pro Football

Only after he cleared me to play football again in April of 1963 did Dr. Farber admit that he originally thought I would be out at least two or three years, maybe forever.

"Tom, this is one of those times when I'm glad to be wrong," he said. "The spot on your lung is gone and I see no reason why you can't play football."

He thought I recovered so quickly because I was young and in such good shape. However, I had to continue to get regular checkups and take the same medicine for another five years.

During the one year I didn't play a lot of things happened to the Raiders, most of them bad. The losing streak we started at the end of 1961 was continued for another 13 games, setting a franchise record that may stand forever, 19 consecutive losses.

After five games in 1962, Marty Feldman was released as head coach and Red Conkright finished out the season. The only win of the year came on the final game by 20-0 over the Boston Patriots at little Frank Youell Field, in Oakland. As a sportswriter, I was one of only 8,000 who watched that win in person. And that little group of fans sounded like 50,000 after the game as they honked their horns and started a parade of cars into the Oakland streets.

There were fears after the 1962 season that the Raiders might be sold or move. They lost $500,000 or more in each of their first three years. Groups from Portland, New Orleans and Seattle were interested in buying the struggling AFL franchise that had a combined 9-33 record in its initial three seasons.

Historians might consider it an ironic touch that the Raiders might have moved out of Oakland in the early 1960s if it weren't for one man—Al Davis.

In 1963 Wayne Valley was looking for a new head coach and asked me if I had ever heard of Al Davis. I had heard his name once when some assistant coaches at COP were talking about this guy who was an assistant at USC. I didn't remember much, but I did recall hearing the word "ruthless" several times, as well as a few other words that aren't necessary to repeat. Even from what little I heard that day at COP, I was curious how this Al Davis guy could create such an emotional reaction. I figured he must be one hell of a competitor.

I told Wayne Valley about the little conversation I overheard about Davis and that he sounded like a hell of a fighter who would do anything to win.

"Sounds like an interesting guy," said Valley.

Two weeks later the Raiders named Al Davis as head

coach and general manager. Within a few days of his hiring, Davis summoned me to his office.

He seemed to be curious about everything from my bout with tuberculosis and the welfare of my family to the personnel of the team and my grasp of football strategy. I had heard that he loved to talk personnel and strategy, but I was surprised when he spent so much time talking about non-football things such as my illness and my family and my background.

Eventually he was standing at the chalkboard drawing Xs and Os all over the place, talking faster and faster and saying how the bottom line was throwing the ball deep. Then he suddenly turned around and saw me smiling.

"What the hell are you smiling about, do you think this is funny?" Davis said.

I was startled because he was acting as if I were laughing at him, which was hardly the case.

"No, not at all," I said. "I'm smiling because this is what I always thought football was all about, throwing the ball deep. That's the one thing I know I can do, throw the ball."

Davis then sat down and leveled with me about my place on the team. He said that some people in the organization believed I wouldn't be able to make it back from my illness. That's why the team went out and signed some other quarterbacks.

At the time I admit I wasn't in the best of shape. I couldn't do much until the doctor gave me clearance and then I went out and played in College of Pacific's Spring Game. My arm felt great, but I was a little overweight so I think some people in the Raider organization panicked.

Al Davis: *Tom was tall as quarterbacks went in those days. He was bright and he could put the ball up top. But the main thing about*

Tom was he was courageous. When I was with the Chargers in 1961, Oakland's center Jim Otto mouthed off that he would handle defensive tackle Ernie Ladd and Ladd said he would make mush out of him. But it was Flores who took the beating by Ladd that day. We won by 44-0 and Tom was sacked six times for 72 yards. I remembered how he kept coming back and standing right in that pocket. I knew I could get him better protection on the inside so he could see downfield. He had the ability to get that ball out there. He was a quality player.

Al said he had faith that I would come around. He said he was going to go easy on me at the start of training camp to let me break back into football a little easier after being out for a year with my lung condition.

I made only one mistake. I believed him.

When we got in training camp I thought I was going to die. He worked me at least as hard as everybody else, probably harder. At first I thought he forgot about what he told me because I kept waiting for him to take it easy. I thought if this is what he calls breaking me in easy, I wonder what it would be like if I hadn't been ill.

We moved our training camp to Santa Rosa in 1963, so it was much hotter during our practices in Sonoma Valley than it had been in the coastside town of Santa Cruz. We stayed at the El Rancho Motel, which also provided us with two football fields for practice.

Then there was the food. It was better than at the Palomar in Santa Cruz and the motel in Holyoke, Mass. Still, it wasn't anything that made you rush to the chow line. I guess mom just spoiled me with those cheese enchiladas. But I had no complaints. At least I was back in pro football.

To say that Al Davis had fascinating ideas about football strategy is like saying the Bible is a pretty good book on religion.

It seemed that Al had an uncanny ability to apply everything he saw, learned or experienced in life to football. So it was that his football theories were much like his life. Different.

His was not the story of a poor kid who struggled from the bottom. The son of a successful but demanding garment-maker, Al was raised in Brooklyn with more than the average amenities.

Still, he grew up street-tough and refused to be insulated from reality by his parents' money as he went through school. For him sports were concentrated reality. It was a single arena in which he could grapple with the physical, mental, emotional and even financial aspects of life.

Al always seemed to have a different perspective on sports. Some of his memories of competing as a youth are the same as mine and everybody else's. But judging by what he still remembers to this day, he always looked beyond his individual battle and even the individual games or seasons. He always seemed to be looking at a bigger picture.

Instead of going to any of the private schools in his own neighorhood, Al traveled across town to Flatbush to attend Erasmus Hall High, well known for its great sports teams. He played football, baseball and basketball there. But, of course, he did more than play. He absorbed.

His basketball coach was local legend Al Badain, who scoured the summer camps in the Catskill Mountains and the asphalt courts of Brooklyn to find players to plug into his system. Badain would take anybody, regardless of color or reputation, if they could help the team. He became famous for making championship teams from kids who were shunned by others because they were incorrigibles or renegades. Does any of this sound familiar?

Al managed to watch baseball and basketball and somehow convert what he saw to football strategy. He admired the tenacity of Eddie Stanky, a pugnacious infielder for the Brooklyn Dodgers and New York Giants who went on to manage several major league teams. Stanky always gave his players the green light on the bases, which was unusual in those days. This kept pitchers and catchers uneasy. Al was tremendously influenced by UCLA coach John Wooden's zone press defense, which, even before the Bruins had great players, would rattle bigger, more talented teams into submission.

At times Al would talk about those and other things that somehow contributed to his football concepts. Watching Stanky's teams raise hell on the bases planted a seed in Al that grew to become his love of the constant threat of a long touchdown. Wooden's zone press was the genesis of the Raiders' famous bump-and-run defense.

"Fear and pressure," Al would say. "That's the key. You make sure that the opposing defense goes to bed the night before a game knowing, fearing, that they will be facing somebody who can beat them deep on any play. Let them stay awake all night worrying about it. And their offense should go to bed knowing that nothing will come easy, not even short passes. They know that we will pressure them with bump and run coverage all over the field."

Before coming to the Raiders, Al had the good fortune to be an assistant coach for the Chargers' Sid Gillman, who may be the most knowledgeable man in the history of football on the passing game. As a receivers coach for the Chargers, Al broke down films on every receiver and every quarterback in the league. He absorbed everything Gillman said and everything he saw on those films.

Of course he would need all the help he could get considering the Raiders lost 25 of their previous 28 games over two years.

Al urged us to go for the home run. If the bomb is there, go for it. A lot of teams looked for the bomb, but didn't go for it as frequently. Davis told us to always go for the deep six, even if what we called in the huddle was a good play. Like Stanky, he gave his players the green light.

To make this a real threat, Al wanted that one great wide receiver that opponents knew they would have to double team. So he went out and signed Art Powell, who had played out his option with the New York Jets. Al knew Powell had already signed with the Buffalo Bills under the table, but Buffalo had not submitted the contract to the league office because they thought they would have to compensate the Jets. Al didn't care. He went to Powell's home in Toronto, signed him and sent the contract to the league office.

I knew we had the kind of receiver who would keep defensive backs awake the night before a game. I still had nightmares about covering him in college. He went to San Jose State and as a cornerback at College of Pacific I had to cover him. The only reason he didn't embarrass me was that San Jose didn't throw to him a lot, thank God. I even had an interception covering him once. He slipped and fell and the quarterback threw the ball right into my chest. I was about eight yards away from Powell. Great coverage.

Powell wasn't a speed merchant type of receiver, but he was so good that defenses always had to double him or pay the consequences. So we spun everything around him. We'd send him across an area and pfft, it was cleaned out so another receiver would be wide open there. Everybody was trying to play man coverage in those days and he made it damn near impossible.

If they paid too much attention to him, we could always go deep to somebody else. That's mostly what we did with Bo Roberson, a world class sprinter who really wasn't that great of a receiver. But when he stretched a defense, they couldn't ignore him. Soon defenses found that between Powell and Roberson they were being stretched beyond the point of being able to cover.

Next Davis introduced "East Formation," which slotted Powell inside Roberson, usually on the right side. Teams were so stubborn about changing in those days that they usually tried to cover Powell with a safety on that side while leaving the cornerback on the weak side. When they finally did wise up and bring a corner over to cover the slot receiver, Al threw something else at them, a great pass-catching halfback.

Clem Daniels wasn't the kind of halfback that a defense could cover successfuly with a linebacker. So when defenses reacted to our East Formation by putting both cornerbacks on one side, we sent the halfback out on the other side. When defenses finally realized they needed to cover Daniels with at least a safety, we sent him deep to occupy the safety and then forced them to cover one of our tight ends, either Bob Mischak or Ken Herock, with a linebacker.

Until the early 1960s, tight ends had been slow, plodding guys who were used mainly for blocking. But the Chicago Bears were using tight end Mike Ditka as a big play receiver and the Baltimore Colts had the great John Mackey. In 1964 Davis upgraded the tight end position by getting Billy Cannon, a former Heisman Trophy winner from LSU who was disenchanted as a running back with the Houston Oilers. He was the first of a series of great tight ends the Raiders would have, including Raymond Chester, Dave Casper and Todd Christensen, who like Cannon was formerly a running back.

By 1964, using Al's offense and new players, we stretched defenses to the breaking point. That year Powell caught 76 passes for 1,361 yards and 11 touchdowns. Roberson caught 44 for 624, Daniels 42 for 696 and Cannon and

Herock totalled another 60 catches for more than 800 yards and 6 touchdowns.

Al's defenses were just as innovative. I'm just glad I didn't have to play against them.

All the changes we went through in 1963 brought the change that Al wanted the most, in our record. The Raiders pulled off the biggest turnaround in pro football history, going from 1-13 in 1962 to 10-4.

Thanks to our wide open passing game, I was able to do the one thing I like the most, throw the ball. I finished third in the AFL, completing 113 of 247 passes for 2,101 yards and 20 touchdowns, despite splitting time with another quarterback, Cotton Davidson.

The season began the opposite of that horrible 1961 season when we lost the first two games by 99-0 and coach Eddie Erdelatz was fired. In 1963 we opened in Houston with a 35-13 win, then beat Buffalo, 35-17, in Oakland. It was obvious that Davis wasn't going to get the Erdelatz treatment.

However, we did have some problems after that, losing four games in a row. This didn't surprise anybody because the Raiders were picked to finish dead last and those first two wins were as many as we were expected to have all season.

So we surprised everyone except ourselves when we finished off the season with eight consecutive victories, including two classics over the Chargers, who went on to win the AFL Championship that year with an 11-3 record.

If Barron Hilton wanted a rivalry, he sure as hell had one. We beat them for the first time ever, 34-33, in San Diego, then swept the series with a 41-27 win at a sold out Frank Youell Field. Of course sold out was only 20,249, but that was the noisest 20,249 anyone ever heard. We gave the

AFL champions two of their three losses. They went on to dominate the Boston Patriots in the title game, 51-10.

After our second win over the Chargers we had only two games left, against the Denver Broncos and the Houston Oilers. Until then I had a pretty good year, but I split a lot of playing time with Cotton Davidson. The next two were all mine and turned a pretty good year into a damned good one.

First I warmed up against the Broncos by completing 11 of 21 passes for 272 yards and five touchdowns. That set the stage for the last game of the season, against venerable old George Blanda and the Houston Oilers.

Old? What am I saying? George was *only* 36 years old when we played that game in 1963. It was *only* his 14th season. But I was only 26 years old and in only my third season, so George seemed plenty old to me. Little did I know that George would go on to play 26 seasons, including nine for the Raiders and four while I was an assistant coach.

I should have realized on December 22, 1963, how much spunk Blanda still had when we ended the season with some fireworks in one of those classic, whoever-has-the-ball-last-will-win, AFL games. At halftime the score was 35-35 and I can still hear Blanda bitching and moaning as he walked off the field.

"Thirty-five lousy points and we're still tied with these son of a bitches," he screamed at nobody in particular and everybody in general. "Shit. Crap. I can't believe it. What the hell is going on out here. We've scored enough points to win two games."

I learned later that George was such a competitor that he never accepted anything short of a victory. He didn't accept mistakes by others, but he was hardest on himself. I recall being in the locker room years later when he missed a field goal that would have won a game and a reporter made the mistake of asking him what happened.

"What happened?" he screamed. "You saw what the hell happened. I kicked the bleeping ball and it didn't go through the uprights. I missed, that's all that matters. I have no damned excuses, if that's what you want to hear. I'm supposed to make the bleeping field goals and I missed. That's what happened."

I can only imagine what Blanda was like in the locker room after our game in 1963. He completed 20 of 32 passes for 342 yards and 5 touchdowns. But I had the best game of my career, completing 17 of 29 passes for 407 yards and 6 touchdowns. Still, the hero of the game turned out to be our kicker, Mike Mercer, who went in with about 20 seconds left and made a field goal that gave the Raiders a 52-49 win.

So I finished the season with 11 touchdowns in the last two weeks and I was third in the AFL in passing. I thought that was a pretty good comeback for me as well as the Raiders. l felt I should have gone to the AFL All-Star game that year. Cotton Davidson won some games for us and played quite a bit, but I finished the season as the clear-cut starter and I finished third in the league in passing. His statistics were almost exactly half of my numbers right down the board and he was eighth in the league in passing.

However, when the season was over our public relations manager Scotty Stirling called me in and said that Chargers' Sid Gillman, who was coaching the West All-Stars, wanted one of our quarterbacks and he got Cotton Davidson on the phone. I immediately thought that was totally wrong because there was no question I deserved to go. I started more games and I had the better year.

Cotton and I were roommates and close friends. After Gillman called him, Cotton called me and said "Tom, you deserve to go, but hell, I don't want to just turn down a big opportunity like this." He was calling me from his home in Texas and I'm in the Raiders office in Oakland. We decided to be fair and flip a coin. We flipped and I lost and I was pissed, really upset. Cotton went and had a great game, throwing the ball all over the place and winning an MVP award.

I went to my own bowl game, the bowling alley. After we flipped the coin, I went home and told Barbara what happened, then went to the bowling alley. I bowled all by myself for a long time, trying to get rid of the anger.

I never did. I still get pissed when I think about it, but until now I don't think I ever really said anything publicly. I don't want to be somebody who goes around griping about something that happened in the past, but that was hard to take. It was a lousy way to end such a great season.

After the Raiders' great finish in 1963, we didn't sneak up on anybody the next season. In fact, we managed only one win and one tie in our first nine games as I continued to split time with Cotton Davidson.

We finished with a 5-7-2 record, Al's only losing season as a head coach and the Raiders last losing mark for 25 years. But despite the bad record, we did finish on another upbeat note that firmly established a winning tradition. In our final five games, we had four wins and one tie, including victories in the last two games over the teams that would play for the AFL Championship.

The most dramatic game in that stretch drive was a 16-13 last-play win over the Buffalo Bills. Trailing 13-10, we got the ball on our own 25 yard line at 1:55 for one last try to pull it out. I completed six consecutive passes to put us on the Bills' one-yard line with four seconds left.

By this time everybody at the game was crowded around the sidelines, and there were more than 18,000 at Frank Youell Field that day. And I think the whole place new what we were going to do. Art Powell, our big play receiver, was being covered by Butch Byrd, who was a tenacious cornerback. All eyes were on that matchup.

Art ran into the end zone, broke to the outside and I threw it high so he could go up in the air for it. He went up and muscled it down and the place went crazy. They picked up Art Powell and carried him around the field. I tried to run to get off the field and somebody had a hold of me and I was slapping the guys hand. He was holding my waist and I was dragging him and I turned around and saw he was a buddy of mine from Sanger.

So we won 16-13 and because of all the people on the field there was no way we could even try a PAT, but because that was the last play it didn't matter.

That was one of only two losses the Bills had that year as they went on to beat the San Diego Chargers, 20-7, for the AFL championship. But not until after we beat the Chargers ourselves, 21-20, in the last game of the regular season.

As a young coach Al Davis was more intense, more focused on every little detail, than anybody I ever saw before or since. The remarkable thing about it was that he never had a game plan or a list of plays in his hand. He just ran the show, the offense, defense, everything without anything to refer to but his own mind.

His intensity was so overwhelming that sometimes he got carried away trying to control things. I mean sometimes there are things that you just can't control. One day I was throwing in a drill after practice and I stopped in the middle of a throw because a receiver fell down. I felt a pop in my bicep and it was like I had been shot. I felt my arm and there was a hole in my muscle, a hole in my bicep.

George Anderson, our trainer, saw what happened and was next to me within seconds. He told me I tore the bicep from where it connects near my shoulder. He immediately took me in and encased my arm in ice. I'm sitting there wondering if I'll ever be able to throw again and all of a sudden Al comes in.

"Is that the coldest ice you have?" he asked.

I looked down at George and saw him grit his teeth.

"Al," he said, "this is the only friggin' ice we have."

Here I am in pain and wondering if I'll ever be able to throw again and I'm trying to stop from laughing. Maybe I was in shock from the injury. But at that moment Al's intensity, his desire to do things above and beyond normal, struck me funny. Colder ice? What the hell was he thinking about, dry ice or something?

Another time we were playing the Jets in Shea Stadium and somebody missed a block and we fumbled. As I'm coming off the field, Al confronts me. I tell him we missed an assignment because our center missed a line call.

Jim Otto is our center and he rarely made those kind of mistakes, but he did this time. He needs to make calls to the other linemen when the defense switches. That way each guy knows exactly whom to block, so you don't get two on one and nobody on another.

Anyway, that's what happened. A simple mistake by the center, which is what I tell Al.

"It's not my fault that the center misses a call," I said.

"Then *you* make the damn call," Al screamed as he walked away.

I couldn't help but chuckle because I tried to picture a quarterback calling the signals and making line calls at the same time. What am I supposed to do, stop right in the middle of calling signals, lean over and tell the linemen "you block him and you block him?"

But that's how intense Al is during a game. And I believe that deep inside he expects the quarterback to be an extension of his thinking and take care of everything. That's why a lot of players get nervous just being around Al.

I remember one time I became extremely nervous. It happened during a wet and muddy game in Houston's Jepperson Stadium.

We're on about Houston's five yard line and I throw a pass that's intercepted. This guy starts running it back up the sideline in the mud and I figure I better catch him because I threw the damn ball. I take an angle and get as close as I can at about the 40 yard line and make a dive for him. I miss and go face down, splashing mud everywhere.

When I finished sliding I'm staring at these two black shoes. I know who they belong to without looking up. Al. Not only did I throw an interception when we were so close to a touchdown, but the ball was returned for a score the other way because I also missed the tackle. And when I did, I splashed mud all over Al.

I didn't even look up. I scrambled to my feet and walked over to the bench. After the game somebody asked him about all the mud and I heard him say 'Oh, that freaking Flores.' I thought that he was more angry about the interception than the mud, but I never asked.

The Raiders got back on the right track in 1965 with an 8-5-1 record that they repeated in 1966. That was the year we had a famous game against the New York Jets in Shea Stadium, which is so close to LaGuardia Airport that you can't hear a thing when the planes are revving up to take off.

With the final seconds ticking off—and I mean 14, 13, 12—we were on the Jets' one yard line with no time outs left, trailing 21-17. But at that moment the Jets that bothered me most were the ones at LaGuardia.

The planes are revving up while I'm at the line trying to call a play as I look at the clock—11, 10, 9 . . . Our halfback, Clem Daniels, says "What?" He couldn't hear me above the planes. So I make the call a second time, but between the 58,000-plus fans and the planes I can't even hear myself. This time three players scream "What?

Now my insides are really churning as I scream the play a third time and look at the clock—8, 7, 6. Otto snaps the ball, I hand to Hewritt Dixon and he scores the winning touchdown. Two seconds left.

"There were still two seconds left, we had plenty of time," guard Wayne Hawkins explained to a reporter after the game. "Tom wasn't a bit nervous. He acted like he had all day out there. Hell, he was so cool he even called the play three times just to make sure we got it right. That's why they call him 'The Ice Man.'"

By 1966, Al's intensity and ability to turn things around were so well known that he was named Commissioner of the AFL, which was at war with the National Football League and its commissioner, Pete Rozelle.

After Al joined the Raiders, our weekly agendas would say "We Go to War" for the time of our kickoffs. Most teams would just say "Game time" or "Kickoff" but Al thought "We Go to War" set the proper tone.

The NFL soon found out what it meant when Al Davis would Go to War. He was named AFL Commissioner on April 8. On June 8, NFL Commissioner Pete Rozelle signed a merger agreement with the AFL. Al's tactics were as blatant as his offense. He went right for the jugular.

He got the AFL to sign as many of the NFL's starting quarterbacks as possible. They received contracts that included big signing bonuses and huge salaries. Quarterbacks who still had contracts in place were offered deals that secured their services as soon as their existing NFL contract ran out.

The NFL had to merge or it would lose its biggest attractions, quarterbacks. This, of course, was the event that laid the foundation for the animosity between Al Davis and Pete Rozelle in later years. Under terms of the merger, the two leagues would have a common draft and a common schedule and, of course, only one commissioner. Rozelle got that job. Davis didn't want to be a lame duck commissioner so he returned to the Raiders.

When Al became commissioner, John Rauch was given the Raiders' head coaching job. Wayne Valley, the Raiders owner who suggested to the AFL that Al would be a good commissioner, believed Davis would return to coaching. Like many others before and since, Valley misjudged Al.

Davis returned to the Raiders in August as a managing general partner on a ten-year contract that gave him complete control of the operation. He was also given 10 percent of the franchise for the sum of $18,500, which turned out to be one hell of a deal considering the San Diego Chargers were sold later that year for almost $10 million.

Still, there was a feeling among many of us on the team and in the organization that Al would return to coaching. After all, it was his choice. He kept that belief alive by coming to practices. But when the Raiders crawled out to a 1-3 start and he made no move to become head coach, some of us quit thinking he would coach.

So we played the 1966 season with John Rauch as head coach. We rebounded from that bad start to finish 8-5-1 for the second year in a row. I had my best season, completing 151 of 306 passes for 2,638 yards with 24 touchdowns and 14 interceptions.

I was one of 12 Raiders who made the All-Star team, which shows how much respect we had in the AFL. Looking back, I probably didn't know how much young potential that team had. Among the guys who made the AFL All Star game alone were center Jim Otto, as usual, guard Wayne Hawkins, wide receiver Art Powell, running back Clem

Daniels, defensive linemen Ike Lassiter, Tom Keating and Ben Davidson, linebacker Dan Connors, and defensive backs Kent McCloughan and Dave Grayson.

I guess it was appropriate, then, that Rauch coached the West All Stars. Little did I know that would be my last game wearing a Raiders helmet.

We had a lot of fun in the off-season. I was looking forward to making a big run for a championship. I was so into it that when it was time for the college player draft, I was really curious to see who we would get. I felt that the Raiders were on the brink of greatness.

On March 15, 1967 I got a call from Scotty Stirling, who was the team's general manager.

"Hey, Scotty," I said. "How did we do in the draft?"

"Tom," he said in a soft voice. "We just traded you to the Buffalo Bills."

"Right, Scotty, quit joking around," I said, totally believing that this was just another typical Raider joke.

"No," he said, his voice more firm now.

"You're not kidding, are you Scotty?" I heard myself say.

"Nope."

You talk about a shock. One minute I'm giddy because I think the Raiders are on the verge of being a championship team with me as their quarterback. The next moment I'm not a Raider. I'm shuffled off to Buffalo. I was stunned, hurt, sad, angry, maybe every negative emotion. I was with this team from the very start in Santa Cruz and now that we were ready to reach the top, I'm sent away, banished to Buffalo.

I went through the motions for the rest of that day, answering phone calls from long-time teammates who were pissed off, from the media in Buffalo, from the media in the Bay Area, and from Al Davis, who wished me well and said his door was always open to me. At the time, of course, I thought it was just a kind gesture. I also thought that was more than John Rauch gave me. He didn't even phone.

I finally ran into Rauch at a function in May when I was presented with an award. I felt kind of hollow because all the Raiders were there, laughing, happy and optimistic. I felt like I was on the outside looking in. When it was time to accept my award, I couldn't hide my feelings.

"I wish you all good luck," I said from the podium. "But don't have too good a year because if you do they'll trade you."

I could see some of the people with the Raiders cringe. I was bitter. I didn't feel that a trade was justified. At the time it looked like a great deal for Buffalo. The Raiders gave up me, Art Powell, and a second round draft choice for Buffalo's Daryle Lamonica, wide receiver Glenn Bass and the Bills' third and fifth round picks. Powell and I were both starters who made the All-Star team. Lamonica and Bass were backups on the AFL championship team.

As it turned out, I went to Buffalo and beat out Jack Kemp for the starting job only to hurt my knee in the opening game against the Jets. I spent the season as a backup. I completed only 22 of 64 passes for 260 yards, no touchdowns and eight interceptions.

What I didn't know before the trade was that people in Buffalo were down on Jack Kemp and liked Daryle Lamonica. They booed Kemp unmercifully. When I didn't get the starting job, they hated me for that, too. I remember walking in downtown Buffalo and somebody yelled "Hey, Flores, go back to Oakland." Hell, I wanted to go back, at least they were winning there.

While the Bills went from Eastern Division champions in 1966 to a 4-10 team in 1967, the Raiders did exactly what I expected. I had mixed emotions as Oakland went 13-1 and represented the AFL in the second Super Bowl. Lamonica led the league by throwing for more than 3,000 yards and 30 touchdowns. To be honest, when they lost to the Green Bay Packers in Super Bowl II, I had a difficult time even watching the game.

Because our season in Buffalo was over early, I was back in the Oakland area for the playoffs. In fact, Barbara and I spent New Years at my favorite place, the Elegant Farmer in Oakland, which was a hangout for a lot of Raiders players. All anybody wanted to talk about was how great the Raiders were.

I remember I was introduced to somebody who said "Tom Flores? Didn't you used to play for the Raiders?" Talk about how soon they forget. I thought of the old saying, "A winner has a thousand fathers and a loser is an orphan." I felt like an orphan that day. When they played Auld Lang Syne the words had a special meaning for me. Happy New Year.

Six years later, when I returned to the Raiders as a coach, another assistant coach told me that he was in the room when John Rauch said he wanted to trade me because I was a trouble maker. What a bunch of crap.

My guess was that Rauch was bothered by the fact that I was a player rep. Every time there was a problem everybody would come to me and I had to relay the complaint to management or the coaching staff. In the All-Star game after the 1966 season the Chiefs players were worn out because they had just played in the Super Bowl. They wanted me to tell Rauch to take it easy because he was having two-a-day workouts. I guess that may have been the crowning blow for this touble maker to tell him to take it easy in an All-Star practice.

I was just representing the other players, but I guess it rubbed Rauch the wrong way and he traded me. In reality I feel deep inside that I helped save his ass in 1966 because at the beginning of the year, when we were 1-3, I wasn't even starting. All due respect to Cotton Davidson, but he shouldn't have been starting because he just came off surgery. When I became the starter we began to win and I finished with my best pro season.

Anyway, all I know for a long time is that Rauch doesn't like me for some reason and he was the one who traded me without even having the common courtesy to give me a phone call. I admit I dwelled on this while I was a backup in 1967 and then when I was sidelined by a freak injury—I ruptured a chest muscle—in 1968. We went 1-12-1 that year and Joe Collier was fired before the season was through.

Next thing I know the Bills hire John Rauch as their new head coach in early 1969. Together again. What fun. Here I am coming off an injury in the option year of my contract and I get a head coach who already traded me away because he doesn't like me. Barbara and I had already decided that she and the kids would join me in Buffalo this year because we already had spent the 1968 season apart. But I told here to hold off until we see what happens.

When I get to Buffalo and Rauch calls me in and asks why I haven't signed my new contract yet.

"Because I don't think you want me to be here," I said.

"Why do you feel like that?" he asks.

"No reason in particular, it's just the way I feel," I said.

He didn't agree or disagree. He just sat there. I felt that confirmed my feelings.

A week before the final cut, I go to Rauch and tell him I want to bring my wife and family out to Buffalo. I tell him I'm a big boy and would understand if he suggested I didn't. He told me to go ahead and bring them out. But for some reason I didn't.

We went into the season with Jack Kemp and I and James Harris, a big, strong, athletic rookie who is obviously the quarterback of the future. Kemp has a no-cut contract and I have no contract, so I have to wonder what my role will be. After the second league game it was obvious I wasn't in line for a raise, so I went in and told Rauch I would sign for the same amount I received the year before.

"Tom," he said. "We have decided to let you go."

Once again Rauch had stuck it to me. I was stunned. The worse thing you can do to a quarterback is keep him through the entire training camp and then let him go early in a season. It's difficult to get quarterbacks to fit into a system without a training camp.

"I don't know what I ever did to you," I told him. "But this time you really screwed me."

As I'm walking out he tells me if no other teams pick me up, then he would like me to stay on the Bills' taxi squad.

Sure as hell, I clear waivers and I'm back in his office two days later.

"No calls or anything, so I'd like to take you up on your offer," I said.

"Sorry, Tom." he responded. "I can't do that for you."

Next thing you know I'm on my way back to California wondering what in the hell I ever did to deserve such crappy treatment from Rauch. By the time I got home, Barbara says she received a couple of phone calls from people who wanted to know how I was. I chalked it up to friends who were concerned that I felt bad emotionally or something.

But when I called Hank Stram of the Kansas City Chiefs, I begin to get the feeling that something is weird.

"Tell me, Tom, how are you?" Stram asks in a way that showed more than the usual curiousity. "Are you in good shape? Is your arm OK?"

I tell him I'm fine and he says to jump on the next plane and get out to Kansas City so he could take a look at me. I flew that night, threw for them the next morning and signed a contract in the afternoon.

When I called Barb to tell her, she said that Wayne Hawkins phoned to see how my arm was. Apparently when Rauch waived me there suddenly was a rumor going around the league that I couldn't throw more than 35 yards because there was something wrong with my arm. I don't know for certain who started that rumor, but it was the kind that can end a quarterback's career and I only know one guy who did a lot to wreck mine.

Suddenly it was clear to me why nobody picked me up on waivers and why Stram was so curious about my health. I talked to Paul Maguire, a friend of mine on the Bills team, and we both agreed who we thought spread the rumor.

About a month later the Chiefs play the Bills and while I'm warming up Maguire stands on the 50 yard line and yells, "Hey, Flores I thought you couldn't throw more than 35 yards," which he thinks is pretty funny. Paul was never one of Rauch's favorites, but Paul probably preferred it that way.

That year I threw only six passes, completing three, including one for a touchdown. It turned out to be the last action I saw as a player because I spent the entire 1970 season on the Chiefs' reserve list. However, my final games in uniform were not only memorable, but historically significant.

The 1969 season was the last for the American Football League. Terms of the merger called for the AFL to become part of the National Football League in 1970. The ten AFL teams plus Pittsburgh, Baltimore and Cleveland became the American Football Conference.

So 1969 marked the last battle for an AFL championship. I am proud that I was one of the original AFL players who stayed for the duration. There were only about 19 players who competed in every season of the AFL's existence. I am not counted because I sat out 1962 when I was ill. I think I should be counted, because I was on the Raiders' reserve list that season, but there's no point in making a big deal about that.

The final AFL championship game, in fact the very last contest between two AFL teams, was the Oakland Raiders vs. the Kansas City Chiefs on January 4, 1970. Len Dawson was our starting quarterback and I didn't play against my former teammates, but I'd like to think I made an impact.

During a quarterback meeting before that game, Stram asked me to take over and describe the Chiefs' approach to the Raiders. I was surprised and pleased that he gave me what may be considered my first opportunity to coach a pro football team.

First I went over the Raiders' personnel, which was pretty impressive. For our offense, I basically said that there were three key people to control, defensive tackle Tom Keating, linebacker Dan Conners and safety Dave Grayson. The Raiders used a four-man line that shifted to both the strong and weak side, but Keating was always over the center and had to be handled. Conners was a big play guy. And Grayson had to be neutralized by the quarterback looking him off.

I gave a couple of tips to our defense that may have been even more helpful. First, I said that whenever the Raiders lined up in their three-wide receiver, East Formation inside the 30-yard line that the man in the slot usually would run a pattern to the corner of the end zone. One of the best battles in the game was expected to be between Raiders tackle Bob Svihus and Chiefs defensive end Aaron Brown. I told Brown that Svihus had a tendency to open up too much against an outside rush, making him vulnerable to a cutback type move on an inside rush.

Svihus was one of my favorites and I felt bad doing

that, but that's life when you "Go To War" in the NFL. Brown had a great game and harassed Lamonica all day. In fact, Lamonica hit his passing hand on Brown's helmet and had to leave the game for a while.

When the Raiders lined up in East Formation inside the 20, we put Emmitt Thomas on the receiver in the slot, Warren Wells. Thomas had two interceptions, including one where he covered corner pattern as if he knew it was coming. Good player that Thomas.

Anyway, the Chiefs won, 17-7, at the Oakland Coliseum, which was quite a feat. The next stop was New Orlans for Super Bowl IV against the Minnesota Vikings. The previous year the Jets and Joe Namath shocked pro football by giving the AFL its first Super Bowl championship with an upset of the Baltimore Colts. The Chiefs upset the Jets in the 1969 playoffs to inherit the job of proving the AFL win in Super Bowl III was no fluke.

This, of course, was the last time any team would play under the AFL flag. We wore patches on our jerseys that said "AFL-10" to represent the upstart league's ten great years. It was a proud, sad moment. I was proud to have been part of that great, gutsy league and I was sad that Super Bowl IV was its last stand.

Recently there have been talks about expansion and realignment. Some theories have been put forth that show no feeling for the great rivalry between the old AFL and NFL. I wonder how many young football fans now even realize that the Super Bowl itself is the result of the wars between the AFL and NFL. Since the merger was finalized in February of 1970 so many teams have changed owners that much of the passion in that deep-rooted rivalry has kind of dissipated.

But for those of us who endured the early years of the AFL, the passion will never die. I guess it's hard to explain, but former AFL players, coaches and even owners still form a fraternity within the order of the NFL. And I am proud to be in that fraternity.

I am happy that I was part of the whole thing when the AFL went out with a bang as the Chiefs defeated the Vikings, 23-7, in Super Bowl IV.

Although I did not get into the game, I am grateful that Stram gave me the chance to be a part of that historical event. I probably should thank Rauch for setting me free so I was able to suit up as a player for a Super Bowl. I'll tell him as soon as he phones.

eight

Coach Flores

Players never anticipate their careers ending abruptly. Unfortunately, that's how they usually end. One day you are a player and the next you are looking for a new line of employment. It's a very lonely feeling.

I spent the entire 1970 season on the Chiefs taxi squad. In 1971, Coach Hank Stram had Lenny Dawson, Mike Livingston and young John Huarte at the top of his quarterback list. At my request, Hank released me in June so I could have time to look for another team.

But the phone never rang. Suddenly I was a former player.

Maybe I could have called around and tried to make it with somebody, but all things considered that didn't seem like the right thing to do. The previous year I didn't get a full salary because I was never active. So I thought it was time to move on.

Barbara had been playing the role of both parents during my four seasons in Buffalo and Kansas City. The kids were getting to be a lot to handle for one person, so maybe it was time for me to settle in with the family and get a real job.

A friend of mine had a plastic company, so I started working for him. Television station KGO, an ABC affiliate in San Francisco, talked to me about doing the weekend sports. I was beginning to think that living a more normal life might not be so bad after all. Hell, I might even enjoy following a football season more if I wasn't taking part in it.

Then the phone rang. The Buffalo Bills wanted me to help as an assistant coach.

My good friend John Rauch had quit the team the day before training camp opened. It seems he unjustly criticized a couple of players rather severely and owner Ralph Wilson was so upset he demanded that the players receive an apology. Rauch refused and quit. What a guy.

So for the second time in three years, general manager Harvey Johnson was pressed into emergency duty as a head coach. Because Rauch had installed the Raiders' offense, they needed somebody familiar with it to help coach. I was that somebody. They offered me $15,000. I asked for $20,000. They said, "OK, there's a plane that leaves at midnight from San Francisco, be on it."

The next morning I was back in the NFL as a coach.

It was a strange feeling to be a coach in charge of a passing game for an NFL team. My only previous coaching experience was for the freshman team at College of Pacific, so I felt a little overwhelmed at first. Fortunately we had pretty good players, like running back O. J. Simpson, quarterbacks James Harris and Dennis Shaw, and wide receivers J. D. Hill, our No. 1 draft choice, and Haven Moses.

With players like that we were able to move the ball pretty good. But the defense was horrible. To make a long season short, we were 1-13. After the season they ran me out of Buffalo again. The Bills had rehired head coach Lou Saban, who came in and fired up the Juice with probably the greatest running attack in NFL history.

In January of 1972 I got a call from Al Davis, who asked if I would scout a few college players. That sounded good to me so Ron Wolf, the Raiders player personnel whiz and a great friend of mine, set up some guys for me to see. I was on the road one week. It seemed like a year.

I went to Morningside College, Yankton, Southeast Missouri, and Montana Tech in Butte, Montana, where the temperature was 25 degrees below zero. I was in Sioux City, Iowa, when the chill factor was 60 degrees below zero. After that I came home, bundled up and slept for 12 straight hours. Hell, it took me that long to thaw out.

The idea of scouting players for a living left me cold, so once again I began to consider the possibility of getting a job in the real world and maybe finally spending more time with my family.

Wives and children of football players and coaches lead an unusual life. For half the year the husband or father is away from the house most, if not all, of the time. What little time he might spend there he might be tired, moody or have his mind elsewhere. The other half of the year, for a player anyway, you have almost all your time free and you probably mess up the normal rhythm of the home.

Barbara did an incredible job through all this, especially during the four years between 1968 and 1971 that I was away for the whole football season. She decided to keep the boys, Mark and Scott, and our daughter Kim in California while my playing career wound down and my coaching career began in Kansas City and Buffalo.

Considering the physical and emotional stress involved with football, I don't know how I would have made it through everything without Barb. She was my confidante, my best friend, my lover, and too often she was both parents to our children. She has one of those upbeat attitudes that always manages to lift everybody around her.

Through the years her knowledge of football grew amazingly. During the two years she watched me play at College of Pacific she didn't even know that I played defense or punted. She knew I was the quarterback and that I passed the ball. Period.

Barbara Flores: *When I was at College of Pacific my entire football background was that I had been homecoming Queen at San Mateo High. When they said "First and ten, do it again," I had no idea what they were talking about.*

By the time I was playing for the Raiders in the early 1960s she began to learn a lot about football. However, there was the time I was injured in a game against the Boston Patriots that she heard a term she had never before encountered. She heard that I got a hip pointer and when I got home she wanted to know how my pointed hip was. The trouble with her asking that was that this particular hip pointer hurt when I laughed.

Little Kim really grew up in a football home, with me off playing in the pros and both her brothers playing in high school. So she began to learn football terminology at a young age. When she was four she heard everybody saying that I had been cut by the Buffalo Bills. When I got home she wanted to see where daddy's cut was because she wanted to put a bandage on it.

When Mark and Scott were about three years old Barbara took them to a game at Frank Youell Field. On that particular day I got whacked in the head pretty good and when I went to the bench I sat there with a cold towel over my head.

When I got home that night, the boys were running around the house with towels on their heads saying they were playing football. They knew that daddy played football and when they finally came out to see me, they saw me with a towel over my head. So they thought that's what you did to play football.

Anyway, by 1971 it looked like I was going to turn in my footballs and towels and join the real world.

Then the phone rang. Raiders head coach John Madden needed a receivers coach to replace Mike Holovak, who left the team to spend more time with his family on the East Coast. On February 15, 1972, I was back with the Raiders, as the receivers coach.

That turned out to be a very interesting year because it was when Ken Stabler first tried to unseat Daryle Lamonica. At wide receiver we had Fred Biletnikoff in his prime and rookies Cliff Branch and Mike Siani. Raymond Chester was one of the top tight ends in the league.

That was also the season that ended with the controversial "Immaculate Reception," by Pittsburgh Steeler halfback Franco Harris. In a playoff game, Stabler replaced Lamonica in the fourth quarter and put the Raiders ahead of the Steelers, 7-6, with 1:13 left. But with 22 seconds left Steelers quarterback Terry Bradshaw threw a pass to John "Frenchy" Fuqua. The ball, Fuqua and safety Jack Tatum all collided at the same time. The ball bounced backward to Harris, who ran it in for a touchdown, giving the Steelers a 13-7 victory as the clock blinked down to zero.

According to the rules at that time, the pass was illegal if only the two offensive players, Fuqua and Harris, touched it. The only way the pass was legal was if it was Tatum who knocked the ball back to Harris. The officials took a long time to figure this one out. They even phoned upstairs, although they never made it clear what it was they found out on that phone call. About five minutes later, they signaled touchdown.

There is one persistent story, the validity of which is unknown, which says the official called security to ask how many guards there would be to usher the men in stripes from Three Rivers Stadium, which was filled with 53,350 maniacal Steelers fans.

"Six," was the answer supposedly given on that phone call.

"Six?" the official responded in fear.

Another official nearby heard that and signaled for a touchdown, six points.

It probably didn't happen that way, but that version of that ugly incident was easy to sell in Oakland, where fans were geared to go to a Super Bowl. They were teased even more the next three years when the Raiders were eliminated one step away from the Super Bowl, in the AFC Championship Games. One loss was to the Miami Dolphins and two were to the Steelers again.

In the 1976 season the Raiders had the best record in football at 13-1 and swept through the playoffs again. But this time they not only won, but dominated, the AFC Championship Game with a 24-7 win over the Steelers.

On January 9, 1977, the Raiders finally became world champions when they totally outplayed the Minnesota Vikings, 32-14, before 103,424 fans in Pasadena's Rose Bowl. Fred Biletnikoff was named Most Valuable Player after three of his four receptions set up touchdowns. Unfortunately, they didn't give a replica of the award to his receivers coach.

As an assistant coach with the Raiders I was able to stay in football and take part in historic games. But it wasn't fulfilling. To be an assistant coach in most places is to work in anonymity. To be an assistant with the Raiders is to be invisible. Except for John Rauch, no Raider assistant has ever been directly hired as a head coach by another team.

John Madden was elevated from a Raiders assistant to Raiders head coach. I followed him in the same manner. Art Shell did the same thing. But I realized when I was an assistant that as far as the outside world was concerned, Raiders assistant coaches didn't exist.

After we won Super Bowl XI, I bumped into an old friend in Oakland. He was surprised to see me and asked what I had been doing since I quit playing. When I told him I had been an assistant with the Raiders since 1972 he was shocked. He said he went to every home game and watched every road game on television, but he never saw me or heard my name.

That night I told Barbara that maybe I should get a second job as a bank robber. Hell, I could hide out as a Raider assistant coach and they never would find me. Since my goal in life wasn't to have a position that was good for being on the lam from the law, I decided it was time to make a career move. I wanted to become a head coach.

Although that's probably the desire of every assistant coach, it is not an easy move to make. After all, the fraternity of NFL head coaches is a small one. Until the league expands again, there can be only 28.

In 1978 Chuck Knox left the Los Angeles Rams to take a head coaching job with Buffalo. I called Rams general manager Don Klosterman, whom I had known since 1957 when he was with the Calgary Stampeders of the Canadian League. I told Don that I was interested in the Rams head coaching job. I think the Rams were already talking to Bill Walsh and had their own assistant, Ray Malavasi, waiting in the wings.

Don told me that I was a good candidate for a head coaching job, but that I had to find somebody to toot my horn. He said I needed more exposure. A great concept, but not an easy assignment. I could streak a game while playing a trombone, but I don't think that was what Don had in mind. Anyway, that probably wouldn't get me any interviews for a head coaching job.

I was interviewed by Monte Clark to be his offensive coordinator with the Detroit Lions. That would have been a slight move upward, but it was also eastward so I decided to stay with the Raiders. I had known Clark since my high school days because he was from Kingsburg, which wasn't that far from my home town of Sanger in the San Joaquin Valley.

On January 4, 1979, John Madden announced his retirement because his guts ached from uclers accumulated during ten years as head coach. I wasted no time in letting Al Davis know how much I wanted the job. Who are you calling a masochist? On February 8 I was named head coach of the Raiders.

A close friend gave me a present that should be a starter kit for head coaches. It contained a bottle of booze and a bottle of Maalox. The booze was for after the losses. The Maalox was for after the wins. I was ready for anything. Or so I thought.

From my earliest days as a quarterback I had learned to watch out for a blitz. That's when the defense sends at least one more pass rusher than you have blockers. The quarterback is supposed to take care of that extra pass rusher by getting rid of the ball. If he doesn't, then the pass rusher takes care of the quarterback.

As a head coach, even before the 1979 season began I knew I was going to be facing a blitz. If the 1978 season wasn't a tipoff, then the offseason was. I knew I was going to be rushed by more problems than a rookie coach would want to see.

Looking back at 1978, quarterback Ken Stabler had a rough year that wasn't entirely his fault. His favorite receiver, Freddie Biletnikoff, was bumped from the starting lineup by younger, faster Morris Bradshaw. His deep receiver, Cliff Branch, had some personal problems and didn't play well. Right tackle John Vella, who protected Snake's blind side, was out with an injury and his replacement, Henry Lawrence, had a rough time. Halfback Clarence Davis, an outstanding blocker, was also injured and his replacement, Arthur Whittington, was more of a runner than a blocker.

I had a feeling things weren't right when we flew to the 1978 season opener at Mile High Stadium in Denver. Flying into Denver is never a treat because the thin air and the Rocky Mountains make the airplane jump around like an off road vehicle in rough terrain. John Madden had been bothered more than usual by his ulcers during training camp and this bouncy flight didn't agree with him at all.

He hated flying anyway, as everyone learned after he retired and began taking trains and, finally, his own bus all over the country. Undoubtedly one of the reasons John disliked flying was that when he was a student coach at Cal Poly-San Luis Obispo the team plane crashed, killing 16 players, including some who had been his teammates only two years earlier. John wasn't on the plane because he was scouting another team.

I remember the crash because it happened in Ohio in October of 1960 while I was a rookie with the Raiders on a road trip to New York. When the news flashed that an airplane carrying a California football team had crashed, the switchboard at our hotel was jammed with calls from concerned friends and relatives. Anyway, that probably had a lot to do with John preferring to take trains and buses after he retired from coaching.

Our rough trip into Denver was an omen for that 1978 season. The Broncos beat us, 14-6. It was the first time the Broncos beat the Raiders in Denver since that horrible 1962 season and it was the first time since 1975 that we had failed to score a touchdown.

With all the changes around him, Stabler was having a rough time getting the offense to move consistently. Always the competitor, he tried everything, including some sleight of hand. In our second game, we were trailing 20-7 before Stabler threw a 44-yard touchdown to Bradshaw with 8:26 left. Then, trailing 20-14, Stabler was being chased out of the pocket on what was certainly the last play of the game. He made an underhanded motion and the ball went rolling toward the goal line. Running back Pete Banaszak sort of goosed it along without picking it up, then tight end Dave Casper hovered over it like a mother bird until it got into the end zone, where he fell on it.

The officials ruled the play a fumble by Stabler and a touchdown. The media gave that play such names as the "Immaculate Deception" and the "Holy Roller." It led to a rule change the next season that became known as the Stabler Rule, where, in the last two minutes of either half, a fumble cannot be recovered for an advance by anybody except the player who fumbled it.

Stabler knew all the rules, especially the unwritten one that says you should never criticize your teammates.

Not in the middle of an emotional season, anyway. He told the coaches that he missed Biletnikoff, Vella and Clarence Davis. But when the media asked what was wrong with the sputtering offense, Stabler at first said that he wasn't playing very well. Then, after our fifth game of the season, a 25-19 win in overtime at Chicago, he quit saying anything to the media.

The plot really started to thicken in the 13th week of the season when the Seattle Seahawks pulled out a 17-16 victory on a 46-yard field goal with two seconds to play. That marked the first time a team had beaten the Raiders twice in the same season since the Buffalo Bills did it in 1965, way back when Al Davis was still coaching and you know who was the quarterback.

After this loss, Al did an uncharacteristic thing. He criticized his quarterback and he second-guessed his head coach in the media. Again Stabler had done everything he could to win. He threw a 31-yard touchdown pass to Dave Casper that gave the Raiders a 16-14 lead with 5:29 left. But the PAT was missed by Errol Mann, who was having such a rough year that he tried only three field goals in eight weeks. This missed PAT set the scene for what became very controversial strategy.

With little more than a minute left we had a third and one on the Seahawks' 38-yard line, still leading by two. Stabler went for it all, a surprise bomb that could have put the game away. But it was inches long, incomplete. On fourth down a run came up short. Seattle quarterback Jim Zorn hit on five passes for 51 yards to put the Seahawks in position for the winning field goal.

"Going for the touchdown pass on third-and-one was like going for a home run when you need a sacrifice fly," Davis told the media. "I've got nothing against running on fourth down, but I would never have thrown that pass on third-and-one. And it wasn't Kenny's fault."

Oh, my.

This didn't do much to heal John Madden's ulcers.

"If Ken connects, the game's over," said Madden. "But he didn't, so now I'm the jackass."

Things were pretty icy between Madden and Davis for a few weeks. They spoke very little, if at all, for almost a month. After Stabler throws three interceptions in a 23-6 loss in Miami, Al tells a reporter that Snake is "Like a 24-8 pitcher who is having a 17-10 season."

Actually we finished 9-7 that year, missing the play-offs for the first time since 1971. Snake threw for almost 3,000 yards and 16 touchdowns, but he also had 30 interceptions and was sacked 37 times. A lot of stories were written about how Stabler's off-season life down in Alabama's Red-neck Riviera left him out of shape going into 1978.

"One year they're writing about how I'm a folk hero who carouses in the honky-tonk's at night and wins football games on Sundays," Stabler said. "Then all of a sudden when we don't make the playoffs it's because I drink too much and I'm out of shape. I'm not all that surprised. Like the man said, winning is the only thing."

I remembered when I was Al's quarterback how much he expected of me. I recalled the day he told me I should have made the center's line calls. So I wasn't surprised when Al took on Kenny when the lousy season was over.

"You've got to point to someone, so blame Stabler," Davis said to the media. "He makes the most money. He gets paid to take the pressure. I'm certainly not going to make excuses for him, but he doesn't do any work in the off-season. I'm dissatisfied with the condition of the team and with the coaching staff for allowing the players to get out of shape. . . . It's been our offense that has controlled the game. The defense played the same this season as it always had. But this year Cliff Branch caught only one touchdown pass. If you can't get the long ball to your wide receivers, you can't win. It all starts with the left-hander."

Not long after Al said that, Madden announced his retirement. Stabler was always close to Madden and became even more so during that 1978 season. Back home in Gulf Shores, Alabama, Snake reacted to the criticism to a long time friend and reporter for the *Birmingham News.*

"I have lost all respect for the organization," he said. "I don't want to stay where I'm not appreciated. I have contractual obligations to the Oakland Raiders and I will fulfill them. I'd be letting down my teammates if I took a powder."

By now I had heard more bickering than I wanted and was hoping that Stabler would just mellow out in the offseason and come back ready to play. But he was a hot topic. People wouldn't leave him alone. Next thing I know a reporter who went to Gulf Shores to see Snake is arrested and sent packing when police find cocaine in a keybox under the fender of his car.

As soon as the reporter gets back home he writes a story that implies that Stabler set him up. Stabler later admitted that he believed he thought one of his friends, who has since died, framed the reporter as part of a good old boy type prank. They have a strange sense of humor on the Redneck Riviera.

None of this does anything to calm the storm between Snake and Davis and pretty soon Stabler tells his agent to demand a trade. At about the same time, a national magazine comes out with an interview in which Snake spews venom everywhere. He was especially pissed at Davis.

"I wouldn't talk to him if he walked through the door right now," Stabler said in the article. "Davis wanted to talk to me when he came to the Blue-Gray Game in Montgomery, Alabama, and he called my lawyer, Henry Pitts, to set up a meeting. He wanted me to come up to bury the hatchet.

I'd like to bury the hatchet—right between Al Davis's shoulder blades."

Boys, boys. There's no need for violence. I should have guessed those two would get carried away. What else should I expect from the two most intensely competitive people I have ever known? But Stabler wouldn't stop there. He was on a roll.

"Henry Lawrence didn't play very well, and sometimes when I went back to pass, it felt like I was standing in the middle of a freeway. he got me banged around a little, which I guess resulted in my throwing the ball before I wanted to. And we had problems with our outside receivers because another one of Al Davis's brilliant moves was to bench Fred Biletnikoff. 'The Genius' went to a youth movement and put Morris Bradshaw in there. Well, Morris doesn't play very well, and Cliff Branch didn't play very well either last year."

This did not sound like Stabler, who is a great team guy. If he was upset with a player, he told that player. He did that in 1978. He told the players and he told the coaches. But in order to keep himself from complaining to the media he even quit talking to the press for most of the season. Soon after these quotes hit the streets they were picked up by every wire service and newspaper in the country. Snake told me later that he was sorry he said anything about his teammates in the media.

But the damage was done and I was just wondering if I would head into my first year as head coach without Stabler. His agent, Henry Pitts, told Davis that Snake wanted to be traded. Al gave Pitts permission to shop Snake around to other teams. Al put a price tag on the deal—two first round draft choices and two quality players. That riled Snake even more because he and Al both knew nobody would pay that much.

"First the media is told that I'm an out-of-shape,

My classmates in second grade at Granville Elementary School were farm kids. I'm in the top row, third from the teacher.

I met Barbara at College of Pacific. Here we are on our engagement night.

This family photo was taken in 1965. Barb is holding Kim, Mark is in the middle, and Scott is on my lap.

My mom, dad, and my brother Bob and I get together in 1979 at Checkmates, Bob's restaurant.

Bob Dougherty (44) and I were the first co-captains in Raiders history.

Fellow quarterback Cotton Davidson and I are looking forward to a successful 1966 season on the first day of training camp.

Jim Otto (00), Clem Daniels (36), Al Davis, and I watch our defense at work. Al Davis led the Raiders to a 10-4 season in his first year as head coach and general manager.

Jim Griffin (77) of the San Diego Chargers walks back to his huddle after chalking up a sack against me and the Raiders.

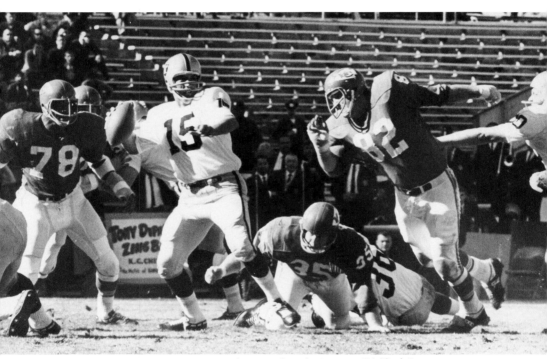

My offensive line gave me good protection during our 34-13 victory over
the Chiefs in 1966.

Ralph Baker (51) and Gerry Philbin (81) of the Jets made my last game as a Raider quarterback a difficult one. We did manage a tie, 28-28.

Being traded to the Bills in 1967 was tough on me. It didn't make it any easier when we struggled to a 4-10 record, while the Raiders went to their first Super Bowl.

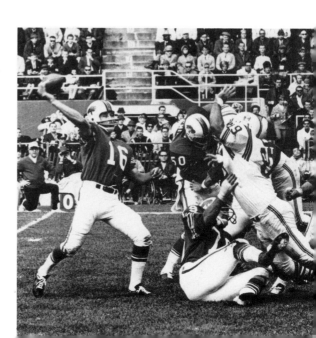

Super Bowl week is a media circus, but after beating the Eagles I enjoyed talking to Bryant Gumbel in the locker room.

Just suiting up for the Kansas City Chiefs in Super Bowl IV was a thrill. Our victory over the Vikings, 23-7, sent the AFL out winners. In 1970, the NFL and AFL merged.

Dan Pastorini was to be our starting quarterback in 1980. When Dan went down, Jim Plunkett stepped in and led us to the Super Bowl.

I was in my first year as coach of the receivers when we drafted Cliff Branch out of Colorado. Without question, his speed on the football field was the best I've ever seen.

Playing in bad weather can sometimes limit what a team can do. I hadn't yet had to abandon my game plan in this game.

Who says I can't put on my game face when things aren't going well, as they weren't during this game at Denver between the Los Angeles Raiders and the Broncos. With me are two top running backs, Marcus Allen (32) and Frank Hawkins (27).

The celebrating begins as the last seconds tick off the Superdome clock in Super Bowl XV.

The Raiders were truly number one after beating the Philadelphia Eagles, 27-10, in Super Bowl XV.

It will be a very long time before I forget that the Sugar Ray Robinson Youth Foundation named me its man of the year in 1984, and that Sugar Ray made the presentation.

I am probably demonstrating in front of comedian Arte Johnson that I can miss short shots with the best of them.

There they are, five NFL head coaches in a row. Or, more accurately, there they were, at a 1984 AFC West coaches meeting: From the left: Don Coryell, San Diego; Chuck Knox, Seattle; Dan Reeves, Denver; John Mackovic, Kansas City; and me.

We all took a turn at coaching the Raiders. I succeeded John Madden (center) and in turn was succeeded by Mike Shanahan (right).

My professional relationship with Al Davis goes back more than 20 years. He changed the Raiders, he changed my life and, more importantly, he changed pro football itself.

Here's the press conference where, on Feb. 22, 1989, owner Ken Behring (left) announced my appointment as the new Seahawks president and general manager with Coach Chuck Knox (right) looking on.

This is what I missed and this is what I'm back doing—working with the Seahawks one-on-one.

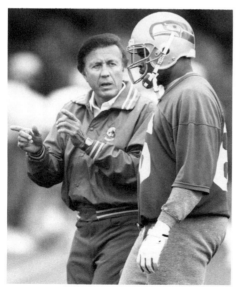

We're counting on Travis McNeal to be a potent part of our offense at the key tight end position.

Did we draft well for this season? Ask me or Gary Wright, Seahawks vice president, administration-public relations, later on—after the season. But we may not even know then.

My ideas on offense are a little different than those of Chuck Knox. Not necessarily better, just different. We'll see if the long bomb still works once in a while.

Barbara's been at my side through the good times, and, especially, through the not-so-good times.

over-the-hill, booze-guzzling geezer and then they're told that somebody should hock their farm to get me in an auction," said Snake. "Now I ain't no Wall Street genius, but either that's pretty bad marketing or some serious overpricing."

While all this fussing and feuding is going on, other problems begin to show up on the horizon. Two of Snakes favorite receivers aren't exactly ready to invite Al over for dinner.

Tight end Dave Casper, who spoke up for Stabler and against Al in the offseason, isn't in much of a hurry to sign a new contract and says he is willing to sit out the whole year if he doesn't get what he wants. He talks about quitting football and doing a television series about fishing with celebrities. Even among the Raiders, Casper was a little different. Sometimes a whole lot different. There was very little he did in a conventional way. But he did just about everything pretty damn good. So when he said he wanted to quit football to do a television series about fishing, you couldn't ignore him. But I did hope he would decide to catch passes instead of fish that year.

In 1978 we eased Biletnikoff out as a starting wide receiver. In 1979 one of my first jobs as head coach was to tell Fred that he shouldn't bother coming to training camp in Santa Rosa because he probably wasn't going to make the team. As I dialed the phone I remembered that I threw Fred his first touchdown pass back in 1966, his second year on the team.

I thought of all the incredible, one-handed catches he made over the years. In 14 seasons with the Raiders he set every receiving record the club had, 589 receptions, 8,974 yards and 76 touchdowns. He shared a league record of 10 consecutive seasons with at least 40 receptions. He was always his best in the big games, which is why he had another 70 catches for 1,167 yards and 10 touchdowns in postseason play. Hell, those are career totals for some receivers. And, of course, he was the Most Valuable Player in the Raiders first Super Bowl Championship when he set up three touchdowns against Minnesota. He even caused a rule change by using so damn much stickum that you couldn't shake his hand, or touch him anyplace, after a big play.

"Hello," said the voice on the other end of the phone.

Damn, how would I tell him it was all over. What a shitty way to start a coaching career, by firing one of your best friends. After exchanging the usual pleasantries, I dove into the ugly stuff.

"Fred, your chances of making the team this year are pretty damn slim. Basically, you have three options. You can retire, you can come to camp and probably get waived, or we can release you right now."

"Shit, I'm not through playing," he said. "You go ahead and release me now and I'll see if I can catch on someplace else. At the very least I can play in the Canadian League a little bit."

That was my first big move as an NFL head coach. I thought to myself, "Geez, it can't get much worse than firing a close friend, so maybe the job will seem easier after this." Boy was I in for a rude awakening.

nine

Bedlam in Raiderville

I learned quickly that head coaches must be ready to change their plans. When I was named head coach of the Raiders I told the media we would open up the offense and that there would be no massive roster changes.

In my first season we used a two tight end offense and the next year we traded away the biggest names on the team. The media would have crucified me for lying except that we also managed to do the one thing that exonerates you from sin in pro football. We won.

Not right away. First we had to go through a few adjustments. And there was one conspicuous difference in 1979 that players, coaches, media and even fans had to accept.

Me.

I'm not John Madden. In his ten years as the Raiders' head coach, Madden won far more than 112 games and one Super Bowl. He won hearts. He's a big, funny, outgoing, talkative, entertaining, Irish red head.

I'm not.

That's not to say that I shouldn't win a few hearts. Hell, I'm a very compassionate, caring person. But I do things differently than Madden. I don't flail my hands around on the sideline and scream at officials or run through chalkboards. That works for John. That is John. I'm sure I disappointed everybody who thought that is how a head coach is supposed to act.

I had to laugh at some of the conclusions people drew because I was not as demonstrative as Madden. Some of the media and maybe even a few of the players thought that because I am a mild-mannered, even tempered, relatively quiet guy, that the team would run roughshod over me.

After all, the Raiders had a reputation that made it sound like they needed a prison warden instead of a coach. And there were times that may have been close to true. But Madden wasn't the tough guy that a lot of the media and fans thought he was. And I wasn't the softie that a lot of people thought I was. Basically I think that although Madden and I approached things differently, we got about the same result. The players respected us and we won.

That's what I always believed, anyway. Quarterback Jim Plunkett verified those beliefs in his book, *The Jim Plunkett Story*.

"Tom had a tough time his first year as Raiders head coach. . . Because he wasn't a vocal, cheerleader-type coach, people thought Tom couldn't get the job done. He had a tough act to follow.

"Madden was so visible on the sidelines, pulling his red hair, bellowing at the officials. Flores was invisible,

standing passively, arms folded, staring. When he talks, it is closer to a whisper than a shout. People interpreted this as a sign that Tom wasn't a strong leader. Those people were wrong.

"Tom never gets rattled. He remains cool regardless of the situation. . . . He has a temper too, we discovered. Tom will hold it back until he can hold it back no longer, and then the players feel its lash. Tom is a tougher disciplinarian than Madden was, but on the Oakland Raiders there can only be so much discipline."

When I opened my first training camp in Santa Rosa as a head coach, Ken Stabler and Dave Casper weren't there. Snake was still fuming and wanted to be traded and Casper wanted a better contract. Plus now he was beginning to think he could be a country singer.

I like Dave and even he will admit he looks a little, well, different doing a lot of things, including playing football. His arms are bent so he looks like he's imitating Popeye except that he's built more like Bluto. Big. Still, he played smoother than he looked. But the thought of him on stage as a country singer is a little too much. I tried to imagine this big, red-headed, fair-skinned guy with a cowboy hat singing country songs and it just about turned my brown eyes blue.

The media was keeping track of Snake's every move as if he were the president. About one week into training camp, he was spotted driving his Porsche out of Alabama. Good news. The next day I heard he got a flat somewhere in Texas and decided to kind of party there. Bad news. Then I heard he was in the Bay Area, at Casper's house. Great. But he was so pooped that he would stay the night. The next day the entire Bay Area knew he traded in his old Porsche for a new one and said he was headed to camp.

About a dozen newspaper, radio and television reporters stationed themselves around the El Rancho Tropicana Motel to wait for Snake. It was quite a scene. But by the time I went to our usual 7 p.m. team meetings I knew he wouldn't be in until at least curfew. If I were waiting for Stabler, it wouldn't be someplace where he either had to go to a meeting or be subjected to curfew.

Between 11 and midnight Snake drives up in his brand new Porsche behind the coaching office at the motel. Sure enough, he had stopped at Melendy's, a Santa Rosa pub that was popular with the veterans. By the time he got to the motel, all the reporters were gone. Only one guessed correctly and went to Melendy's to wait for Stabler and get his story first. I know their job is competitive, but watching reporters manuever for a story is amusing sometimes.

"Snake, it's about time you showed up," I said as Stabler entered through the back door of our office. "I hope you're ready to go. And just one favor for me, will you drop the damn trade talk? It's not doing any of us any good."

Maybe it was because he was well rested or maybe it was that his competitive urges were taking over, but Snake seemed to have that sparkle in his eye when he showed up. He agreed it would be better for all concerned if he quit the trade talk and just went to work.

The next morning Snake told his tale to a huddle of reporters. Team player that he is, Stabler said he was wrong for maligning teammates and explained gingerly why he quit talking to the media the year before. He even apologized to Henry Lawrence, who said he didn't mind it too much because it's hard for an offensive lineman to get that much publicity.

Then Stabler suited up, went out and threw a few of his nice, soft, catchable passes, including one long one to Morris Bradshaw, the wide receiver he complained about.

"Not bad for a gray-haired geezer," said guard Gene Upshaw.

Most the players were glad to see Stabler back, but

I'm sure Jim Plunkett was not. We signed Jim a year earlier after he was physically and psychologically torn to shreds while with the New England Patriots, who drafted him in 1972, and the San Francisco 49ers, who waived him in 1978.

I still have strong visions of the first time I saw Plunkett play in 1971, when he was leading Stanford to a Rose Bowl championship. He was an impressive, big guy, with a powerful arm and a great passing touch. During the hype and buildup to the Heisman Trophy voting his life story was in all the newspapers and magazines. It was eerie how much we had in common.

Plunkett is basically a quiet person whose calm demeanor in no way reflects his competitive instincts. He is a Mexican-American, the son of poor, blind parents, and was raised in San Jose, California. An outstanding scholar and athlete in high school, he earned a scholarship to the university I originally wanted to attend, Stanford. Shortly after getting the scholarship, however, an 18-year-old Plunkett was told that a cancerous tumor on his neck would have to be removed and that he would never be able to play football again.

The tumor turned out to be benign and Plunkett went on to a storybook college career, setting NCAA passing records by the dozens, winning the Heisman Trophy in 1970, winning the Rose Bowl and then becoming the first player taken in the 1971 draft.

With Plunkett's heritage, his modest upbringing, the life-threatening discovery and even the way he conducted himself in public, it was easy for me to identify with him. The similarities were almost scary. Except for the scholarship to Stanford, the Heisman Trophy and the draft, of course. That shows you the value of taking the right courses and getting good grades in high school.

When Plunkett came out of college, it was known as the Year of the Quarterback. Among the top college stars were Joe Theismann at Notre Dame, Rex Kern at Ohio State, Bill Montgomery at Arkansas and Ken Anderson at little Augustana College. The pros were more interested in Plunkett, Archie Manning from the University of Mississippi, Dan Pastorini from Santa Clara, and Lynn Dickey from Kansas. Plunkett was the first player taken, by the Patriots. Then Manning went to the New Orleans Saints in the first round and the Houston Oilers took Pastorini in the first round and Dickey in the third.

In a way, I felt sorry for all of them. Although they made it into pro football easier than I did, they were fighting an uphill battle. Everybody expected them to perform miracles because they were high draft picks. But the nature of the draft, where the teams with the worst records pick first, dictates that good players go to horse shit teams. So they all go the hell beat out of them that first year, except Dickey, who watched from the bench while Pastorini got the hell beat out of him.

Manning got the worst of it. Although most people in football recognize that he may have been one of the best quarterbacks ever to play the game, Archie suffered through his entire career with bad teams at New Orleans.

Plunkett was in on every offensive snap his first season and was named the NFL's Offensive Rookie of the Year. When I became an assistant coach with the Raiders we played against the New England Patriots and I got to see first hand how atrociously they were treating Plunkett. Here was a guy perfectly suited to be a strong, drop-back passer and Patriots coach Chuck Fairbanks was using Plunkett to run the option. Not a run-pass option, mind you, but a run-run option, where the quarterback elects whether to pitch to a back or keep it himself.

That stuff was popular at Oklahoma, where Fairbanks coached college football, but it was generally regarded as pretty damn stupid in the NFL, where quarterbacks were the most important commodity on a team. To put them in a position to be manhandled by 275-pound defensive linemen is sheer lunacy. Of course, that is the opinion of a former quarterback.

I remember one game the Patriots had against the Raiders at Oakland when Plunkett ran the option and was wide open with nothing but field in front of him and suddenly he pulled up like he was shot. He pulled a hamstring and had to go out of the game. He was beating the hell out of us, but he spent the rest of the game on the bench and the Raiders pulled out a victory, Eventually he injured and then re- injured his shoulder running that stupid option play. His confidence and his effectiveness were also injured.

In 1976 the 49ers, under the new ownership of Eddie DeBartolo, Jr., got Plunkett from the Patriots for quarterback Tom Owen and four draft choices, two firsts that year and a first and second in 1977. Then the Niners, who were trying to rebuild, put him on the field with very little real help and things got even worse.

By 1978 Plunkett was a remnant of the guy I watched win the Rose Bowl for Stanford. You could see his passing motion was altered and his confidence was gone. He didn't throw the ball so much as he pushed it, kind of like a shot putter. In a preseason game against the Raiders he threw 11 consecutive incompletions, some of them so far off target it was difficult to tell who was his intended target. Not long after that the 49ers waived him. The former Heisman Trophy winner and Rookie of the Year was not even claimed and became a free agent.

Ron Wolf, one of the best personnel men in the league, scheduled Plunkett to work out for the Raiders at our facility in Alameda. John Madden asked me if I would work him out. So Al Davis, Wolf and Madden stood on the edge of the field while Lew Erber, another assistant coach, and I put Plunkett through the usual hoops, looking for movement, throwing on the move, scrambling, throwing for distance, touch.

After watching his horrible performance against the Raiders in that preseason game, I was curious about his physical ability. Before that workout, I admit I had my doubts.

When I'm working out a quarterback I like to stand downfield about 25 or 30 yards to see if there's any zip on the ball. Sometimes you can be misled if you don't catch it. That's my way of getting a feel. Sometimes the ball is thrown too hard, sometimes too soft and sometimes just right.

There are some guys you would hate to play catch with. I hated to catch Daryle Lamonica's passes because, for some reason, his passes hurt my hands. My passes were always kind of soft, although they traveled at good speeds and got their quickly. Snake's were the same way, soft and easy to catch. Plunkett's were kind of in between, good velocity but not hard to catch. I was impressed.

"There's nothing wrong with him physically that I can see," I said.

Davis wanted to sign him, Madden wasn't so sure. We decided to sign him and just let him sit for the rest of the year behind Stabler and Humm. We thought he needed to regroup psychologically and get back his confidence. At the time even his facial expression and tone of voice made him seem down.

Although it was difficult for Jim to sit on the sidelines in 1978, I'm sure that was a key reason he was able to come back and play. By the second game of our 1979 preseason I thought Jim had undergone a major transformation. In that game, against the Los Angeles Rams, he completed a couple of key third-down passes, including one for a touchdown to tight end Derrick Ramsey that tied the game at 14-all after we had been behind 14-0. That day we lost the game, 20-14, in overtime, but we gained a quarterback.

However, Stabler was also back and ready to play so there was no doubt who would be our starting quarterback. Stabler had done it all and taken us to the top of the mountain. Jim actually had a better preseason than Snake but there there was never any second-guessing on the coaching staff about changing starters.

All things being equal, there would have been times during the 1979 season that Plunkett would have replaced Stabler. But all things weren't equal. Yes, it was obvious that Jim had regained his passing touch. But Stabler was the team leader.

Stabler seemed a little lost in training camp. I finally realized it was because all his closest buddies were gone, Biletnikoff, and Pete Banaszak.

It was easy for me to understand how Snake felt. I missed seeing a few familiar faces during my first training camp as head coach. Biletnikoff was trying the Canadian League; Banaszak, Willie Brown and special teams captain Warren Bankston retired; Skip Thomas was done because of injuries and Clarence Davis and Willie Hall failed their physical; Neal Colzie and Dave Rowe were traded; and George Buehler was released.

In Santa Rosa, Snake and Biletnikoff roomed and ran together. When I say ran, I don't mean they jogged or sprinted. There were about two hours of free time between the end of our evening meetings and curfew. The veterans knew how to make the most of those two hours, especially Snake.

As a player and sometimes as an assistant coach I was able to go out and enjoy Santa Rosa at night. By the 1970s the players had a couple of annual traditions. One was the Air Hockey Tournament. The other was so-called rookie night.

The Air Hockey Tournament became famous in Santa Rosa as an event not to be attended by the timid, especially the year San Francisco topless star Carol Doda presided as the tournament queen.

According to the official rules, cheating and verbal abuse were highly encouraged. Biletnikoff was always a hit at this event. One year he wore a T-shirt with obscenities written all over it. He also sailed through three victories before it was discovered that he was covering his goal with a piece of clear plastic. He did it so well that nobody noticed until an unmolested shot right down the middle bounced away.

Maybe you had to be there to understand it, but that air hockey tournament epitomized the personality of the Raiders: tawdry, bold, physical, confident and most of all competitive. Assistant coaches even took part in these events. Defensive coach Bob Zeman became so adept at air hockey that they named one of the sneakier shots after him, the Zeman toss. If an opponent left the puck untended in front of his goal, Zeman would fling his hockey "stick" across the "ice" and knock the puck into the goal.

There was also the (Mike) Siani single-hand, head-and-shoulder fake reverse, but it defies description. If Melendy's is still open in Santa Rosa, I know they must talk about those tournaments to this day.

The rookie parties were often even more bodacious. Those, however, were closed to the public. It was an eye opener for some of the rookies, like quarterback Marc Wilson, a well-mannered Mormon from Brigham Young. Wilson was astonished when defensive end John Matuszak got carried away at a rookie party.

The Tooz, as he was affectionately known, hoisted a cocktail waitress onto his shoulders and began dancing around. He failed to notice a beam in the ceiling and smacked the poor waitress's head on it.

I was concerned about Tooz because in 1978 his life style wasn't exactly condusive to making him the best football player possible. Then again, it never was and he would be the first to admit it. Like Plunkett, Tooz was the first player picked in the draft. That and the fact that the best years of their careers were with the Raiders may have been the only things they had in common.

To put it simply, Tooz liked to party. Those of us who knew and loved him are sure that he partied a few years off his life. He all but predicted his own sad fate in his book, *Cruisin' With the Tooz,* written in 1987, four years after his retirement. When he died in 1989 at the age of 38 the cause was given as heart failure.

The Raiders signed Matuszak in 1976 after the Houston Oilers, Kansas City Chiefs and Washington Redskins waived him for reasons that weren't necessarily related to his ability to play football. In Kansas City he was caught in the team's jacuzzi with a bottle of champagne and a girl friend. The Redskins signed him, but didn't give him much of a chance. We were short of defensive linemen in 1976, so we took the chance.

When we went to a three-man line, Tooz had the kind of size and strength you like to put at left end. He was about 6-8, 290. Because that is the side teams run to most often, it is as important that the defenders over there are as good against the run as they are as either pass defenders or pass rushers.

During the 1978 season big John really didn't get a place to stay. If he had a girl friend he stayed at her place. If not, he stayed in his car. That was good enough for him. He didn't feel a need to rent an apartment. That's probably why he had the biggest car on the team, a yacht-sized Lincoln. But that's still not a comfortable place for a giant of his proportions to sleep.

At the end of training camp in 1979 I wanted to

make sure Tooz had better accomodations during the season. I knew Snake usually got a place all by himself, so I asked him if he might room with the Tooz. I know a lot of people might have thought that was a gamble. Considering that Snake already liked his night life, maybe I would lose him altogether if the Tooz began to influence him. I knew Snake better than that. I was hoping he would have a steadying influence on the Tooz.

So Snake agreed to room with Tooz. Overall, it worked pretty good. There was one time during the season that it kind of backfired. After one of our usual Tuesdays off, Stabler and Matuszak missed the Wednesday practice. They said their car broke down in Tahoe and they couldn't get back. Hell, I know better than that. Those two guys were such great cons they could have talked a Chevy dealer into buying them a Ford.

Because of the fact that we share the Oakland Coliseum with the baseball-playing A's, our first four games of the season are on the road. After opening with a win over the Los Angeles Rams, we lose the next three games and Bradshaw, who replaced Biletnikoff, dislocates a hip.

So by the time I coach my first home game, we are using a two tight end alignment as our base offense. We still had a deep threat in Cliff Branch, and our two tight ends were both outstanding receivers, Casper and Raymond Chester. In fact, they both made the Pro Bowl that year. Chester caught 58 passes for 712 yards and 12 touchdowns and Casper, who reported during the last week of training camp, had 57 for 771 and three touchdowns.

We took advantage of our first home stand to win three in a row to move above .500 at 4-3. But on Friday night, October 19, there was bad news waiting for us when we arrived in New York to play the New York Jets.

Carol Davis, Al's wife, had a stroke during the previous night in their Piedmont Hills home. She was in a hospital clinging to life and Al was by her side. There wasn't much hope. Fortunately Dr. Bob Albo, one of our team physicians, is a neighbor of the Davis family. When Al discovered Carol in the middle of the night, he summoned Dr. Albo, who was there within a couple of minutes.

But her heart was not beating. She was clinically dead. Dr. Albo began cardiopulmonary resuscitation and told Al to call an ambulance. Dr. Albo kept her heart beating until the ambulance arrived, but she required electro shock treatments to restart the heart three times within the next few hours.

Late Friday night Al called me at the hotel. He spoke so low I could barely hear him. We were on the phone only a matter of seconds.

"You know what you have to do and I know what I have to do," he said.

I was crying as I hung up the phone. I knew how much Al adored Carol, or Carole as he called her. This dear, sweet, vital woman was well-known and loved by most of the players, coaches and their wives.

When I told the team on Saturday morning most of the players hung their heads. Henry Lawrence was so choked up he couldn't talk and Monte Johnson and Cliff Branch were almost in tears. I was not surprised when we played a terrible game. We really weren't in sync. I guess the players felt the same as I did, that the game was meaningless relative to a loved one fighting for her life back home.

Al literally moved into the hospital, setting up makeshift sleeping quarters in a little room near Carol's bed. He sat by her side, held her hand, talked to her, read to her as she lay there motionless, in a coma, for 17 days. Doctors had little hope that she would even come out of the coma, let alone recover.

On the 17th day she opened her eyes and spoke. After months and years of work, Carol is the same amazing woman she was before the stroke. All things considered, I think she's even more amazing.

An NFL season has no feeling, so this one plodded on. When a loss to the Kansas City left us at 6-6, chances of going to the playoffs looked slim, especially with our next two games on the road. Even a 14-10 win at Denver didn't give us much more hope, especially after we found ourselves trailing the New Orleans Saints, 28-14, at halftime in of a Monday night game in the Superdome.

In the third quarter Stabler was intercepted by linebacker Ken Bordelon. Snake already had thrown one interception and fumbled to set up two Saints scores. He wasn't going to let Bordelon stroll to the end zone. Stabler took off in pursuit but defensive tackle Barry Bennett put a block on Stabler, whose head bounced hard on the artificial turf.

Snake staggers to the sideline, pretending he's OK. I ask him what year it is and he doesn't have a clue. I ask him where we are and he doesn't respond. I ask him who I am and he just shrugs.

"Plunkett," I said. "Get ready to go in."

Jim warmed up quickly. When we got the ball back, he jogged onto the field and was ready to call a play. Suddenly I see Snake running out there, pulling his helmet on. I look at trainer George Anderson.

"I think he's OK because he knew the score," said Anderson.

And, with only 18 minutes left to play, that score was 35-14. Stabler soon changed that. He kept moving the team for touchdowns and the defense switched from a three-man line to a four man line and kept getting the ball right back as the Saints picked up only one first down in the second half.

Stabler threw two touchdowns to Cliff Branch, who didn't even start that game because he missed another practice that week. But he was a hell of a substitute that night. Anyway, we pull out a 42-35 win that was the biggest comeback ever on a Monday night game.

Unfortunately, that was the highlight of the season. We closed out the year with a 29-24 loss to Seattle again, eliminating us from the playoffs with a 9-7 record. Not good, but not terrible considering all the changes in the roster and the distractions. I hoped that the next season things would be less hectic and we would win more games.

Fat chance. I was only half right. I had to learn to live with hectic for the rest of my career with the Raiders . We did that well enough in 1980 to win big.

ten

Super Bowl XV

Stabler soon learned to appreciate that old adage, be careful what you wish for because you might get it. In March of 1980 Al Davis worked out a trade with the Houston Oilers. We swapped starting quarterbacks, one-for-one, Stabler for Dan Pastorini.

I didn't want to make the deal. I didn't think Pastorini would enhance our future because he would be 31 before the 1980 season began. I felt good with Snake as our starter and I thought Plunkett was ready in case of an emergency. What we needed was a young quarterback for the future, not Pastorini.

Al and I argued back and forth about it for a couple of days after the Oilers made the offer. Al said sometimes you have to do something before it becomes an emergency situation. By then you might not have any alternatives. So if you know you're going to make a move anyway, it's intelligent to do it while you have a choice.

Looking back, Al may have had a good point. But I wasn't concerned about being intelligent at that time, I was thinking of my own security. I felt secure with Snake. I also thought Al was letting his personal feud with Snake enter into his decision. In the end, I still didn't like the trade, but Al had the final say and he thought it was time to move on.

Snake had two more productive years in Houston, where he loved coach Bum Phillips, then ended his great career with the not-so-great New Orleans Saints. I saw him at a Raider reunion years later and he admitted he was sorry he asked to be traded.

"If I had just shut my mouth, maybe I could have collected a little more jewelry with the Raiders," Stabler said, referring to Super Bowl rings. "I never again had as much fun playing football as I did with the Raiders. I knew I didn't have the big arm that Al wanted, so he was looking for an excuse to get me out of there anyway. Bum was fun, but if I had it to do over again I would have kept my mouth shut and finished my career as a happy man with the Raiders."

Maybe.

Al wanted that stronger arm at quarterback. He wanted to get back to a more vertical passing game. During Madden's last year Al complained that the offense was stretching things across rather than down the field. In my first year as head coach, we had to go to a two tight end offense. If Stabler had stayed, it is conceivable that he may have had to battle Plunkett for the starting job.

That wasn't the only position that concerned Al. He wanted a better combination of speed and size at running back, a younger free safety and a receiver who could take advantage of the open areas created when Cliff Branch stretched a defense.

The Buffalo Bills had just such a receiver in Bob Chandler, a nifty little zone wrecker. Al worked out another one-for-one player trade to get him. Then he called linebacker Phil Villapiano, one of our most fanatic players, and asked him what he thought of Chandler as a receiver.

"He's a great player," Villapiano said. "He can catch anything that's near him and he would be a big help in trying to score inside the 20. Why, do we have a chance to get him?"

"Yes, we do," Davis answered.

"That's great," Villapiano raved.

"There's only one problem," said Davis. "They want you in Buffalo."

It was quiet on the other end of the line for a while.

"Oh, no," said Villiapiano.

Phil was a second round draft choice out of Bowling Green in 1971 and had been a starter since his rookie season. He was only about 6-2, 225 pounds, but he had an uncanny feel for playing linebacker that you just can't coach. He was a natural. He epitomized the Raiders. He played hard off the field and he was a maniac on the field and sometimes vice versa.

We also traded Jack Tatum, who I believe is one of the best free safeties in NFL history, to the the Houston Oilers for second year running back Kenny King. To replace Tatum we gave the New York Jets a sixth round draft choice for veteran safety Burgess Owens. Defensive end Cedric Hardman, a pass-rush specialist, came from San Francisco in another trade.

In the first round of the draft we took Marc Wilson, a 6-5, 200-pound quarterback with quick feet who showed incredible touch and accuracy at BYU. I thought for sure he would be our quarterback of the future. In the second round we got a 6-1, 260-pound defensive tackle from Penn State named Matt Millen and switched him to inside linebacker, where it didn't take him very long to become a standout.

We had so many new faces at Santa Rosa that we should have worn name tags around the El Rancho.

Al also set in motion something that would change more than the names on the roster. In January he signed an agreement to move the Raiders to the Los Angeles Coliseum. Since 1977 Al tried to get improvements in the Oakland Coliseum, which was the second smallest stadium in the AFL. The only smaller one was the Astrodome.

Many people do not realize that in 1980 Al accepted a deal to stay in the Oakland Coliseum that was put together by Kaisar Aluminum executive Cornel Maier and Oakland Mayor Lionel Wilson. But the Alameda County board of Supervisors yanked that offer, and embarrassed Maier and Wilson by repudiating their right to negotiate in the first place.

Maier, who was considered one of the top executives in the world, was so bitter about his treatment by the Oakland Coliseum and the Alameda Supervisors, that he withdrew his services. I know for a fact that Al was happy about the deal Maier and Wilson offered. He was disappointed, then outraged when it was yanked. About a week later he signed an agreement to move to the Los Angeles Coliseum.

Of course this became all entangled in the courts with a series of suits, injunctions and counter suits. I was trying to do my best to insulate the team from this incredible distraction. We were having enough trouble with things like figuring out our quarterback situation.

When we got Pastorini I made it clear that we traded a starter for a starter. Pastorini was our No. 1 quarterback unless he lost the job. I knew this wouldn't sit well with Plunkett, who came to camp in great shape and ready to compete for a job. He actually outperformed Pastorini in training camp. But Plunkett already knew our offense, so we made an allowance for that. Jim didn't.

With about a week left in the training camp, Plunkett told me he was frustrated because for the second summer in a row he played well enough to be the starter but he knew it wasn't going to happen. He wanted to be traded.

I told him that I understood completely, but we weren't going to trade him. I told him to try and relax a little and see how it works out. But Jim was in a bad position. He was 32 years old with a 31-year old starter in front of him and a first round draft pick sitting in the wings. That doesn't leave a lot of leeway for a guy to squeeze in the remainder of his career.

The fact that Pastorini was the other quarterback made matters only worse for Plunkett. Those two had been antagonists since their high school days in San Jose, where Plunkett attended James Lick, a public school, and Pastorini starred at Bellarmine Prep, a high-profile Catholic school known for its great football teams.

They were still in relatively the same neighborhood in college when Plunkett was at Stanford and Pastorini at Santa Clara. Finally, they were both first round draft choices in 1971.

However, their personalities were as different as they could be. Pastorini was a high-profile type who drove fast cars, fast boats, dated and even married movie stars. Plunkett was quiet, conservative and didn't like Pastorini very much.

I admired the way Plunkett handled it. He didn't get into a feud with Pastorini, complain to the media or even whine to me. He was just honest and up front with me about what he thought. And he thought he should be the starter.

He was probably right.

I pointed out to Plunkett that that Dan was still learning the offense and really had not done anything to lose his spot as the No. 1 quarterback. So we opened the season with Pastorini as the starter and Plunkett as an uneasy rider on the bench.

We have a great opener at Kansas City, where the weather was hot and we were hotter. Pastorini threw for 317 yards and we won easier than the 27-14 score appears. But in the second week we blow an early lead in San Diego and the Chargers appear to be heading for victory, especially when defensive lineman Gary "Big Hands" Johnson knocks Pastorini out of the game with less than a minute left. We trailed, 24-17.

Pastorini hurts his knee and is helped from the field. Plunkett takes over with only one shot. We're on their 23 yard line with a fourth and 17 and 39 seconds remaining. Plunkett steps up to the line and draws the anxious Chargers off sides. He changed the inflection in his cadence and they fell for it. As a former quarterback I appreciate this subtle trick. As a coach, I appreciate the five-yard gain.

Fourth-and-twelve from the 18. Plunkett's one shot is a pass to tight end Raymond Chester in the back of the end zone. Touchdown Raiders. The PAT ties the game and the players mob Plunkett, who is as happy as I've seen him since he joined the Raiders.

As we got ready for the sudden death overtime, I felt like the Grinch who stole Christmas. I told Plunkett that Dan might go back in. He looked shocked. I had a bit of a dilemma. Pastorini was saying that his knee was good enough to allow him to play, which was debatable. If I yanked him when he said he was healthy, it might hurt his confidence as the team leader at a critical time. I couldn't explain all this to Plunkett, so I just told him to stand by.

I had to wince when Pastorini went in and threw an interception on his first pass. I could hear the media already. "Plunkett had the hot hand, why didn't you stay with him rather than gamble with an injured Pastorini?" Ah, then I thought Chargers quarterback Dan Fouts made it a moot point. He also threw an interception. But after we had a field goal attempt blocked, Fouts tossed a game-ending touchdown pass to give the Chargers a 30-24 win.

For the next week the big topic was whether Plunkett should have played in overtime. The media was brewing up a coach's worst nightmare, a quarterback controversy. We quieted it somewhat when King, our new running back, made some big plays in a 24-21 win over Washington at home. However, his two fumbles inside the the 20 helped us bobble away a 24-7 decision to the Bills in Buffalo.

The newspapers, television sportscasters and radio talk shows are having a field day. By now I've become accustomed to controversies about quarterbacks. But at this point there's a controversy about an old quarterback. Me. There are rumors that my job is in jeopardy. With a 2-2 record and a very unsettled team, it's difficult for me to ignore these rumors, especially the one that says Sid Gillman is already lined up to replace me.

When he was at San Diego, Al was an assistant under Gillman, who is an expert in the passing game. And it is the passing with which Al is upset. He wants to pressure defenses, stretch defenses with more long passes. That's why he traded Stabler for Pastorini. But Pastorini had thrown so many deep passes in the first four games and our offensive linemen were beginning to say we needed to balance the offense with some running.

It was just one of those times when nobody was happy.

Then, in the first quarter against the Kansas City Chiefs, Pastorini breaks his leg. Defensive lineman Dino Mangiero fell on Dan's leg, breaking the tibia. As Pastorini lay on the ground in pain, a large group of the fans at the Oakland Coliseum actually cheered. It was probably the only time I was ashamed of the fans in Oakland. Sure they were frustrated because the team was talking about moving. Sure they were upset with the offense and maybe even with Pastorini.

But to cheer an injured player, even on the opposing team let along your own starting quarterback, is about as classless as you can get.

Plunkett warmed up quickly and did his best in that game. We were already behind, so his job was not an easy one. He set a team record by throwing 52 passes, but completed only 20 for 238 yards. He also threw five interceptions, lost one fumble and was sacked four times. Even one of his completions, to Casper, was stolen by a defender and returned for a touchdown.

Kansas City rocketed out to a 31-0 lead in the second quarter and eventually won by 31-17.

After opening the season at 2-1, we had slumped to a 2-3 and I'm really not looking forward to my usual post-game conversation with Al. He was upset before the game. I wondered if my coaching career would end right there in the locker room that evening, five games into my second season.

Al was brief, cold and to the point. He said I was the coach and I should take control or . . . .

"Or what? Or what?" a voice screamed inside me. "Or you're fired?" The "or what" part was left up to my imagination. And my imagination thought the worst, especially after Al said he would talk to me the next day. I didn't like to hear that. Did he want time to contact Gillman?

Usually I relax and enjoy a couple of hours with Barbara after the game. Poor Barb. She had some terrible company that night. All I could do was wonder what the hell would happen the next day. I knew we weren't playing well. We had so many new players I knew it would take time. I could only hope that I would get the time.

Barb and I went to dinner with some friends in La-
fayette, then I went home and tried to get some sleep. Late
that night Al called and changed our meeting from first
thing in the morning to later in the day. I didn't like the
sound of that at all. Did it mean he needed more time to set
up a press conference to announce Gillman as the new head
coach? There was no sleeping that night.

I got to the office about 6 in the morning. At 8 I
talked to the coaches. I tried to make it kind of a pep talk,
but without much luck. I just told them we had dug one hell
of a hole and we had to climb out. We were doing the right
things, we just weren't doing them well enough. We needed
to execute better individually and as a team.

I was a nervous wreck by the time Al and finally
talked. Al is not a guy to beat around the bush, so when we
started talking about a lot of things I knew I wasn't
fired. . . . Yet. But he did make it clear that he had considered changing coaches.

"Listen, you've got to find a way to get those guys to
play better," he said. "I don't think I made a mistake in hiring you. You're the coach and you have to take charge and
turn this thing around."

I was glad that he didn't end it with "or" that time.
But I still felt the "or" hanging over my head.

Gene Upshaw called a players-only team meeting after the Kansas City game. He and Art Shell apparently
talked about pulling together as a team. Casper, who had
become a real loner since Snake left, gave his opinion at
that meeting and it was not well-received.

Casper obviously wasn't happy, either with himself,
life in general or the Raiders. Maybe all the above. Nor-
mally you could treat him as an eccentric and everything
would work out. This season his aloof ways were alienating
players. He had a bad back and didn't practice often or hard.

That automatically bothers the players who work hard all week and in the game. But for the first time in his career, he wasn't playing that well in games, either.

Al managed to get the Houston Oilers to trade a first and a second round draft pick in 1981 and a second in 1982 for Casper. We had three other tight ends on the roster, Raymond Chester, Todd Christensen and Derrick Ramsey. The day before the trade deadline, we sent Casper to Houston where he could be with Stabler.

So Pastorini was out, Plunkett was in, Casper was gone and I felt like I was on probation. It was time to put it all together, or.... Hell, I didn't want to even think about the "or."

Plunkett's first start as a Raider was against the San Diego Chargers. It was important that he did not feel like the weight of the organization was on his shoulders. After watching him regain his emotional and physical equilibrium, I didn't want to see it destroyed in one game.

Fortunately we played well as a team, so Jim didn't have to feel any undue pressure. Kenny King ran for a couple of touchdowns and we rushed for 214 yards. Jim threw for 164 yards, including a 43-yard touchdown to Cliff Branch.

Al was pleased to see a touchdown to Branch. He thought Cliff was the key to unlocking the potential of our offense. Our next game was in Pittsburgh on a Monday night, when the Raiders had a 16-1-1 record.

Plunkett had a great game that night. What I liked was the way he shook off a poor start, completing only one of his first eight passes. After that he completed 12 of the next 13 for a total of 247 yards and three touchdowns.

We knew that the Steelers would try to blitz Plunkett because he was a new starter and because that's what they like to do. Plunk made them pay dearly. He answered their blitzes with touchdown passes of 56 and 34 yards to Branch. His other TD pass was for 45 yards to Morris Bradshaw.

After that game I felt a little more secure in my job. We had won two in a row and I felt I could withstand a loss without worrying about Sid Gillman again. That didn't mean I thought it was OK to lose. Hell, no.

We went into Philadelphia riding a six-game winning streak. We left with a one-game losing streak. Plunkett completed only 10 of 36 passes with two interceptions. One of his passes was an 86-yard touchdown to Cliff Branch, but that's all we got in a 10-7 loss.

Plunkett was sacked eight times, injured his left shoulder but kept playing. The shoulder would bother him for the rest of the year, but he was able to play with the help of anti inflamatory and pain-killing shots. He had waited since 1978 to regain his role as an NFL starting quarterback and it would have taken something pretty serious to get him out of there.

Anyway, Plunkett's rough treatment in the Eagles game was followed by some criticism about our offensive line. A couple of the offensive linemen blamed Plunkett for dropping back too far, thereby giving the outside rushers an easier trajectory to get him. The truth is that the line and Plunkett shared the blame. At times Jim did drop back too far and at times the linemen did not sustain their blocks.

After Philadelphia we were at home against Denver for a Monday night game. Oakland fans organized a boycott in protest to the team's decision to move to Los Angeles. I couldn't blame the fans for that. Many had been great fans since 1960 and 61 when they had to go to Kezar and Candlestick in San Francisco to see us play. And then there were those fond memories of Frank Youell Field. The idea of the

Raiders moving to Los Angeles left many fans understandably hurt and angry.

So for the first five minutes of our Monday night game against Denver, the fans stayed out of the Stadium. For almost the whole 60 minutes our offense boycotted. Kicker Chris Bahr missed four field goals and a PAT. The defense helped out with three interceptions and three fumble recoveries, so we were able to win, 9-3.

Somewhere in the middle of the season, the defense began to jell. In 1979 Myrel Moore coordinated the defense. He had been the architect of Denver's Orange Crush, 3-lineman, 4-linebacker defense that beat us in the 1977 AFC championship game. That, and blind officials who missed running back Rob Lytle's fumble, beat us.

In 1976 the Raiders defensive line was so beat up we went to a base defense that called for three linemen and four linebacker. We called it Orange, no relation to the Crush, although it did use the same alignment. After the 1977 season Al hired Moore, which didn't thrill the Broncos. Al wanted Moore to fine tune our Orange Crush. Instead, he began complaining in 1979 that the team wasn't helping him get the right kind of linebackers for the 3-4 defense.

In our great 1979 come-from-behind Monday night win in New Orleans game, we went with a four-man line in the second half and held the Saints to only one more first down. Moore was strictly a three-man line guy. Al wanted more flexibility and, most important, more pressure on the quarterback. He didn't give Moore a new contract in 1980.

Charlie Sumner rejoined the staff when I became head coach in 1979. He was a take-no-shit kind of guy who knew how to put pressure on offenses. He wasn't partial to a three or four man line. He was only partial to getting the job done. His key change to our defense in 1980 was to use outside linebacker Ted Hendricks on every down.

"He may be the best damned defensive player in the league, so why put him on the bench," said Sumner.

Hendricks had an outstanding year and Matuszak and cornerback Lester Hayes had the best seasons of their careers in 1980. Lester led the league with 13 interceptions, with an assist to gobs of stickum, and Matuszak gave us a great combination of run-stopper and power rusher at left end.

The defense was made up mostly of players other teams traded, waived or just plain overlooked. Tooz, of course, we signed as a free agent after Houston, Kansas City and Washington gave up on him. Hendricks played out his contract at Green Bay and signed with us as a free agent, although he wasn't exactly free because the rules dictated that we give the Packers two first round draft choices. He was well worth it.

As a tribute to our personnel director, Ron Wolf, two defensive starters were 12th round draft choices, outside linebacker Rod Martin and nose tackle Reggie Kinlaw, both key players for us in the 80s. Martin literally grew into his posititition after coming to us as an undersized rookie out of USC in 1977. Kinlaw was an outstanding player at Oklahoma, but most teams rejected him because doctors said he had a bad leg. Wolf had our own doctor check Kinlaw's leg, which was good enough to take a chance on in the 12th round. At times he played like a first rounder.

We had three quick defensive ends that year. The starter on the right side was Dave Browning, a second rounder out of Washington in 1978 who, at 245 pounds, was a little undersized and had trouble adding weight. He was late to a minicamp one year because the day he left home in Washington to drive to California, Mt. St. Helens erupted. Willie Jones, our second round pick out of Florida state in 1979, was also undersized at 245 but he was cat-quick. In his first couple of years he jumped offsides all the time. Willie should have been a great player, but drugs ruined his career and he was gone after 1982. Veteran Cedric Hardman, a long-time star with the 49ers, was another situational pass rush for us in 1980.

At linebacker we really pieced together an unusual group, beginning with Hendricks and Martin. On the strong inside position was Matt Millen, a defensive tackle at Penn State who was perfect for linebacker emotionally and physically. Matt was so sharp that he started as a rookie and was able to make defensive calls in his first two seasons. On the weak inside was Bob Nelson, who was rejected by several teams before Sumner hand picked him to fit into our 1980 group.

In the secondary along with Hayes there was cornerback Dwayne O'Steen who we signed as a free agent after he sat out 1978 with the Rams because of a knee injury. At strong safety there was the always vocal Mike Davis, a big hitter we drafted No. 2 in 1977. At free safety Burgess Owens was an outright steal from the New York Jets in a trade for a sixth round pick.

That defense was the lone bright spot on our team for a three-week stretch when the offense went into a slump, scoring only 7 at Philadelphia, 9 against Denver and 13 versus Dallas. Thanks to our defense, we only lost to Philadelphia by 3 and Dallas by 6, and we won the Denver game, 9-3. So we were 9-5, on the fringe of making the playoffs as a division winner because San Diego had the edge in tiebreakers. We had a good shot at a wild card spot, however. Wild card playoff berths go to the teams with the best records that didn't win a division title. Fortunately there were two in each conference beginning in 1979. But we missed getting even one of them in 1979 by one game.

In the fifteenth game of the season, at Denver, the offense finally got back on track, thanks to the pass-catch combination of Plunkett-to-Chandler, which hooked up for touchdowns of 11 and 38 yards against Louis Wright, one of the best cornerbacks in the league. The Broncos were already eliminated from the playoffs so they played like it was the Fourth of July. They put on a fireworks display. They passed 42 times for 507 yards but we turned one into a touchdown when Owens returned an interception 58 yards to the end zone.

My goals in the final game were to win and to stay healthy because the way I figured it we would be in the play-offs one way or the other. We were tied with the Chargers, who played Pittsburgh Monday night. We did our part Sunday, beating the New York Giants, 33-17. The game wasn't as lopsided as it seems because our last score came in the final seconds when Derrick Jensen scooped up an onsides kick and ran 33 yards for a touchdown. However, we didn't stay totally healthy. Plunkett hurt his knee a little and had to wear a knee brace to finish the game.

That gave us an 11-5 record and front row seats in front of the television Monday to see the San Diego-Pittsburgh game. Chargers quarterback Dan Fouts, one of the best ever to play the game, had a sensational year in 1980, setting an NFL record by passing for 4,715 yards. He collected 308 of those against Pittsburgh that Monday night, ending our hopes of winning a division title. The Chargers won, 26-14.

So we were a wild card team. I had no complaints. Hell, after five games I was just satisfied to keep my job. I thought back to that nightmarish week I feared I might get fired. Who would have thought then that we would make the playoffs? No wild card team had ever won a Super Bowl, but I wasn't concerned about that. At least we were still in the hunt.

For our first playoff game we had a class reunion, complete with the Ghost of Playoffs past. To be precise there was

Ghost, Snake and the Assassin, an ominous sounding group if there ever was one.

Funny how things worked out. We traded Stabler, Casper and Tatum to Houston and we got Pastorini and King from the Oilers. As usual each team claimed the trades would help them make the playoffs. Sure enough, here we both were—facing each other in the first round of wild card playoff action.

All of the players involved in our trades would play in this game, except Pastorini. His leg was healed and he wanted to be put back on the active roster, but we didn't think it would be wise because he wasn't ready to compete anyway. He hadn't played since the injury. Marc Wilson was only a rookie, but he had a great arm and very quick feet.

Dan was angry and frustrated when he learned we would not activate him. I guess I would be, too. But I wouldn't have gone out and smashed my car into a tree, which is what Dan did. He cut up his face a little and injured an ankle.

I felt confident about our game plan against the Oilers. On offense we felt we could do a few things, especially when they tried to cover our backs with linebackers. On defense Sumner was positive he could harass Stabler with blitzes against certain formations.

When the Oilers lined up with two receivers on one side, they had a bad habit of not protecting the quarterback from blitzes on the other side. Sumner seized that opportunity to make Snake's reunion with the Raiders a close encounter of the worst kind. We sacked Stabler seven times in that game, two each on blitzes by left cornerback Lester Hayes and strong safety Mike Davis. Hayes also returned an interception for a touchdown.

We won easily, 27-7. This was the third straight year the Oilers lost in the playoffs. The previous two years they lost the AFC Championship Game. Coach Bum Phillips said he was tired of knocking on the door and in 1980 he set out to "kick the door in." On that day he came to the wrong door. We slammed it in his face again. About a week later Bum was fired, which I thought was stupid considering he put the team in the playoffs three straight years.

Next stop was Cleveland, where the temperature was one whole degree above zero. A wind off Lake Erie lowered the chill factor at Municipal Stadium to minus 39 degrees. Where's the Astrodome when you really need it?

Al requested that the Browns get heated benches and offered to pay for them. But when we got to Cleveland we found out they had not ordered them. Al got them himself. According to NFL rules, if one team has something, the other team must be provided with the same thing. So we got the benches, with big heaters and blowers. Although the Browns said they didn't want them, we noticed that their players were all huddled up on those benches during the game.

Anyway, this game ultimately came down to one, big play. It was so big it was labeled with a nickname, just like the Immaculate Reception by Franco Harris and the Holy Roller by Snake. This one became known as The Mistake by The Lake.

With 5:58 left in the game, Mark van Eeghen scored a touchdown that gave us a 14-12 lead. But with only 49 seconds remaining the Browns were perched on our 13 yard line. Trailing by two points, they needed only a field goal to win. If the line of scrimmage was the 13, a field goal would be 30 yards. That's not a chip shot when the chill factor is minus 39 degrees, making the ball not only slippery but hard as a brick. The Browns were also going into the open end of the stadium, into the teeth of a wind off Lake Erie.

On second down, Browns coach Sam Rutigliano told his quarterback, Brian Sipe, to try for the end zone just once. Sam was obviously wary of the chances to make a field goal. They were zero-for-three in field goals and PATs in that direction that day, with one being blocked by Ted Hendricks. Sipe had led the NFL in passing and was particularly good at avoiding interceptions. He had 30 touchdowns and only 14 interceptions that year.

As Sipe went back to pass, Hendricks put pressure on him and obscured his vision. Sipe threw towards tight end Ozzie Newsome in the end zone, but Mike Davis jumped in front and made the interception. I've never heard 77,000 fans get so quiet so fast. We had locked up a trip to the AFC championship game.

Next stop, San Diego.

Our defense was feeling pretty good after stopping Snake and then snuffing Sipe. But the Chargers were something else. That year they set an NFL record with 6,410 yards in total offense.

When I got up the morning of the game, I thought we might be in for some good luck. It had rained. The field would be wet and that might give the Chargers' great passing game some problems. Early in the game we had some more good luck. Plunkett's pass over the middle bounced off King and into the hands of Chester, who ran for a 65-yard touchdown.

I knew that wouldn't be enough. Before the game I told the offense that we could not have enough points against a team that had Dan Fouts at quarterback. Fouts didn't wait long to prove me right. He came right back and tied the score at 7-7 with a TD pass to Charlie Joiner.

But Plunkett answered with a broken play touchdown run and a 21-yard touchdown pass to King. Punter Ray Guy damn near kicked the ball to Mexico in that game, averaging 56 yards, including one for 76 yards. Against a team that can eat up yards in big chunks, every little bit helps.

Fouts kept firing but we still had a 34-27 lead, and

the ball, with 6:43 left. The Chargers had a great front four, three of whom were All Pros—Louie Kelcher, Gary "Big Hands' Johnson, and Fred Dean. They made life miserable for Plunkett that day, sacking him six times and re-injuring his left knee.

But with 6:43 left and holding a 34-27 lead, we knew the best way to handle a hard-charging line was to charge right back at them. The idea was to eat up the clock and keep the ball away from Fouts. I remembered that years before, the Chargers original owner, Barron Hilton, was responsible for Oakland getting a franchise in the AFL because he wanted a natural rival on the West Coast. If it weren't for Hilton, the franchise would have been awarded to Atlanta.

Anyway, we sure as hell had a rivalry going with the Chargers, much to the dismay of the owner at that time, Gene Klein, who disliked Al Davis intensely and was especially angry about our plans to move to Los Angeles. But the job of his team at the time was to stop our offense from moving. It didn't happen.

Our mission was to keep our offense on the field either until we scored or until the clock ran out. Inch by inch, yard by yard, second by second, we managed to run out the clock. It was a Super drive.

And, finally, we were a Super team. My wild, wild, wild card team was headed to New Orleans for a rematch with the Philadelphia Eagles in Super Bowl XV.

There's no teacher like experience. I learned a lot about Super Bowls in January of 1977 when we went to No. XI. Everything went so smoothly in that one, that I already knew what needed to be done in January of 1981.

First, I made sure the players took care of all their ticket requests, family travel plans and all that during the first week of the two week buildup to the Super Bowl. Then we did a lot of film work at home that first week because it's difficult for players to study during all the the hype and hoopla the week of a Super Bowl.

The week before Super Bowl XI, the players actually requested they have a curfew. When the players arrived in New Orleans, I gave them Monday night without a curfew. The rest of the week they had to be in by 11. The minimum fine would be $1,000, to be changed at my discretion.

There have been a lot of exaggerations about how the Raiders partied before that Super Bowl. To hear some people tell it, all our players were out all night every night before the Super Bowl. One book even said that the players paid $25,000 in fines. Not true.

Yes, Matuszak did go out on Wednesday night, which he calls Tooz-day. He is too big to hide, even on a busy Bourbon Street. By morning everybody knew he had been out. Even if they didn't see him out that night, it sure as hell was obvious the next day when he showed up almost two hours late for a press conference. His big sunglasses did not hide his weary looking eyes.

I wasn't amused at the time, but looking back it was kind of funny I guess. A couple of days earlier Tooz announced to the media that he was going to work hard and get to sleep early all week because this was a big game. He said he would be "The Enforcer" and watch for other players who tried to sneak out.

When he finally got to the press conference, he told the media the reason he went out was to check the streets for other players. He said he checked everywhere all night. He did that, I'm sure. It cost him $1,000.

There were only five other players fined in New Orleans. One was hit for $1,000 for leaving his playbook, with the game plan and everything, where somebody could have picked it up. To be honest, I was much more pissed about that than I was for Tooz going out. The other four fines were for only $500. Four players were late to practice because they got in a car with our team doctor and he got lost. I took pity on them, but told them it was their job to get to practice. No excuses.

Eagles coach Dick Vermeil was the darling of the media before that Super Bowl. I remembered how he originally was going to attend College of Pacific, but because I was already at quarterback he would have been switched to halfback. Instead he switched to San Jose State. I had my best college games against San Jose State.

The press was reporting how hard Vermeil worked as a head coach. He often worked 20 hours a day and rather than waste time going home he would just stay at the office and sleep in a cot. Give me a break. Hell, give him a break. I believe in hard work, but being obsessive is not the best way to get good results.

But Dick maintained a business-as-usual approach during Super Bowl week. Work, work, work. One day, I think it was the Thursday before the game, he even had two practices. Two-a-days are not recommended four days before the Super Bowl. It's damn near February and these guys have been at it since July. They're worn out. But Dick ran his team his way and I ran mine my way. I don't think his way would have worked with the Raiders. He was asked what he would have done about Matuszak's mid-week outing.

"I would fine him $10,000 and send him home on the next flight," Vermeil said.

If I took that approach during the season, I would have to activate myself by December so we would have enough guys to play. Our players laughed at Vermeil's comments. I was glad he said it. All week it seemed to me that Vermeil and the Eagles were getting too tight and we were staying nice and loose.

On Tuesday I was real loose. Everything in me was coming out of every opening. I had the flu. But it was Super Bowl week, so I couldn't phone in sick. That morning I was late getting to the bus that was heading to picture day. It took off without me.

I wondered if anybody noticed I was missing. With all the attention Vermeil was getting that week, the media almost didn't know I was there. In a way I liked that and in a way it made me feel overlooked. All the attention was going to Tooz and his night out, Plunkett's great comeback, Vermeil's work ethic and the conflict between commissioner Pete Rozelle and Al Davis.

At one of the press conferences the media talked to Vermeil for a long time and finally when it was my turn, I stepped to the podium and introduced myself by saying, "I'm the *other* coach, Tom Flores." I thought it was kind of funny, but nobody laughed. I laid an egg with that one, but I just kept talking so not many people noticed.

Anyway, Davis had the wheels in motion to move the Raiders to Los Angeles and Rozelle was once again his adversary, just as he had been before the American League merged with the NFL. Some people thought that if the Raiders won that Rozelle would have somebody else give the trophy to Davis. Some said that even if the Raiders lost, Al would figure out a way to get the trophy from Rozelle anyway.

That was a funny comment, but I was confident we would not lose. Our players remembered the 10-7 regular season loss to the Eagles. They kept telling each other "Remember November 23," which was the date of that game. So on January 25, I felt we were ready.

My only concern going in was the zone pass coverage that Eagles defensive coordinator Marion Campbell used. It used man-to-man concepts within zones and was very effective. Fortunately, the Eagles remembered November 25, too.

They remembered the 86-yard touchdown that Branch scored. They were determined not to give up a long score in the Super Bowl, so they played their cornerbacks well off Branch and Chandler.

That was an example of the Raider philosophy at work. The Eagles obviously went to bed before the game thinking about the prospect of Branch burning them deep. As it turned out they would go to bed the next night having nightmares about Plunkett and Branch on offense and Rod Martin on defense.

Martin intercepted the first pass thrown by Eagle quarterback Ron Jaworski, who apparently was under the misconception that Martin was vulnerable as a pass defender. Not on that Super Sunday he wasn't. Martin went on to set a Super Bowl record with three interceptions.

After his first theft we marched 30 yards and scored on the seventh play, a two-yard pass from Plunkett to Branch. Both of them made the play work by staying alert. Branch was covered at first, but worked back toward the quarterback like he is supposed to. Plunkett had begun to run, but when he did that a linebacker decided he would try to tackle the quarterback. That left a throwing lane for Plunkett to hit Branch.

Late in the first quarter we came up with a play that I think broke Philadelphia's spirit. Appropriately, it was a broken play. Plunkett was supposed to hit Chandler on a crossing pattern, but Chandler was covered. So Plunkett scrambled around and finally threw the ball about ten yards in the air to King. What appeared to be a short gain became a Super Bowl record 80-yard touchdown as King outraced everybody down the left sideline into the end zone.

I think the game really ended for the Eagles on that play. Plunkett threw another touchdown pass to Branch, for 29 yards and Chris Bahr kicked two field goals as we won easily, 27-10.

Quite honestly, after the close game we had against San Diego, the final moments of the Super Bowl were anti-climactic. But as I watched the clock blink down to zero I finally was able to feel satisfaction for the first time. When you win games during the season you have to just move on to the next game. But our next game wasn't until August.

In one season we had gone from being the maligned to the magnificent, from the valleys of dispair to the peaks of celebration. We were Super Bowl champions.

I hugged Jim Plunkett, who was named the Most Valuable Player after completing 13 of 21 passes for 261 yards and three touchdowns. I saw pictures of us hugging and smiling ear-to-ear. We were a couple of merry Mexicans, all right, even if neither of us could speak Spanish very well.

In two years he had gone from oblivion to Super Bowl MVP. His was quite a story. And to think that in the fifth week of the season he was on the bench and I was in jeapordy of being fired. Remembering all that made the Super Bowl that much sweeter.

In the locker room the media was prepared for the long-awaited Rozelle-Davis confrontation. In reality, these are two class men who both love football. Neither one would spoil this special moment because of their personal feud.

First, I addressed the team. I told them they won because they were the best team and they deserved to be World Champions. I said it was the greatest moment in my life. And it was.

After Rozelle presented the trophy, Davis gave one of his succinct speeches.

"You know when you look back on the glory of the Oakland Raiders, this was our finest hour," he said. "To Tom Flores, the coaches and the great athletes, you were magnificent out there.... Your commitment to excellence and your will to win will endure forever. You were magnificent."

eleven

Moving South—The Vagabond Raiders

In my first five years as head coach, we changed almost the entire roster, endured a player strike, won two Super Bowl championships and moved the franchise from Oakland to Los Angeles.

You might say it was an eventful experience.

Some people have asked how I kept the players focused on football while Al Davis was waging a major battle against the NFL to move the Raiders during that five-year period. Actually, all the commotion about moving may have been a blessing.

It didn't intrude into football matters and with so much attention being given to Al and the move, maybe less attention was given to all the changes we were undergoing as a football team. I'm not saying we were able to operate in secrecy, but maybe the media didn't have as much time, energy or space in the newspapers to be as critical or analytical as usual.

So despite all the events in 1980 surrounding the move, the operation of the football team was relatively unaffected.

It is frustrating to hear people blame Al Davis for taking the Raiders out of Oakland. The blame should be given to Oakland politicians and Coliseum officials, who all but drop-kicked the Raiders.

Although Al has been depicted as a complicated and devious man in business dealings, I think the opposite is actually true. He is basically simple in what he wants and direct in how he goes after it.

So was Rocky Marciano. I don't think his opponents liked the results, either.

People must always remember that the prime motivation behind everything Al does in business is to win. Second, when Al says he wants to do something, you damn well better believe he will do whatever it takes to accomplish his goal. With that in mind, let's remember what was really behind the Raiders' move from Oakland.

At first, Al didn't want to move. All he wanted was a better stadium situation to help maintain a winning organization. He believed that players would be granted some form of free agency in the 1980s and he wanted to be able to compete financially for talent. The Oakland Coliseum was the second smallest stadium in the AFC, larger than only the Houston Astrodome, and offered no income from luxury suites.

So he asked for a better lease and a renovated stadium. If the Oakland-Alameda politicians and Oakland Coliseum officials had worked half as hard to accomodate the Raiders' initial requests as they later did to try and lure an expansion team, then they would have saved millions of dollars as well as the team itself.

Some people have accused Al of using Oakland while he negotiated a new deal in Los Angeles, but I know that's not true. In February of 1980 he was happy and excited when Oakland Mayor Lionel Wilson and Kaiser Aluminum executive Cornell Maier offered him a proposal to stay in the Oakland Coliseum. Al felt the details could be worked out. It called for a loan to build luxury suits, among other things. The Raiders would have built and leased out the suites themselves. As I recall the whole deal would have cost Oakland about $12 million.

As soon as he agreed to that proposal, Al visited Tex Schramm of the Dallas Cowboys, to see the luxury boxes in their new Texas Stadium. While Al was gone, there was a phone call between NFL Commissioner Pete Rozelle, who was in Hawaii for the Pro Bowl, and Bill Moorish, who was head of the Oakland Coliseum board's football committee.

There are conflicting reports as to what was said in the phone call. Rozelle said Moorish phoned just to keep him up to date on the proposal. In court, Raider attorney Joe Alioto got Moorish to acknowledge that Rozelle may have pointed out that the Raiders needed a three-fourths approval of owners in order to move. It was also brought out in court that the NFL objected to the Raiders moving to Los Angeles because it was prime expansion territory, meaning it would earn millions for each owner if an L. A. franchise bought into the league. So the league had reason and opportunity to stop the Raiders from leaving Oakland. But we may never know what was really said in that Rozelle-Moorish phone call.

I do know that Wilson and Maier were allowed to negotiate. I do know they and Davis thought there was a deal, or at least the possibility of one. I do know that there was a conversation between Rozelle and Moorish and after that the Wilson-Maier deal was yanked off the table.

When Al returned from the Super Bowl in Pasadena in January of 1980, Wilson and Maier came to visit him and were embarrassed to say that the deal was off and they were no longer empowered to negotiate with him.

The next thing I hear is that Oakland sent a revised offer to the Raiders' office. Al LoCasale, the team's executive administrator, threw it in a dumpster without looking at it. Davis was pissed. That was February 4, 1980. On March 1, Al signed a Memorandum of Agreement with the Los Angeles Coliseum.

In the interim, on February 22, the City of Oakland filed an eminent domain action to take over ownership of the Raiders. I thought that was both ludicrous and funny. Here they don't think enough of the team to keep a $12 million offer on the table, but they file a suit based on the fact that the team in indispensible to the community. Now that's talking out both ends of your mouth.

Anyway, can you imagine the precedent such an eminent domain case would set? Any time a business that serves the public wanted to move—to change landlords—the government could take over that business so the public wouldn't be deprived of its service at the original location. Scary. Even more scary is that such a ridiculous suit stayed alive in the courts long enough to cost the people of Oakland millions of dollars.

Meanwhile, in Los Angeles the NFL sent notices to major banks warning against loans to the Raiders based on the fact that they were moving there because such a move required a vote of approval by the owners. So even if there is a shred of doubt that the NFL interfered with Al's ability to do business in Oakland, there can be no doubt that the league tried to torpedo him in Los Angeles.

Over the next three years there would be up to nine

major legal actions on state and federal dockets in northern and southern California. There was an injuction that prevented the NFL from stopping a move, a stay of that injunction, and then a temporary restraining order that held the Raiders in check. For a while.

On June 14, 1982, the courts finally issued an injunction that prohibited the NFL from interfering with the Raiders' move to Los Angeles. On July 5, Al finalized a 10-year agreement to play in the Los Angeles Coliseum. By August 29, when we played our first preseason game in Los Angeles against the Green Bay Packers, we had sold 53,000 season tickets.

Hell, after all that success, if we didn't win a Super Bowl the football season would have been anti-climactic.

In April of 1983 the courts threw the NFL for a bigger loss, totalling about $60 million to be paid to the Raiders and the L. A. Coliseum when all was figured in. The court fixed the Raiders' loss at $11.5 million and the L. A. Coliseum's at $4.86 million. Because this was an anti-trust case, the losses were trebled to $34.650 million for the Raiders and $14.580 million for the Coliseum. That didn't count Raiders' attorneys fees of $10.6 million, which had to be paid by the NFL, or the league's own legal expenses, estimated to be about $20 million.

All things considered, everybody would have been better off if Oakland just followed through on the deal that Al accepted.

We gave them a first class team and they thought we should be happy with a second rate stadium. Look at the other teams in the AFC West division. Seattle's Kingdome seated about 65,000. Denver renovated Mile High Stadium into a great dual-purpose facility that seated 75,000. Kansas City's beautiful Arrowhead Stadium had 78,094 seats. San Diego has redone its stadium to accomodate more than 60,000.

The whole thing left me sad and angry. I was sad to leave Oakland, where I had been the franchise's first quarterback. And I was angry with the politicians and officials who didn't cooperate.

In 1992 San Francisco's baseball Giants failed for the fourth time in five years to get voter approval to build a ball park in the Bay Area. They were trying to get something built in San Jose. That made me remember that when the Raiders had to move out of Oakland I thought that we somehow should have built our own stadium somewhere down the peninsula, probably in Santa Clara near Great America. There's a lot of land and we could have built the stadium of our dreams. We would have kept all our Oakland fans, gained more fans from the San Jose area and had total control over our own stadium, like the Dodgers do theirs.

But like everything else the Raiders had in Northern California, that idea is now just a faded memory and it makes me sad.

After winning Super Bowl XV, the 1981 season was not a good one. The age on our offensive line and our lack of depth in several areas began to take a toll. Jim Plunkett got beat up and we used Marc Wilson at quarterback a lot.

Another problem that was prevalent in the league in 1981 was drugs, especially cocaine. It was an insidious drug but we didn't know yet how bad it was or how widely it was being used. I think the Raiders were a little more aware of how to deal with drugs than some teams, but I was to learn in later years that in 1981 many teams had more problems with cocaine than anybody suspected at the time.

The team that wins a Super Bowl has a shorter off-season than anybody else. First, they are one of only two teams that played in the final game. Then, when the loser takes off and goes home right after the Super Bowl, the winner goes back to the city or the stadium. There are parades, speeches. And after that there are offseason dinners, awards.

Some guys aren't even through celebrating their Super Bowl victory when they find themselves suiting up for a minicamp.

The short offseason really bothered Plunkett. He was so banged up in 1980 that he tried to heal up after the season. Usually he jogs, runs in distance races and stays in great shape. But this time he just rested and showed up in training camp about 15 pounds over weight. He started six games, then gave way to Wilson for nine games after he threw nine interceptions and only four touchdowns.

Wilson was not only too inexperienced to step right in, but he was using those quick feet to escape pass rushers as often as he was his strong arm to hit pass receivers.

The offensive line lost two Hall of Fame starters, and a big piece of Raider history, as left guard Gene Upshaw and left tackle Art Shell went to the bench that year. Another great offensive lineman, center Dave Dalby, followed. Dave had been only the second starting center in Raiders history until 1981. Twenty one years, two centers. That's impressive stability. Double D, as he was called, was the man who replaced the original Raider, Double O, Jim Otto.

Tight end Raymond Chester seemed to slow down and lost his job to Derrick Ramsey. Cornerback Lester Hayes showed up looking more like he was ready for his old college position, linebacker. After a big 1980 season, he obviously had a big offseason. He weighed almost 230 pounds. The other corner, Monte Jackson, had knee and weight problems and never did prove to be worth the three high draft picks he cost us.

And then there was the drug damage. As far as I'm concerned, cocaine sidetracked wide receiver Cliff Branch and defensive end Willie Jones in 1981. I'm sure it affected several others, as well.

Needless to say the season was a nightmare. Not only did we have the first losing season in 17 years, at 7-9, but we went three consecutive games without scoring a point. Nada, zilch and zip. Yuk! To make it even worse, the fans were not that friendly in Oakland because we already were fighting to leave for Los Angeles.

So we were one very lame, lame duck team.

Perhaps the best reason for optimism coming out of the 1981 season was that we did have a good rookie crop, with seven of our nine draft choices making the team. That included future All-Pro Howie Long, who led the team in sacks.

In the spring of 1982, when the anti-trust case was really heating up, Al Davis spent more time in court than he did with the team. He wasn't even with us during the draft. He phoned as often as possible and we kept him up to date. I didn't know how things were going in court, but in the draft we we did great.

I had coached in something called the Gold Bowl that year and had the opportunity to see USC's Heisman Trophy winning running back, Marcus Allen. After a couple of runs it was obvious to me that he was something special.

For a change, we even had a high draft pick, which is the only good thing that comes out of a lousy 7-9 season. Usually it's new coaches that get to make the high draft selections because the guy that earned it with a lousy season is gone. Anyway, we had the No. 10 pick and I wanted to take Allen. Some people said he lacked the speed necessary for pro football. I didn't agree. He was fast enough to gain 2,342 yards, an average of 212.9 per game, his senior season.

I knew the Minnesota Vikings and Atlanta Falcons

might take a running back and they were ahead of us. I just hoped they thought Allen was too slow. The Vikings took Stanford running back Darrin Nelson in the seventh spot. One down. Picking ninth, right ahead of us, the Falcons took Arizona State running back Gerald Riggs.

So Marcus Allen was a Raider. OK, there was the formality of signing him. But we didn't usually have trouble with that. In our usual search for veteran help, we acquired defensive end Lyle Alzado, who had been with Denver and Cleveland, and running back Greg Pruitt, who was also an outstanding punt returner despite being a 10-year veteran. So the future began to look a little brighter.

After the courts prevented the NFL from interfering with our move, we became the Los Angeles Raiders on July 7, 1982.

The team opened a ticket office in Los Angeles, but we opened our training camp at Santa Rosa, the same as usual. Our first two regular season games were on the road, at San Francisco and at Atlanta, and we knew the Players Associations was preparing for a strike. We had a pretty good idea that if there was a strike it would be after the second league game. So rather than move everything south for the start of the season, we would go back to the practice field in Alameda after we broke camp in Santa Rosa. Then we'd wait to see what happened.

But you can imagine the chaos it caused for players and coaches who didn't know where they were going to live.

Our first regular season game as the Los Angeles Raiders was against the San Francisco 49ers, who had just won Super Bowl XVI. Because we had won the previous Super Bowl, this season opener was tabbed as Super Bowl XVI1/2. It was unfortunate to break up the geography of the cross-bay rivalry at this point in history. Within a ten-season period of 1980-89, those two teams would win six Super Bowl Championships.

We won our first league game as the Los Angeles Raiders, 23-17, over the 49ers with Marcus Allen rushing for 116 yards in his pro debut and the defense sacked quarterback Joe Montana five times, including two by a rejuvenated Alzado. The next week we went to Atlanta and beat the Falcons, 38-14, with the help of seven sacks and three interceptions.

Then we were stopped cold. The players went on strike, just as we figured. We were in limbo for 57 days. I didn't know what to do with my time. I saw a college game at Cal for the first time in my memory. I even saw my daughter Kim do some cheerleading at Ygnacio Valley High. She was also a princess at homecoming, taking after mom, who had been the queen at her San Mateo High homecoming a couple of years earlier. When the strike was over it was already November. Seven games were lost and we still had not played a regular season contest in our new home. That finally happened on Monday night, November 22. No matter how long the Raiders stay in Los Angeles, it will be hard for their real fans to forget that first game.

With 36 seconds left in the first half, we trailed the Chargers by 24-zip. We scored just before the half, then came back and introduced Los Angeles to a classic Raider comeback. We pulled it out, 28-24.

Because so much of the season was lost during the strike, we continued to work out in our old Alameda facility and fly to all games. Despite all these distractions, we finished 8-1 in the regular season and then beat the Cleveland Browns, 27-10 in the first round of the playoffs. Now Los Angeles was turned on to its new football team. Some 90,688 fans show up at the Coliseum for our playoff against the New York Jets.

That was on January 15, 1983, but the warm southern California weather made it feel like the middle of summer. Except for the turnovers, it was a great game. Very physical and a treat for the fans who packed into that old Coliseum.

John Robinson, who was Marcus Allen's coach at USC and a former assistant with the Raiders, was our guest on the sidelines. He had just resigned at USC a few weeks prior to our playoff season. He later became head coach of the Los Angeles Rams. Later he would tell me that standing on the sidelines that day is what got him back into coaching. "The excitement, the roar of the crowd, the players on the field," he said. "I realized I had made a mistake in getting out of coaching."

A few years later I would understand what he meant.

But on that day I was up to my eyeballs in being a coach. The Jets ended our season, 17-14. But under the circumstances nine wins and two losses wasn't bad for a team that played every game on the road.

Before the 1983 season I spent a lot of time checking out our new headquarters, which was formerly El Segundo Junior High. Our old facility had about 16,000 square feet of office space, one full sized football field and some extra field for practice. El Segundo gave us 55,000 square feet of office space, plus two grass football fields and 80 yards of artificial surface. This was a nice setup.

For my family the move south would be an easy transition, although we wouldn't all be moved in down south until 1984. Barb's mother lived in Long Beach and her brother and sister-in-law lived at Sunset Beach. Our two sons were attending southern California colleges, Mark at U. C. Irvine and Scott at U. C. Santa Barbara. Kim was just getting out of high school and would attend El Camino Junior College.

The summer of 1983 was our last at the fabled El Rancho Tropicana Motel in Santa Rosa. We planned it so that when we broke camp, the Raiders would say good-bye to northern California. We had big trucks at camp for the players to ship their cars to Los Angeles. So we broke camp, flew down, stayed at the Airport Hyatt overlooking Century Blvd. With most families still in transition that year, most of us lived at the hotel, which we nicknamed Mother Hyatt.

That move was pretty hectic because we had to take everything from our offices in Santa Rosa and Alameda and move them into El Segundo. We thought it was important that the players believe everything was totally organized. Realistically there's no way you can make a move like that and account for everything. We had plenty of surprises. But we never let the players know when we became frustrated. We refused to allow this to deter us as a football team.

Most of the coaching staff lived at Mother Hyatt. My home address was room 533. It was convenient in that you didn't have to worry about cleaning or cooking or making beds. But the routine did become a little monotonous. One night after a game I got tired of the hotel food and drove around looking for someplace to eat.

I saw a Bob's Big Boy and pulled in. I didn't want anything fancy, just a change of scenery. I went in and ordered a cheeseburger. As I waited I looked around and suddenly realized I didn't quite fit into this place because I wasn't wearing chains or carrying a knife. I obviously had driven into a pretty rough neighborhood. I slipped my wallet into my shoe, gulped down two bites, paid the tab and got the hell out of there. Months later I was showing Barb around town and I drove by that place to show her where I celebrated a victory one night. She couldn't believe I stopped the car in that neighborhood.

We also had something to learn about how the other half lived. I was invited to a fund-raising banquet by the Starlight Foundation on Valentine's Day. As I was to learn, this is a great group of celebrities that helps grant the wishes of children with terminal illnesses. This was a black tie affair, so I called Barb and asked her to join me. I knew we were in for an experience when they sent a limo to pick us up.

We thought we were dressed nicely until we walked into the place. Suddenly we looked like faded wallpaper. Those Hollywood types really know how to put on the beads, bangles and sparkle. There were too many stars to name. We met Jane Fonda and her husband Tom Hayden there and since then Tom and I have become pretty good friends.

Before we sit down to eat, Barb notices a dog sitting at a table next to ours. I almost choked on my drink when I saw that, but somehow managed not to make a fool of myself. This was verrrrrry Hollywood, I guess. Then I saw Odis McKinny, one of our players. I asked him if he saw the dog.

"Oh, yeah," he said, as if nothing were unusual. "That's Benji."

I did a double take and, sure enough, it was the dog I had seen in those Benji movies. He was just sitting in a chair at a table like everybody else. Well, not exactly everyone else. His head was on the table and his rear was on the chair. And he didn't check his fur coat at the door. His trainer, or date, or whatever, was a guy dressed up like an old seaman. Or maybe he was an old seaman. Hell, you can never tell about those Hollywood types.

After a while I accepted Benji as just another one of the guests. After all, he was served tournedos of beef just like the rest of us.

I eventually became an honorary trustee with the Board of Directors for the Starlight Foundation and I like the work they do all over the world. There is always a fundraiser or benefit for something in the Los Angeles area so you have to be choosy. I did receive several honors that I am proud of from the southern California community. In 1984 the American Lung Association of Los Angeles selected me as Humanitarian of the Year. Imagine somebody giving a Raider coach an award for being a humanitarian.

There are so many Hispanics in southern California that you get fan mail from them all the time. They were extremely proud that the Raiders, with me as head coach and Jim Plunkett as quarterback, had moved to Los Angeles. In 1985 I received a Golden Eagle Award from NosOtros, a presitgious Hispanic group started by Ricardo Montalban. I was the first sports personality to receive this award, which previously went to entertainment celebrities.

At first I felt a little out of place in the Los Angeles area. We eventually built our own home in Manhatten Beach, which is about as southern California as you can get.

In 1983, for the first time since I became head coach, we didn't have some kind of a a catastrophy in the first few weeks of the season. In 1979 we lost three of our first four games. In 1980 we lost three of our first five games and I almost lost my job. In 1981 we lost four of our first six games. And in 1982 we had a 57-day strike after the second game and didn't know where to call home.

But in 1983 we had a home, even if it was a hotel for some of us, and opened the season with four wins before losing to the Washington Redskins, 37-35. But we were to have the final say in that duel at the end of the season. A big play in that game was a screen pass from quarterback Joe Theismann to running back Joe Washington for 67 yards.

This mere footnote of a play was to be rewritten later as a major chapter in Super Bowl history.

We finished the regular schedule with a 12-4 record. Plunkett opened the year as the starter, but when he looked worn out I replaced him with Marc Wilson as the starter against the Dallas Cowboys. Wilson looked like the heir apparent to the Raider quarterback job. in his first start he completed 26 of 49 passes for 318 yards as the offense totalled 519 yards. We won, 40-38, when Chris Bahr kicked a field goal with only 20 seconds left.

But two weeks later Wilson injured his shoulder trying to make a tackle after an interception. Plunkett, who healed physically and emotionally once again while sitting on the sideline, was ready for another Cinderella year. He came in and pulled out the Kansas City game by completing 5 of 9 passes for 114 yards and we won, 28-20.

That was the first of five consecutive wins that clinched a division championship.

We opened the playoffs at home against the Pittsburgh Steelers, the team we met in the playoffs five times in the 1970s. An AFC record crowd of 92,434 was at the L. A. Coliseum for this one. Led by a defense that featured Alzado's pass rushing and a Lester Hayes interception, we held them to 123 yards passing and won easily, 38-10.

That brought the Seattle Seahawks to town for the AFC Championship. Two of our four losses that year were to the Seahawks. Later in 1984 they would split with us in the regular season and oust us in the first round of the playoffs. But we were in charge on January 8, 1984. We jumped on them big time, getting ahead 27-0 on the way to a 30-14 win.

It was on to Tampa Bay for a rematch with another team that beat us in the regular season. We would meet the Washington Redskins in Super Bowl XVIII.

One of the first things I saw after landing at the airport in Tampa Sunday before the game was a big billboard that had the Raiders logo and "Committment to Excellence" written on it. A chill ran through me and it felt good. I had arrived a day ahead of the players. I knew when they landed the next day they would see that sign.

It was a symbol of how completely we prepared to be in the Super Bowl, on the field and in the front office. Unbeknownst to me, Al Davis and Al LoCasale had once again purchased such signs all over Tampa, on bus benches and billboards. We had done the same thing two years before in New Orleans when we won Super Bowl XV.

To some this may have come across as a sign of cockiness or overconfidence. But for those of us who had fought for this from the El Rancho to El Segundo, it was a declaration of our determination.

The previous week we had taken care of tickets and travel plans, as usual. We also practiced a lot of things we knew would be useful against the Redskins. On defense, we faced every type of counter-gap, trap, o-t, play that was imaginable. That was the basic Redskin play, featuring running back John Riggins behind a pulling guard and tackle. He set an NFL record with 24 touchdowns that year. We must have run that play 100 times until our defense was probably more familiar with it than the Redskin offense.

It certainly appeared that way in the game.

The week before the game was usual hype and tripe. The media was everywhere. Our hotel lobby was so inundated with fans that we used back stairways and exits to get around. On Tuesday there were the traditional fines for about five guys who were late for picture day—$1,000 apiece.

On Thursday we had our traditional fight. On Thursday before Super Bowl XV, Matt Millen and Gene Upshaw got into a little scuffle. This time one of our coaches told Millen to hit guard Mickey Marvin on an unexpected blitz. Smack, the two were rolling around in one of those nobody-could-ever-get-hurt fights.

On Friday or Saturday I learned that Willie Brown was selected to the Hall of Fame. That reminded me of the

Raiders first Super Bowl victory, when Brown set a record with a 75-yard interception return against the Vikings.

Because of all the fans in our hotel, I took most of my meals in my rooms. I had a limousine and driver at my disposal, so I told Barbara to go out in it with some of the family or her friends. So she went shopping with friends in the limo. When they got hungry, she and the kids had the driver pull into a Jack in the Box. That must have been something to see, somebody ordering from the back of a limo at Jack in the Box.

I had a couple of unusual things happen, too. I got a phone call from a pay phone in a bar in Stockton. A guy I had known in college had bet his friends that he could get me on the phone. I think I surprised him when I accepted the call and even got him a couple of tickets for the game. It might shock some people to learn that if you do it correctly you are not buried in work the last few days before a Super Bowl. If you are, then you probably are in trouble.

By the time we get to Super Sunday, I'm ready for everything except the excruciating wait. Because of television, the game didn't begin until 4:15. If they tried to start any later I think our players would have started by themselves. I mean they were ready. I was a little jumpy, too, which I displayed during our first big play.

That came when Washington tried to punt on its first possession. Our special teams coach, Steve Ortmayer, thought he saw a weakness in the Redskins blocking scheme the week before. He overloaded one side in such a way that Derrick Jensen, our special teams captain, might be able to get free on an inside charge. And that's exactly what happened.

Jensen blocks the punt and there is a mad scramble for the ball near Washington's goal line. Everybody on our sideline is going nuts and I'm worried that nobody is thinking about the correct thing to do. So I start yelling "goal line offense, goal line offense," but I notice nobody is paying much attention. In fact a couple of players looked at me as if I had just lost my mind. Then one player finally said, "Coach, we scored a touchdown."

"Oh," I said, trying to act like I knew what was going on. "PAT team, PAT team." I looked up at the big screen and was happy that the TV cameras didn't catch my mistake. With all those wide bodies jumping around in front of me, I couldn't see where we recovered the ball. As it turned out, Jensen not only blocked it but recovered it in the end zone.

In 1983, scoring in the NFL reached an all-time high of 21.8 points per game. That led to a misconception that offenses were taking control. In fact, the opposite was true. Defenses scored on 49 interceptions, up from 30 in each of the four previous seasons, and also pressured offenses into numerous turnovers that set up short scoring drives. So, in a perverse way, defense was the reason that scoring was up in 1983. Teams were abandoning their zone defenses and the trend was toward attacking on defense. This would reach a peak in 1985 when the Chicago Bears dominated pro football.

But in Super Bowl XVIII it was the Raiders' attacking defense that gave an object lesson in pro football's latest trend. The key was the great man-on-man coverage ability of cornerbacks Lester Hayes and Mike Haynes. They got on the Redskins wide receivers so tight that they could have qualified as tatoos. They denied everything, short, medium and long.

Theismann found out he had no targets to hit when his first three passes—the short type that are usually gimmes—were either incomplete or broken up by Haynes and Hayes.

Because those cornerbacks were able to handle that difficult chore without help, the Raiders defense did not have to use zone coverage. That freed the linebackers to close down the running game. Inside linebackers Matt Millen and Bob Nelson walked right up to the line of scrimmage and got facemask-to-facemask with guards Russ Grimm and Mark May.

If either guard pulled to lead one of those counters, the linebacker went right in and pursued the play. Our linebackers were also strong enough to get a pretty good stalemate right at the line of scrimmage. Because of our linebackers' proximity to the line of scrimmage, the Reskins had trouble using their usual array of traps and counters.

This worked especially well because Millen, who weighed about 260 pounds, was strong enough to play much like a defensive lineman, which he had been, of course, at Penn State. So Riggins, who had rushed for at least 100 yards in his previous six games, was held to 64 yards on 26 carries.

With both guards preoccupied by our linebackers, that left Washingrton's center, Jeff Bostic, one-on-one against nose tackle Reggie Kinlaw, who had a sensational game.

This was all the design of defensive coach Charlie Sumner, who recalled that we used a similar approach against another tricky offensive line to get us into Super Bowl XI. Even though Charlie wasn't with us in 1976, he remembered that in the AFC championship game against the Pittsburgh Steelers, the Raider defense deployed inside linebacker Monte Johnson eyeball-to-eyeball with guard Jim Clack, who became so confused that he didn't pull on running plays when he was supposed to.

"Well, I didn't think I should because that linebacker or tackle or whatever he was was right in front of me," said Clack. The Steelers rushed for only 72 yards in that game.

So history repeated itself in Super Bowl XVIII.

There were two more major plays in the first half.

The first was one of the most remarkable plays I've ever seen in football. We were on the Redskins 42 yard line with a fourth and seven and Ray Guy was back to punt. Our snapper, Todd Christensen, let fly with one of his rare bad snaps. The ball sails a good 12 feet above Guy's head. If anybody else had been the punter—anybody else!—the ball would have sailed back inside our 20 yard line.

But Guy jumped up and made a one-handed catch that would have made Fred Biletnikoff proud, only without stickum. Then, in one smooth motion, Guy boomed a punt into the end zone, about 60 yards in the air. Instead of the Redskins getting an easy score or getting the ball close to our goal line, they start on their 20. They gain only four yards then punt to us on our own 35.

Three plays later, including a 50-yard pass from Plunkett to Branch, Plunkett connects for a 12-yard touchdown to Branch and we're ahead 14-0.

With 12 seconds left in the first half, the Redskins had the ball on their own 12 yard line. It was at this time that Sumner made one of the greatest sideline calls in Super Bowl history. Intuitively, he recalled that 67-yard screen pass in a similar situation during our regular season loss to the Redskins. So Sumner grabs linebacker Jack Squirek, who we sometimes use in our nickel coverage on passing downs. He calls a defense where everybody plays zone, except he tells Squirek to watch for the screen pass to Joe Washington.

Squirek goes in and tells Matt Millen he's out. Millen was out, all right. Out of his mind with anger because he didn't want to leave the field. He is frothing at the mouth as he gets to the sideline. He begins yelling at Sumner, who tries to ignore the linebacker as he watches the play. Millen raves on and the play begins.

Theismann looks downfield and sees zone coverage.

Without looking he throws a screen to his left. Even if he did look he might not have seen Squirek closing in on Washington because defensive end Lyle Alzado sensed a screen and peeled off. Alzado was in position to obscure Squirek even if Theismann had looked.

So Theismann throws and Squirek arrives right on time for the interception and runs it in for the touchdown. With seven seconds left in the half, the Raiders were ahead by 21-3. If Washington had any hopes, they were squashed with that play. Technically, the game was still within reach, but that interception demoralized the Redskins.

Meanwhile, as Squirek crossed the goal line, Millen quit yelling at Sumner, picked him up and said "Great call, great call. . . ."

The one play everybody remembers from that game was Marcus Allen's 74-yard touchdown. That play was also one with historical significance for the Raiders. It was a Bob Trey-O, a simple power play off tackle. We used it in Super Bowl XI when Art Shell manhandled Jim Marshall and fullback Mark van Eeghen took care of the linebacker so halfback Clarence Davis could gain 137 yards on 16 carries, including a 35-yard run on third and seven from our own six yard line. That run kept alive a drive that went 90 yards and led to the first score of the day.

But Allen would give this play a twist that nobody would forget. When he got to the spot behind left tackle where he would usually decide to cut in or out, he did neither. Intead he reversed his field. This is a major no-no under normal circumstance. But Marcus Allen with a football in his hand is not a normal circumstance. The guy some people thought was too slow for the NFL proceeded to cut up the middle, then veer to the outside and outrun everybody for a Super Bowl record 74-yard touchdown.

Allen finished with another Super Bowl record 191 yards on 20 carries with 2 touchdowns and was named Most

Valuable Player. Considering the way our defense played, I'm not sure Marcus was the most valuable player in that game, but he sure was the most entertaining.

As the clock is ticking off the final tedious seconds I see Alzado on the sidelines with tears flowing down his cheeks. Two years earlier he was in my office at training camp saying he thought he should retire because he wasn't sure he could contribute.

Ha! Alzado was a force on our defensive line, showing our young stars, Howie Long, Bill Pickel and Greg Townsend, what it took to be great. This intense man from little Yankton college played 13 years with three different NFL teams and finally he was experiencing a Super Bowl. Some great players never get that chance. O. J. Simpson, Jim Brown, Dan Fouts, Archie Manning and so many others never got to play in a Super Bowl. But we gave Alzado a chance to realize his dream and here this tough guy was crying on the sideline.

I had to turn away to prevent from breaking into tears myself. God, it was a touching moment. A little more than eight years later, in the spring of 1992, Alzado was taken from us because of a brain tumor. But when I think of him I will always remember that moment on the sideline when he was so proud to be a world champion.

Just as in Super Bowl XV, one of the big moments after the game for the players was to see Rozelle hand the Lombardi Trophy to Al Davis. Their long and bitter battle in the court room made this a charged moment. But once again both showed their deep love for football and did not use the moment to further the personal feud.

Rozelle would later admit that the presentation of the Lomardi Trophy in Super Bowl XVIII was by far his most difficult. I thought he was gracious in the presentation.

Rozelle congratulated the team and said that I was a

great coach in the National Football League. Al took him one step further.

"Just win, Baby," he said, initiating a phrase that has become synomous with the Raiders. "I think today that this organization, this team, this coaching staff, dominated so decisively that two things must be said. Not only, in my opinion, are you the greatest Raider team of all time, I think you rank with the great teams of all times to have ever played any professional sport. Tom Flores isn't just a great coach in our league. With all due respect, he's one of the great coaches of all time."

Finally I felt like I received some acknowledgement. I feel fortunate that everything went right so that team could fulfill its potential. In 1980 we had a good team that played great at the right moments. But the 1983 team had much better talent, a trully great team.

After Super Bowl XV I didn't get to speak to the president, which is a custom, because we had just received the American hostages who had been released and he was too busy. But after Super Bowl XVIII President Ronald Reagan congratulated me on the phone in the locker room.

"I just think you ought to know, thought, that you've given me some problems," he added. "I have already had a call from Moscow. They think that Marcus Allen is a new secret weapon and they insist that you dismantle it. Now they've given me an idea about that team I just saw of yours. If you turn them over to us, we'd put them in silos and we wouldn't have to build the MX missile. It's been great. You proved tonight that the good defense can also be a pretty good offense."

I thought that remark about the defense was awfully perceptive of the President. I know a lot of people in the media that missed that point. Of course, they aren't exactly presidential material.

I partied with the team until 3 a.m., then did Good

Morning American at 5 a.m. We flew back to Los Angeles for a big reception in front of City Hall. That night Barb and Kim went back to the Bay Area and I went back to my room at Mother Hyatt. The next morning I was on my way to a scouting combine meeting to look at potential draftees.

Like I said, the off season is short for Super Bowl champions. Short, but very, very sweet.

twelve

People and Peeves

Everybody who was an American adult on November 22, 1963, remembers where they were and what they were doing on that date.

I was a quarterback on the Raiders' practice field. We were waiting for our head coach to come out on the field. It was Al Davis' first year on the job. That day we learned that something mattered more to him than winning: Life and death.

You could tell something was terribly wrong when Al walked slowly onto the field.

"President Kennedy has been assasinated," he said.

Like everybody in the country we were stunned. Al was visibly shaken. His voice was shaky. There were tears in his eyes. We had never seen this side of him before. Most of us couldn't have imagined then that Al was anything but tough and possibly oblivious to any emotions that didn't have to do with winning or losing.

We were getting ready to play the Denver Broncos. It was a Friday, which was our final day to practice in full gear before the game. I remember watching Al, wondering how this intensely competitive person would reconcile preparing men to play a kids game in the midst of a national tragedy. I mean we are talking about the President of the United States being killed.

Kennedy was such a dynamic speaker that whenever you thought of him it was easy to recall little pictures of him or part of one of his dynamic speeches. In my adult life I have not experienced any other event that gripped the consciousness of our entire country as much as Kennedy's assasination. It's sad that it takes such a monumental tragedy to bring us together. But on that weekend our country grieved as one.

The players, coaches and Al stood there for a long time without saying a thing, as if we were in shock. Maybe we were.

"That's it, guys, let's go in," Davis said. "I don't know how you guys feel or what you're going to do, but I ain't going to be there."

He was choked up and really couldn't say much more, so he turned and walked in. We stood there for a while then slowly walked into the locker room. I really didn't know what we were supposed to do. The game was scheduled to be in Denver. Did Al mean that he wasn't going to be at the game?

We soon learned that's exactly what he meant. Word got around the locker room that Al wasn't going to the game and didn't think it should be played. It wasn't a time for games. It was time to mourn the death of the leader of our country.

The next day the American Football League cancelled its games for that weekend. The National Football League chose to play. To this day I am proud of the AFL's decision to do the right thing.

That was the first of many times that I saw the side of Al Davis that you never hear about. I remember the first description I ever heard about Al. Ruthless was the word. And when it comes to football I guess you might say he is ruthless. But I also remember what he said when asked what was the primary thing in his life.

"To win," he said. "Outside of life, health and death — to win."

I always believed that comment spoke volumes about Al Davis. In fact, I think the ultimate challenge for Al is not to win football games. I think it is to win a battle between life and death.

To the best of my knowledge he remained true to those words. The story is well known about how he stayed by the side of his gravely ill wife, Carol. That happened during my first year as head coach, in 1979, and I've already mentioned it. What I didn't mention was that my wife, Barbara, wrote letters to Carol and Al read her the letters as she lay there unconscious.

"I know she can hear me," he would say.

That was the most dramatic dedication of time, energy and money that Al expended in a matter of life or death. But it was by no means an isolated example.

Al has helped friends, players, even people who had been his adversaries, whenever a major illness or other tragedy struck them. He handled these things discretely. Some times he helped people who didn't even know where the help was coming from.

And whenever Al became involved there was only one way to take care of things. The best way possible. I will always remember the time I hurt my arm and Al yelled at the trainer, George Anderson, "Is that the coldest ice you have?" That's an example of how intensely Al wants to get the best care.

In every case I know, whenever Al learned somebody was in a life-threatening situation he made sure they were able to get the best doctors or the best treatments available.

When I became an assistant coach in 1972, Del Courtney was struck by a mysterious illness that left him in a coma. Del was the Raiders' original band leader, and one of the nicest men on Earth.

When Al learned of Del's problem he was on the phone finding out everything. He was relentless. As is always the case with Al, he didn't want a doctor that somebody said was pretty good. He wanted the doctor that everybody said was the best.

I remember that somebody told Al there wasn't much hope and he might be wasting his time. That made him furious.

"A man's life is at stake," he said. "How in hell can you say that I am wasting my time?"

He wasn't, of course. I am reminded of that every time I visit Hawaii. Del and his band play for tea dances at the Royal Hawaiian Hotel. Del is well up in his 70s now and living a full, rich life. The last time I visited Del, we talked about the time we feared he would leave us.

"You showed how tough you were, pulling through that one," I told him.

"Yeah, but I had one tough guy helping me pull through," Del said. "He saw to it that I got the best of everything, otherwise we might not be here today talking about it. When Al does something, he only knows one way, full speed ahead. I can remember him sitting next to me when I was paralyzed. He said "Del, you're a Raider. Raiders don't die.' "

Al's dedication to football, to friends, to whatever cause he undertakes, should not be surprising. He does not spend a lot of energy doing the kind of things that most of us think are very normal. He doesn't play golf. He doesn't watch television, unless, of course, it's a football game. He does not go to parties unless they are important to his business or unless Carol wants to go.

I remember after Carol worked so hard to rehabilitate herself after the stroke that Al was so proud of her they attended one or two of the big parties at the Owners' winter meetings.

Carol greeted people, talked to them in detail about what they had been doing. She even talked to some of the sportswriters and asked about their spouses and children by name. She is an incredible woman and Al knows it. He stayed in the background and you just see him beaming with pride. He never told anybody this. It was just obvious to those who knew the situation.

When Tony Conigliaro had his stroke in Boston, Al visited him in the hospital back there. He also talked to Tony's family and told them everything he learned through his experience with Carol. Conigliaro was the great baseball player who lived in the Bay Area and became a sportscaster for a local television station.

He was visiting his family in Boston when he suddenly had a stroke. He clung to life in a hospital and his family, which was very close, was by his side all the time. When Al heard what happened he once again wanted to do whatever he could. Tony already had the best medical help that could be found. So Al went there and tried to give a boost to his family.

Al is obviously the subject of a lot of public curiosity. There have been two or three unauthorized biographies.

I glanced at a couple of them. Neither showed great insight into the man. One was written by an East coast author and reflected a lot of research and had many interesting, little known facts. The other was by a Bay Area sportswriter and seemed to be written off the top of his head. Not only was it biased, but it was factually incorrect in numerous places. Dates, names, the kind of things that can be looked up were wrong. It's no accident that I will not mention the name of that book.

Al does lead a fascinating life, but I think its funny how so many people depict him as something like the second coming of Howard Hughes. Al is different, but he is not weird, like Hughes was.

Al is kind of simple in his living style. He does not touch liquor. He is a creature of habit who likes a few, specific restaraunts. He eats about the same thing at about the same time every night. If he does frequent a restaurant he arranges to have the same table every time. And the table must have a phone, which he usually installs and pays for.

The only times he seems to be lavish is when it concerns his team or the health or welfare of somebody he knows.

Wells Twombly was a columnist for the *San Francisco Examiner*. Somehow it seems crass to refer to Twombly as a columnist. He was an artist, an essayist who happened to write for the sports section. He had a way with words like no sportswriter before or since. But at a young age, not even 40 years old I believe, Twombly became extremely ill with a liver disorder.

He was hardly what you would call a close friend of Al's. In fact, Twombly was more of an adversary. He mocked the Raiders often, at times likening our operation to the Soviet Union's KGB. But he cut us to ribbons with such artistic strokes it was difficult not to appreciate his work. I remember Al saying something about how gracefully this

writer was slicing us into little pieces. I'm sure Al appreciated Wells Twombly's remarkable ability in much the same
way he would appreciate Joe Namath as a quarterback or
Jim Brown as a running back. They're the enemy, but you
have to admit they are damn good.

Twombly tried to keep his illness a secret, but when
Al found out he reacted as if Wells were a close, personal
friend. Al knew that Twombly had a wife and a large family,
about six children as I recall. Al inquired around and found
out that some doctors gave Wells only a few months to live.

"That can't be," Al said. "There has to be something,
somebody, somewhere who can help this man."

There was. Al learned that doctors in another country had performed successful operations that cured people
with similar liver problems. At the time, such operations
were not performed in the USA. I don't know the details because Al did not do these things in a public way. But I know
that Al tried to persuade Twombly to go wherever it was to
get the operation that might save his life. Twombly was
stubborn. He declined. A few months later he died.

"It didn't have to be this way," Al said. "He was a
great man in his field. He has a wife and a growing, young
family. Damn, it just didn't have to be this way."

After I became head coach, one of the most difficult
things I had to do was let Lew Erber go as an assistant
coach. Lew had joined the Raiders in 1976 and we soon became best friends. He was a prince of a man who also helped
many people. But when Lew left after the 1981 season, he
and Al were not on the best of terms.

A few years later Lew was diagnosed as having a
rare virus that led to grand mal seizures. Even when he
seemed well, Lew did not have his short term memory. His
speech was affected. He would ramble on, talking so fast
you could barely understand him. He had been such a
smart, vital human being. Even in his forties, Lew had the

body of a man in his twenties. He ran all the time. He always had a smile. After he became ill, it hurt to see him in such bad shape.

When Al found out that Lew was in trouble, he searched for the best doctors. For a while Lew improved. I remember when it dawned on him that Al had helped find the doctors and pay the medical bills. He couldn't believe it.

"Tom, Al and I didn't even talk the last few years I was with the team," Erber said. "I can't believe that he would help me after the way we didn't get along. He is a difficult person to understand."

That he is. But he is an easy person to appreciate.

The Tooz. Just mention that name and anybody who knew him will smile. John had the effect on people. Everybody has some outrageous Tooz story. His public image was that of this huge, fun-loving, hard-living, one-step- over-the-line guy. The Tooz was all of that and more.

I still get a chill whenever I see a video or a rerun of his first big movie, North Dallas Forty. In it, he played a football player, which didn't take any imaginative casting. But he makes one speech near the end of the movie that is considered a classic by pro football players. It expresses the contradictary nature of this game that we call a business . . . or vice versa.

In this scene, The Tooz, as O. W. Shaddock, is fed up with the way Coach Johnson's is yelling at another offensive lineman, Jo Bob Priddy, who has just been humiliated in a game. Coach Johnson is yelling at Priddy in the locker room, saying he didn't study his opponents "facts and tendencies."

Shaddock: "Aw, shit, you never give us anything to bring to the game except your fucking facts and tendencies. To you it's just a business, but to us it's still a sport."

Coach Johnson: "You're supposed to be professionals. You go out there to play football."

Shaddock: "Aw, shit. We'll work harder than anybody to win. But, man, when we're dead tired in the fourth quarter, winning's got to be more than just money."

Coach Johnson: "You're hired to do a job."

Shaddock: "Job, job. I don't want no fucking job. I want to play football, you asshole. I want some feeling, I want some fucking team spirit."

Coach Johnson: "This ain't no high school. You don't have to love each other to play."

Shaddock: "That's just what I mean, you bastard. Every time I call it a game, you call it a business. And every time I call it a business, you call it a game. You and B. A. and all the rest of you coaches are chickenshit cocksuckers. No feeling for the game at all, man. You'll win, but it will just be numbers on a scoreboard. Numbers, that's all you care about. Fuck man, that's not enough for me."

He delivers his lines with such passion that you know this is more than acting. He is saying what so many pro football players have felt over the years. The big business atmosphere that has swallowed football in recent years has pushed these passions in the background. Players live like executives now. But I know that in order to put up with pro football, players have to love it for more than the money. It's a passion. That's was what Tooz was talking about.

But before there was The Tooz, there was John Matuszak. Inside that big body and underneath or behind all that loud talk and forever-on-stage act, John Matuszak became lost. I know I've already related some of the wild things The Tooz did. But few people were able to see this man when he dropped the act and allowed his sensitivities come through. . .to let John Matuszak out.

During his final training camp in 1982 he had trouble walking his back hurt so bad. He wanted very much to be able to play. Hell, he even tried to come back the next year, but he hurt himself running alone on the beach, so there was no way. But during that final summer of training camp with him at Santa Rosa's El Rancho Tropicana Motel, I got to know the John Matuszak that was trapped inside The Tooz.

It was a time for this 6-8, 300-pound giant to confront the reality of life without football. He became very introspective. I remember he sat down in my office one day and talked about his constant struggle with life.

"Tom, I only have this one life and I always wanted to make the best of it, but I always screwed things up somehow," he said. "People look at this big man and think he should be invincible. I think I've spent most of my life trying to live up to that stupid misconception. I did everything in a big way. Too big. Only now am I really trying to get in touch with who I really am.

"Sometimes I think I was given this big body as a test. It was a plague, really. Inside I feel like I am a gentle, sensitive guy who just wants to love people and be loved. I even let that come through at times, but I swear people thought I was putting them on. It was no joke, though."

There were many times that people were able to see how sensitive Matuszak was. He was wonderful with kids. He was extraordinary with people who were hospitalized or were in wheel chairs. He did have a remarkable ability to empathize. I think that is what made him such a natural actor. It was intuitive. That's how he lived his whole life. Acting.

After John retired I saw him several times. He's hard to miss. He loved his years with the Raiders.

"Happiest days of my life were thanks to the Raiders," he told me. "I was thrown away like trash by other teams. The Raiders took me in like I was part of a family.

They gave me a chance. I can't say that I didn't screw things up a few times. I did. But Al was always there with a kind word or a kick in the tail, or both. It meant something to be accepted."

In 1986 John said he was having some problems with drugs. He said he had always fooled around with things he shouldn't, more or less, but this time he didn't think he was handling it well at all. I saw him again in 1988 and I thought he looked much better.

"I think I have it licked, now," John said. "I've done too much booze and too much of everything bad for too long. When you are young and tough you think you are invincible. Hell, it catches up to you. I've realized I can't be The Tooz forever. It's time for John Matuszak to enjoy things. Now I get high on life and I feel great. I don't have time for any more setbacks. Life's just too damn short."

A few months later he was dead.

In recent years I've been asked a lot about two well-known athletes, Bo and the Boz. For the uninitiated that would be Bo Jackson, the great running back and baseball player, and Brian Bosworth, the former linebacker.

Both of these men were tremendously gifted athletes whose careers were sadly ended far too early because of injuries. In a weird twist of fate, all 3 of our lives became entwined. I was with the Raiders when we surprised everybody by getting Bo to play pro football. And I was with the Seahawks when the final decision was made to let Boz go.

But all of us were in the same ABC-TV Monday Night spotlight on November 30, 1987. Bo and Boz went head-to-head and I was coaching what was to be my second to last win for the Raiders. Bo set a Raider record by running for 221 yards and scoring 3 touchdowns, including one on a 91-yard run in which he showed his quickness, power, and world class speed.

I became familiar with both Bo and the Boz while preparing for the 1985 NFL College Player draft with the Raiders. Boz was a tremendous undergraduate linebacker at Oklahoma and Bo was an incredible athlete at Auburn who won the Heisman Trophy, was a two-time NCAA 60-yard sprint semifinalist, and was already drafted by Major League Baseball's Kansas City Royals.

Bob Zeman, our linebacker coach, was watching film of prospects and he was so impressed by one player that he got me out of my office to watch.

"Look at this number forty-four for Oklahoma," said Zeman. "He's in on every damn play."

Sure enough, number forty-four was all over the field, making tackle after tackle. He was big, fast and obviously very strong. It was one of the most impressive performances I have ever seen.

"Who is that guy?" I asked.

"Boz," said Zeman.

"Boz?" I repeated. "Is that a first, last or only name, like Dion?"

"I think," said Zeman, "Boz is all we need to remember. There can only be one guy like this."

We didn't know at the time how true that was. By 1987 Boz was a major topic. He was outspoken, had multi-colored hair, a "44" ear ring, and was considered the best linebacker to come out of college in years. Some said the best ever. He was strong as a truck, fast as a sports car and smart enough to have a very high grade point average.

He became available in the supplemental draft and we wanted to get him on the Raiders very badly. He would have fit perfectly, it seemed.

Bo had been the Tampa Bay Bucs' No. 1 draft pick in 1985, but he opted to play baseball with the Kansas City

Royals. In 1987 he not only played in the All-Star game, but in his first at bat he hit a home run, then stole a base and was selected as the MVP. Most people had written him off as a football player. As we know, Al Davis is not like most people.

Others laughed when we spent a seventh round draft pick for the rights to Bo. The Seattle Seahawks got Boz in the supplemental draft.

Bo surprised everybody, except maybe Al, by signing with the Raiders and then reporting for football duty shortly after the 1987 baseball season was over. You could tell immediately this was no ordinary physical specimen. He was about 6-1, 230 pounds and many believe he was the fastest man in football. In 1987 this NFL rookie played in only 7 of the 16 regular season games and still finished second on the team with 554 yards rushing and led the league with 6.8 yards per carry.

That, of course, included that incredible game at Seattle.

We were stuck on our nine yard line with a third down when I put in two tight ends and used Marcus Allen and Bo in the backfield. Marcus lined up as a fullback. We called for the 17 Bob Trey-O, the same play that we used to ruin the Vikings in Super Bowl XI and the one that Allen free-lanced into his remarkable touchdown against the Redskins in Super Bowl XVIII. It is a simple, basic play that calls for the tackle to take on the defensive end, the backside guard to pull and block and the fullback to take on the linebacker.

Every back in Raider history had run this play. But nobody ever ran it the way Bo Jackson did on this Monday night. I was just hoping to get the ball out far enough so our punter was comfortable. Bo gets the ball and runs right behind Marcus, then cuts up field. The first thing I see is we have five, six yards. I think, "Good, we have plenty of room to punt." Then I see Jackson another ten yards down the field and I think, "Great, a first down."

About that time Bo turned on the afterburners. I had never seen such a burst of speed since little Cliff Branch was a young wide receiver. But Bo probably weighed about 50 pounds more. He was amazing. He changed gears and everybody else looked like they had their feet caught in quicksand. Seattle's great safety, Ken Easley, thought he had an angle on Bo, but Bo's speed ruined everybody's angle of pursuit.

He seemed to gain speed with every step. By the time he got to the end zone he was going so fast he couldn't stop. He ran off the field and into the tunnel. I just stood there, stunned. Bo scored two more touchdowns in that game, including a short one where he lowered his shoulder and ran right over the Boz.

Bo was a quiet guy and we were together only part of that one season so I didn't get to know him very well. In a playoff game against the Cincinnati Bengals in 1990 he injured his hip. He tried to make a comeback in baseball, but he finally had to have his hip replaced. He's been told he will never play football again, but he says he will return to baseball.

Athletes like Bo Jackson come along very seldom, less than one in a lifetime. We are fortunate to have been able to see him perform even for a short time in pro football. I know the odds are greatly against him, but I wish Bo well in his attempt to come back and thank him for sharing his greatness.

For me, that 37-14 victory against the Seahawks was less than one week before my final win as a Raider coach. The next Sunday we beat Buffalo, 34-21. We closed out the 1987 season with three losses. In January I retired.

I remember that Boz grabbed a lot of headlines in 1987 even before he signed with the Seahawks. First he said he didn't want to go to Seattle, which I'm sure endeared him to the Seahawks fans. Before he signed he said a lot of things that polarized opinions about him.

Because he was a holdout, he reported late and then had trouble adjusting to the defensive scheme. Within a year he wrote a book about himself, which I thought was pretty presumptuous for somebody who hadn't accomplished anything on the pro level.

His misadventure against Bo in their rookie season is still talked about by fans in both Los Angeles and Seattle. Because of his outrageous lifestyle and outspoken ways, many Seattle fans were anti-Boz. When Bo ran over him, I heard Seattle fans cheer.

Boz tried to tackle Bo too high and then didn't wrap him up. You can't get away with that in an open field situation against an athlete like Bo Jackson. Wait a minute, there isn't an athlete like Bo Jackson. There's only one Bo. Anyway, Boz made a typical rookie error, the kind you can get away with in college but not the NFL. I'm afraid that one play is the only picture many NFL fans have of Boz.

The next thing I know Boz went on injured reserve in 1988 with a shoulder problem. I finally met him in 1989 after I became president of the Seahawks. He was down because he wasn't able to practice, this time due to a knee problem. He also had changed a whole lot since I first saw this brash kid with multi-colored hair on television. He was very quiet and his hair was all one color.

When he did start to play, he wasn't quite right. He had missed training camp and it showed. Then in the second game of the 1989 season he injured his right shoulder. Again he had to be placed on injured reserve. This was a very humbling experience for a guy who had been probably the best defensive player in college before he left Oklahoma.

One time we were talking and he was really down because he couldn't get out on the field.

"All I ever wanted to do was play pro football and now I can't," he said.

I think he realized he created a lot of the resentment towards him. When he was doing all those flashy things he was riding a high created by his ability to come through as a football player. But once that was taken from him because of injuries, he was in a strange new world. He was in one of those situations where you have to put up or shut up. Because he always attracted so much attention, even injured, we told him he didn't have to hang around the facility. We said it would be fine to work out on his own and we would just monitor his progress.

I think he appreciated that. I was reminded of how Jim Plunkett, a great quarterback, had to heal both psychologically and physically before he made his comeback with the Raiders. Boz was overwhelmed and needed something like that. Hell, the way he and his agent, Gary Wichard, built him up, he would have had to be Superman to live up to his reputation.

Unfortunately there are a lot of losers in the world who enjoy seeing someone join their lot. Let's get something straight. Bosworth was not a loser. He was a great college player who could have been a great pro player, but everything just sort of fell apart. Our medical people recommended that he stop playing football. Before the 1990 season we announced he failed his physical.

He had signed a huge contract, worth more than $11 million over ten years. It included a loan for $2.5 million. His salary started at $300,000 and went up $100,000 each year until 1992. As it turned out, he collected the first three years of his contract and we were responsible for $65,000 on an injury settlement because he failed his physical. He also had an insurance policy that covered him for a career-ending injury.

But I don't think any amount of money will compensate him for the career he never had. He created a lot of commotion for a short period of time and then he was gone. He was entitled to act, dress and cut his hair however he wanted. None of that would have mattered if he had been able to play football. But he couldn't, so he will always be remembered as a controversial character. Time heals all wounds, they say. I'm not sure whoever said that ever played pro football. Anyway, I wish Bosworth well.

I hate drugs. All drugs, including steroids and so-called performance enhancing products. I'm glad that the NFL finally installed a strong drug program. As far as I'm concerned you can't make it too strong.

If I had my way the rules would be simple. If you use drugs you are out, period. Whether they want to accept the role or not, athletes on the pro level are role models. What do these role models say to young kids if they are able to take drugs and still compete? It's an ugly message.

I don't believe there is such a thing as recreational use of drugs and I don't think there should be such a thing as invasion of privacy when it comes to drugs. I know this wouldn't go over very well with the American Civil Liberties Union. Too bad. I'd rather step on somebody's civil rights and save their life than let them shoot, snort, smoke or whatever until they are dead.

Remember Len Bias, the great basketball player who didn't even live long enough to collect his first NBA paycheck? Remember Don Rogers, the Cleveland Browns safety who died in his twenties? Do you think they would trade their civil liberties for another chance to be alive? Your damn rights they would.

Sometimes we let bullshit get in the way of reality. We tie our hands and watch our fellow man die. It's so stupid. We're not talking about people reading dirty books in a back room. We talking about people who are endangering their lives and influencing others to do the same. We're talking about the vermin who are out there selling on the street corners, selling to our young children. Maybe your children. Think about it.

There's no excuse for that. If we don't do something dramatic, it will keep getting worse. Instead of passing the buck, everybody should gang up on this insipid monster before it devours another loved one. Families should take charge. The government should keep the heat on. And organizations like the NFL should enforce the harshest rules possible.

I understand that everybody, even NFL stars, can make a mistake and probably deserve forgiveness. But the sad part is that if you forgive an NFL star for doing drugs, it sends out the wrong message to the kids who look up to these players. Look at Steve Howe, the baseball pitcher. He has been busted five or six times yet he was back pitching in 1992 . . . . and he was busted again.

It's a pathetic commentary on sports. If he were a lousy shortstop, or even an average right-handed pitcher, I bet Howe never would have had a second chance, let alone and third, fourth, fifth and counting. But he happens to be a good, left-handed pitcher, something that is difficult to find. So what's the message here? If you are good enough you can do any damn thing you want?

If we allow that to continue, we will cannibalize our own sport. We are condoning things that will kill not only our own players, but the kids that look up to those players. We have to be more responsible for our own well being and to the community we serve.

In 1979 we drafted Willie Jones, a defensive end who was smallish at 240 pounds, but had cat-like quickness. We didn't know it, but Willie already had a cocaine problem when he came to us. We certainly didn't help by giving him a big paycheck at the age of about 21 years old.

The big salary Willie received gave him more money to buy drugs. So his problem became worse and by 1981 it was obvious to everybody on the team. By then there were several players on our team who had developed a problem with cocaine. Getting paid $64,000 in postseason bonuses for the 1980 year didn't help. To somebody doing drugs, more money means more drugs.

Jones spent his playoff money within about two months. He didn't do that much drugs all by himself. No, he suddenly had a lot of friends who hung around him whenever he bought the stuff. They helped him do that much drugs. With friends like that you don't need enemies.

It got so bad during the 1981 season that I had to tell Willie to get out of the locker room. We tried to get him some help, but if they won't make a commitment there isn't much you can do. His last season with the Raiders was 1982. He should have been a star for at least seven or eight seasons. Instead, he was a bit player for three years and he was gone. He tried to play in Canada, but didn't do that well. He heard in the late 80s that he had cleaned up and found peace. I hope so.

The most classic story about drugs destroying somebody is that of Clifford Branch, possibly one of the greatest deep receivers in the history of the NFL. When I was in my first year as an assistant coach with the Raiders, Cliff was a rookie who had so much trouble catching the ball that he was almost booed out of the stadium. One game against Pittsburgh he must have dropped five or six passes.

But by his third season Cliff's hands caught up with his feet, which is a pretty impressive job of catching up because he had the quickest feet in the NFL. Cliff was always an upbeat guy who stayed in great shape and always looked good.

Somewhere between 1979 and 1980 Cliff began to look a little peculiar. He appeared tired and haggard. He acted withdrawn. He missed meetings. He missed practices. These were classic symptoms of somebody on drugs. We has suspected a small problem as early as 1978, but we thought he took care of it. We just weren't very educated on the subject back then.

By 1981 Cliff was paying a big price for indulging in cocaine. He got totally carried away and it cost him his marriage, his house, almost every dime he had. We feared for him and told him so. We begged him to get help and he said he was cleaning up. But if you looked at him, you knew better. Suddenly he didn't show up at the practice field for two consecutive days. His phone was disconnected. Nobody had seen him. We were worried.

Assistant coach Lew Erber and a trainer went to Cliff's house. He was so screwed up he couldn't even answer the door. They broke in the door, pulled him out of bed and dragged him back to the field house. He looked like hell. He had not eaten for at least a couple of days and he was just a total mess. He had been laying in bed, coming off a high and didn't care about anything.

They threw him in the whirlpool, then the shower, then made him go out and run. After that they took him to get a good meal. Here was a guy who had starred in two Super Bowls but he didn't have a dime to his name. He had given away or sold almost all his possessions in order to get more drugs. About the only thing he had was a scrapbook with clippings about all his accomplishments. It was a sad commentary.

Cliff was special to us and we rode him hard. He responded. He cleaned up in 1982-83 and was able to star in a third Super Bowl. He did slip a little, but finally he was strong enough to walk away. Cliff knows that he cannot afford to slip. Once you have become addicted to anything, including drugs and booze, there is no cure except abstinence. You have to fight the fight for the rest of your life.

Branch's case was classic. He was a strong person who had always been able to gain control of himself until he took drugs. Success, money, peer pressure, thrills, women. Those are the things that either lead to or surround drugs. If you let your guard down, drugs will take your life. That's why I hate drugs.

thirteen

All Raiders Team

During my brief retirement I thought about all the players I had either played alongside or coached while with the Raiders. It boggled my mind to think of all the great names, most of which already are, will be, or should be in the Pro Football Hall of Fame in Canton Ohio.

I hope someday we will have as many great years and as many great players with the Seattle Seahawks. But before I even came to the Seahawks I put together a team of my favorite Raiders, kind of an All-Flores team. It's a dream team that I think would hold its own against any lineup anybody could put together.

In picking this team, statistics didn't count, only my opinion.

Quarterback

In the history of the Raiders franchise there hasn't been a revolving door situation at quarterback. I am not naming myself here because I don't think I was the best quarterback to play for the Raiders. The first, but not the best. The picks here are Ken 'Snake' Stabler and Jim Plunkett, two guys who were total opposites in everything except being winners.

Snake played harder than anybody I know on and off the field. The left-hander from Alabama is probably the greatest competitor I have ever known and in my estimation the best quarterback the Raiders ever had. He did things his own way, to be sure, but he usually got the job done when nobody else could have. It seemed the tougher the situation, the more focused he became. He gave new meaning to the term "Two Minute Warning."

I can remember times when all hell was breaking loose and we were talking about a key play in the final moments of a game and he would look up at the stands and say something like "We're sure giving these fans their money's worth today." If there was a way to win, Snake would find it. If it meant a pin-point pass, he'd fire it, as he did to haflback Clarence Davis for the "Sea of Hands" touchdown. If it meant running, he would do that, too, as he did with a couple of seconds left to beat the New England Patriots in a playoff game. And if he had to bounce the damn ball into the end zone, he would do that, as in the so-called "Immaculate Deception" touchdown against the San Diego Chargers.

He threw sidearm, he threw overhand, he'd throw it between his legs and your legs, too, if that's what was necessary. One of the things I really admired about Snake was that he was the same on Sunday as he was on Tuesday, Wednesday, Thursday, Friday, whatever. He was very, very cool; always had that sparkle in his eye; and he loved to play the game. He even loved training camp because it involved all of his favorite things — competing, hanging out with the guys, and going to what he called honky tonks at night in Santa Rosa. According to his book, "Snake", he obviously he liked the night life, drinking beer and meeting the ladies.

But when it was time to play, nobody was ever more ready for a battle than Snake. He set the tone for the whole team during the week before Super Bowl XI against Minnesota. In our Thursday practice he was so hot that none of his passes hit the ground. All were completions. John Madden was so freaked out by this incredible performance I think he wanted to put Snake in a hermetically sealed container until kickoff.

In my mind I will always see Snake as a Raider, with long gray hair flailing from the back of his helmet as he throws a touchdown. Sidearm. It was weird to see him in a Houston uniform after we traded him there in 1980. It was even more weird to see him in a New Orleans Saints uniform.

For those who weren't fortunate enough to see Snake play, he was in many ways like a left-handed Joe Montana. Or maybe Montana is a right-handed Stabler. Snake did get a little bigger in the belly thanks to some of that beer. But they were otherwise the same in that neither had a rocket launcher for an arm, but both became deadlier in the final moments of a close game.

Plunkett's powerful right arm could launch an ICBM, but his confidence had been shattered when he we picked him up after the 49ers tossed him away. His comeback with the Raiders, as our quarterback in two Super Bowl victories, was a remarkable story.

He is a guy who truly did it all in football. He took Stanford to a Rose Bowl championship, won the Heisman Trophy, was the first player picked in the NFL draft and then made Rookie of the Year. Then he had injuries and was traded from New England to San Francisco when the 49ers were in disarray. He seemed to lose his confidence, his touch. He was a man on the brink of being broken when we picked him up in 1978. We hoped he could help as a backup. Little did we realize he would start and win two Super Bowls for us.

I think it's crazy he's not mentioned with a lot of these bozos who have their names thrown around as outstanding quarterbacks. All he's done in his lifetime is win the biggest game in any college career, win the greatest award in any college career and win two of the biggest games in his pro career.

And, unlike Stabler, he was a classic, dropback quarterback who had the size and strength to just stand in the pocket and throw the ball when defenders were hanging all over him. Of course that was before that damned in-the-grasp rule came along. When you looked at him he didn't look quick, and he didn't have a real quick delivery. He looked a little awkward when he ran with the ball, but he got things done.

Unlike Stabler, who had the flamboyant type of attitude, Jim was more serious during the course of a game. Both of these guys would get tremendously upset if things weren't going right. They were both fighters and they'd pick themselves up off the ground and come back with both guns blaring. Plunkett made more come backs than Rocky did in all the Rocky films combined.

As I mention elsewhere in this book, Plunkett's background is very similar to mine in that he he overcame a deadly disease when he was young and he is the son of Mexican immigrants. But he was such a great quarterback that I would have selected him even if he were a Gringo.

Running Backs

In my years with the Raiders, they had a lot of great running backs, but choosing Marcus Allen and Clem Daniels ahead of the rest wasn't difficult. Both were able to do anything you ask of a back, run with speed, power, elusiveness as well as catch and block.

Marcus is one of those rare players who you can enjoy watching play even if you know nothing about football. The running style of this 6-2, 210-pounder is so graceful and smooth that it qualifies as beautiful. Coming out of college the knock on him was that he didn't have the speed of a great back. True, he doesn't get great times when you put him on the clock, but give him the ball and he becomes fast enough to get away from almost anybody, which is all that matters. Great football speed.

The best example of his instinct, grace and football speed came in Super Bowl XVIII when he reversed his field on a sweep to the left, made a great lateral cut up the middle and outran everybody for a broken-play, 74-yard touchdown.

I'm going to put Marcus at fullback on my Dream Team, which is where we moved him after Bo Jackson joined the Raiders. Marcus was a quarterback in high school and played both tailback and fullback at USC, where he won a Heisman Trophy. When we moved him to fullback in 1987, Marcus didn't complain as most backs would have. Those who marvel as the grace of his running and receiving may not realize what an effective blocker he is. He is willing to take on and cut down defenders.

We've had a few guys who were more classic fullbacks, like Hewritt Dixon in the late 1960s, who was a prototype 6-2, 235 pounds and could do everything. Others deserving mention were Mark van Eeghen from Colgate and old fashioned tough guy Marv Hubbard.

For my Dream Team halfback, I will reach back into the 1960s and take Clem Daniels. We stole him in 1961 after he played defensive back for the Dallas Texans, who became the Kansas City Chiefs. By 1963 he was the AFL's Most Valuable Player as a running back. He had good size, at 215 pounds, so he could run with strength inside and still have enough speed to take it all the way on any play. As a receiver he could take little swing passes, break a tackle and explode for a touchdown or he could go deep and catch a bomb over his shoulder.

Wide Receivers

Ever since Al Davis took over, wide receivers have been a key element in making the Raider offense move. Of all the outstanding receivers the Raiders have had, I think three stand above the rest — Art Powell, the team's first great receiver who could do everything, Fred Biletnikoff, who may have had the best hands this game has ever seen, and Cliff Branch, one of the very best deep threats in football history.

In 1963, the first key signing by Al Davis was that of Art Powell. He had gone to high school in San Diego with his brother, Charlie Powell, a defensive lineman who played with the 49ers and Raiders although his only previous experience was as a boxer, not a college football player. That probably told a lot about the athletic ability in the Powell family.

Art played at San Jose State, but left early to play in the Canadian Football League.

Before signing with the Raiders, Art played in the CFL, the NFL, with the Philadelphia Eagles, and the AFL, with the New York Titans. He was traded with me to the Buffalo Bills in 1966 and finally finished with the Minnesota Vikings.

Powell was almost 6-4 and about 215 pounds and had deceptive, ground-eating strides that were so smooth that defenders often miscalculated how fast he was going. In many ways he was much like the 49ers' Jerry Rice, who also has deceptive speed and an uncanny knack of getting to any ball vaguely within reach. When Powell got close to the end zone he knew how to finish off a drive.

I remember vividly a game against Buffalo when we were trailing by three points and had the ball on their four yard line with only enough time for one play. Art was being covered by Butch Byrd, a physical cornerback and one of the best coverage men in the league. Art went straight into the end zone, Byrd made contact as they both went up and battled for the ball. I threw the ball high because Art could jump and had such great hands. Art came down with the ball. Touchdown, the Raiders won and there was no way to try at PAT because about 18,000 fans at Frank Youell Field carried Powell around the field.

The first touchdown pass I threw to Art was in 1963 when we opened against the top team in the AFL, the Houston Oilers. I entered the game in the second half and hit Powell on an in pattern. He had a bad hamstring, but you wouldn't have known it by the way he took that pass and ran away from everybody for an 80-yard touchdwon.

Freddy Biletnikoff is special to me because I threw him his first pass as a pro and then, sadly, one of my first jobs as head coach was to tell him it was time to move on. I'm not surprised that he moved on to the Hall of Fame, where he was inducted in 1988, and to coaching, where he has plenty of knowledge to impart to young players.

He came out of Florida State in 1965 and Al Davis signed him after his last game, under the goal posts on national televison with a representative from the NFL telling him not to sign. Fred actually had some problems catching the ball his first year when he had a lot of pressure on him as a second round draft choice. At 6-1, 190, Fred wasn't big or fast, but he had quick feet and was an absolute perfectionist about everything he did. His footwork, the way he carried his hands, his precision routes were and his concentration were all text book examples of how it should be done.

He could catch the ball in a crowd, stretched out on the sideline, two-handed, one-handed, and he even caught one by trapping the ball on his helmet. In Super Bowl XI, Biletnikoff made great catches to set up three touchdowns and won the Most Valuable Player award. He was such a competitor that when I told him he wasn't in our plans in 1979, he went up and played in the Canadian League.

My last receiver would be Clifford Branch. He was a 24-year old rookie out of Colorado in 1972, my first year coaching the receivers with the Raiders. He was a world class sprinter, finishing fifth in the Olympic trials that year. He wasn't a natural receiver, with his hands kind of reaching for the ball. His speed was incredible, however. Without question, his speed on the football field was the best I've ever seen.

When he signed, Branch was a No. 4 draft choice the same year wide receiver Mike Siani was a No. 1. Cliff dropped several passes in his first year and the unfortunate part about it is that when he dropped a pass it wasn't a five or ten-yard pass, it was usually a 40 or 50-yard pass with touchdown potential. After a while the people got on his case a little bit and we had to sit him down. Interestingly, that was in the first half of a game against Pittsburgh and the passes were from Stabler. Both Stabler and Branch watched in the second half as Daryle Lamonica threw two TD passes to Siani.

So Siani ended up winning back the starting job Cliff won in training camp. Soon we started using three wide receivers, Branch, Siani and Biletnikoff. By his fourth year I think one out of every four passes Cliff caught was a touchdown.

Cliff became one of the most feared receivers mainly because there were people that were fast and then there was Clifford Branch. It didn't matter what you did, at some point in the game he was gonna go beyond you. In one game we designed a play to get Branch man to man on one of their corners. We would motion Biletnikoff across the backfield and then leave Cliff out there with one guy. We'd play action and Snake would pop the ball and Cliff had a chance for six points. We always tried to come up with plays like that.

Tight End

In my first year as head coach of the Raiders we found it necessary to use a lot of two tight end setups as our base formation. Both of those tight ends, Raymond Chester and Dave Casper, made the Pro Bowl that year and are my choices for this Dream Team.

Chester was a surprise first round draft pick out of little Morgan State in 1970, but immediately became an impact player. He was 6-3, about 235, and appeared to be chiseled out of rock. He could run, and the farther down the field he got the faster he went, so he could score from anywhere. If he caught a short pass, defensive backs had a hell of a time wrestling him down.

He was an intense blocker who used every technique known to football, and a few known only to Chester. He endeared himself to teammates by being a policeman, the guy on a team who takes care of cheap shot artists on the other team. He made it a point to let a defender know if he was out of line. So if you were a defensive back and you were a little flagrant and Chester was on, you had to watch out because out of nowhere he would find you. He'd get guys from the blind side. Perfectly legal, but devastating.

In 1973 he was traded to the Baltimore Colts for one-time standout defensive end Bubba Smith. Both players were so big, both in size and NFL stature, that the trade was nicknamed "Godzilla for King Kong." The meaning of that was, there was no way to figure out who got the better superstar and to this day that trade is a subject of debate. It worked out well for the Raiders because we got Chester back in 1978 and he stayed with us until 1981. He finished out his career with the Oakland Invaders in the USFL.

Casper "The Ghost" was clinically as fine a tight end as you wanted. You could almost make a training film with Dave on his blocking. When he came to us he was 260 pounds and had played some tackle in college. At that point we didn't know whether he would play tackle or tight end because he was such a great blocker. He didn't know much about running pass patterns, but was a very intelligent guy, sometimes too much so for his own good. You'd tell him one time and he knew exactly what you were talking about. He was very quick and had deceptive speed and worked like an escaped convict to get free.

At a receiver meeting one time I thought he was goofing off, so I asked him a question. Despite the fact that he had been doodling during everything I said, he was able to repeat it all, word for word. This happened a lot. I think he was so sharp that whenever anything became repetitive, which football does often, he became bored. So I told him to pretend he was paying attention so his doodling didn't distract the other players.

He had the ability to go short, deep, medium and he ran pretty good with the ball. He wasn't a burner, like Chester, but he could take it deep. We had a play called Ghost to the Post, a big play. In the 1977 season playoff game against Baltimore he caught the winning touchdown in double overtime. But his best catch was a long over-the-shoulder grab on a "Ghost to the Post." He made the best catch I've ever seen on a ball that he had to watch sail from going over his left shoulder to over his right. Most people would have just become dizzy and fallen down. That catch set up the field goal that sent us into overtime.

Offensive Line

Here's the beef that makes it possible for all those other positions to get the glory. Smart quarterbacks get close to these guys because they are better for his health than the best doctor. If they treat him right, he won't get hurt in the first place. But their job is an anonymous one, which is why the best adjusted group of guys on any team is usually the offensive line.

Because the Raiders make such great demands of their offensive linemen, it shouldn't be too surprising that three of them on my Dream Team are also in the Hall of Fame — center Jim Otto, guard Gene Upshaw, and tackle Art Shell. The other selections are guard Wayne Hawkins and tackle John Vella, with a nod of recognition to tackle Henry Lawrence.

Otto, Mr. Raider, was inducted into the Pro Football Hall of Fame in his first year of eligibility, 1980. He was the Raiders first center, a slim 218-pounder who snapped to the first quarterback, me, at Santa Cruz in July of 1960. He went on for 15 years, starting 210 consecutive league games and played in 308 as a Raiders. I knew he was a remarkable guy by the end of that first season when he grew to 238 pounds on his way to 255.

Otto is still proud of every minute he played although he is paying a painful price by walking around on constantly painful knees that both underwent surgical replacements. Still, if he had a chance to suit up and play today, he would do it. I remember just before he called it a career in 1985 that he had to get in one more preseason game and get in one more hit. He got in and popped somebody with that size 8½ helmet and then hobbled to the sidelines with a grin that made him look like a kid who just stole some candy.

At left guard would be Gene Upshaw, whom we called The Governor because he was always filibustering in the locker room. He was inducted into the Hall of Fame in 1987, his first year of eligibility. Ironically that was the year he led the NFL Players Association, of which he is Executive Director, on a players strike. Upshaw is the only player in NFL history to play in Super Bowls in three different decades.

As a 6-4, 265-pound player, Uppy was not overpowering but he had good feet, was aggressive and always found a way to get the job done. He especially liked leading runs around the outside and taking on a defender in the open field. He usually buried them.

My other guard would be Hawkins, who played with me at College of Pacific, was in that first Raider training camp at Santa Cruz and was one of only 19 players who survived from the beginning until the end of the American Football League.

By today's standards the Hawk probably would not even be drafted. He's too short at 6-feet and too slow. Hell all he could do was pass protect so you were safe and make big holes for runners. It was interesting to watch him pass block because he had a way to use leverage to handle defenders who were usually so much bigger than him that he would be sticking his helmet in their belly button. Maybe some wouldn't put him on an All-Raider team, but he was my roommate, my friend and this is my team and the Hawk is on it.

Shell is another Hall of Famer, the current Raiders

head coach and just possibly the best tackle ever to play the game. He began with the Raiders as a guard and I remember in old films seeing him pull out and run with great agility. One of Art's biggest loves is basketball, which is where he kept his body nimble. His strength was natural.

Art was about 6-4, 300 pounds and more but he always had great feet. So he had the natural strength to handle power rushers, the great feet to handle speed rushers and was as dedicated as any player who ever played the game. In Super Bowl XI he went against the Vikings Jim Marshall, who was once the Defensive Player of the Year in the NFL. Against Shell, Marshall had no sacks, no tackles, no assists. Zilch. That's a perfomance equal to pitching a perfect game in the World Series.

At right tackle I would go with John Vella, who was a rookie out of USC in 1972. You probably haven't heard much about him because he didn't make any Pro Bowls or All Pro Teams. He just blocked the guys who did.

Although Vella was not a good drive blocker on runs, he was an outstanding pass blocker. His style was a little different because instead of retreating and absorbing hits from a defensive end, Vella would actually strike out and hit first, or take a very short set and hit early. He makes this team because he was able to take Pittsburgh's All- Everything defensive lineman L. C. Greenwood and erase him from a game without help. Every other team would use two people to block Greenwood, but all we needed was Vella.

I have to give honorable mention to Henry Lawrence because he was a unique character and a great person. Killer, as he is called, played on the Raiders' last three Super Bowl teams, two as a starter. He had the physical size and ability to do absolutely anything on the football field. But his most remarkable single ability was singing. During a gathering of former Raiders at Lake Tahoe in 1990, Killer took over a lounge show and pretty soon the place was packed.

Defensive Linemen

Again, there have been a lot of outstanding defensive linemen with the Raiders, but my front four would be Howie Long and Lyle Alzado as the ends and Tom Keating and Dan Birdwell as the tackles.

Long was our second round draft choice out of Villanova in 1981 and a lot of people thought we made a mistake because he wasn't rated that highly by most scouts and scouting combines. But we liked his size, at 6-5, 270, speed and intensity. He can play anywhere on the defensive line, including over the center. Whenever you're double or triple teamed, as Howie has been, it is testimony to your greatness. He's a tough guy, a very sincere guy, doesn't talk a lot, but he has that look that you look for when you're looking for aggressive,tenacious guys, he certainly has that look.

Alzado proved how much of a fighter he was right up until his unfortunate death in the spring of 1992. He had an inoperable brain tumor he said was caused by the use of performance enhancing drugs such as steroids and human growth hormones. In his final year of life he did all he could to warn others of the dangers of such substances.

We first knew Alzado as an enemy when he was with the Denver Broncos and then the Clevleand Browns. Although he never was extremely big by football standards, this little (6-3, 250) guy out of little Yankton College had the aggressiveness, toughness, power and persistence that made him one of the best in the game. We got Lyle in 1982, but he wanted to leave because he felt he wasn't going to contribute. I told him to let us make the decision, and that we thought he could help the Raiders. He stayed, played and the next season we won Super Bowl XVIII. After 13 years in the league, I'm just glad that Lyle had the opportunity to play on a Super Bowl team.

Keating was an undersized tackle (6-3, 247) who was so quick off the ball he would have offensive linemen turned sideways before they got all the way out of their stances. We got him in a trade with Buffalo in 1966 and he played with the Raiders through 1972 before moving on to the Pittsburgh Steelers and Kansas City Chiefs. However, he was never really a dominating force after he tore his Achilles tendon in late 1960s.

Last and hardly least on this defensive line would be Dan Birdwell, who was with the Raiders from 1962-69. Like Alzado, Birdwell is no longer with us. He passed away mysteriously a few years back.

We drafted Danny out of the University of Houston. He was the original bull in a china shop. In the process of walking into your room he would knock over a chair or maybe push over an ashtray, bump a lamp, step on your foot and maybe change channels on the TV all at one time. He was one of the most naturally gifted players I've ever seen.

Birdwell was all arms, toes and thumbs and if you ever sat next to him during dinner you'd find out he was close to uncivilized. He would cut his steak in maybe four pieces and then down it in about 30 seconds. He would be through with his dinner in about 45 seconds. Then he would slap you on the back and laugh and you'd gag as you are trying to swallow.

He had no idea how strong he was. In one game the defensive coaches put him over the tight end and told him not to let the tight end off the ball. He had to hit the tight end before rushing the passer. So in the film, Dan lined up over the tight end and whacked the guy and then to the ball carrier. The tight end took about five steps and then all the sudden without anybody touching him went down. Danny had whacked him a little bit too hard and the tight end had been stunned momentarily so he went to his knees.

Our players hated to play across him in practice because he didn't know but one speed, all out. You would tell him, "this is not live' and he'd say "OK."

Then you'd go through a play and he'd do it properly. Then the next play he'd bat you across the head and when you told him it wasn't live he'd say "Why didn't you tell me, I thought that was only for one play." So if you played against him in practice you had to tell him on every play that you were on his team and that this was just a drill or he would pulverize you.

Off the field he was simply charming. One time he had one dollar and his roommate didn't have any money so he gave the rommate his dollar. Then he came over to me and asked to borrow a dollar. So he would give you his last dollar even if he needed it. Now that's unselfish. We miss him because there wasn't anyone that didn't love Danny Birdwell. He will always be remembered as one of the best defensive linemen we ever had and one of the most unique characters.

Linebackers

My Dream Team would have a linebacking unit that was full of character and characters and very high in ability. On the outside I would put Ted Hendricks and Rod Martin. Inside would be Phil Villapiano and Matt Millen.

When you talk about characters, Ted Hendricks is at the top of the list. He's also at the top of my list as the most dominating defensive player that I've ever seen and I must not be alone because he was inducted into the Hall of Fame in 1990. He came out of college as a standup defensive end who appeared too skinny at 6-7, 225 to cope with the behemoths in the NFL. Originally drafted by the Baltimore

Colts in 1969, he went to the Green Bay Packers and then was signed by the Raiders when he played out his option with the Packers 1975.

He seemed too thin to play defensive end and too slow and awkward to play linebacker, so a lot of teams didn't know where they would play him. We put him at strong outside linebacker, where he did pretty much what he damn well pleased. As it turned out he was faster than a defensive end and stronger than anybody believed, thanks to an uncanny ability to use his long, lean body and arms as leverage.

He was unique in that you would think you had him blocked and all the sudden he would just push you aside and make the tackle. He could see over everybody with his unusual height. He also had one of the best defensive minds that I've ever known. He didn't want to be bothered with meetings and things of that nature, but yet he knew exactly what the other teams were going to do.

Hendricks was a pain in the ass sometimes in practice because he would get bored and do something outrageous. But in the heat of the battle if he wasn't making a tackle, then he was knocking down a pass or intercepting one or rushing a passer, getting a sack or deflecting a ball.

His alertness was recorded by NFL statisticians as 26 career interceptions, 16 opponent's fumbles recovered, four safeties, and I believe he had more blocked kicks and punts than any player in history. Although he was a genuinely funny guy off the field, the book on him as a player was don't piss him off and players around the NFL respected that.

On the other side I'd go with Rod Martin, who we took in the 12th round, the 317th player, in the 1977 draft and then traded away to the 49ers the same year. When San Francisco waived him we re-signed him and Rod stayed with the Raiders through the 1988 season.

He was just a little over 200 pounds when he came to us, but he could run, he could really run. He eventually went up to 220, 225 and then, through his own diligence, he became an outstanding linebacker. He played in two Super Bowls for us and set a record of three interceptions in Super Bowl XV and many people believed he deserved the MVP award.

One of his strengths is his hands. You shake hands with Rod Martin and you're going to go away making sure you have all your fingers and they're not broken. He has powerful hands and uses them very well. At his peak he never came out of the game defensively. He stayed in when we had five defensive backs, passing downs, went in on blocks, played on the kickoff return team, just an all-around great player with a very quiet demeanor.

Rod Martin is another of those guy that had that look in his eyes. I think defensive players share that look a lot more than offensive players. You look at guys like Hendricks and Howie Long, Alzado and Martin. . . . They have that look and you know when they look at you, you better buckle up.

Villapiano played most of his career outside, but I'll put him inside on this team. That's where he finished up his career with the Raiders. I remember talking to Al Davis after 1971 when he told me the reason for drafting Villapiano and Jack Tatum was because the Raiders needed some toughness. We needed to reinforce the squad with toughness. Well, we did that.

Villapiano was not a big guy, and even when he was young his speed could only be called a bit better than good at best. But he had this instinct for playing linebacker and he could hit. Man, could he hit. He was a vocal guy and he was always up. He was piling over people to get to the ball-carrier. When you play with that kind of attitude and enthusiasm you are relentless in what you're doing; this is a characteristic of defensive football. Villapiano was the young guy that the Raiders thought could continue that tradition and he did.

Even when we traded him to Buffalo he was still a Raider. He would get excited when we came to town to play Buffalo. In fact, we beat the Bills in the last 30 seconds of a game back there in 1983 and Phil was so excited he said, "God, that's Raider football, that's the way it should be." He was beside himself. To this day he is still a Raider. Some guys were meant to be Raiders. Villapiano is one of those guys.

Millen was another unsual draft choice in 1980 out of Penn State. He was a defensive tackle in college, but we projected him as an inside linebacker. That's not the first time we did that. In the 1960s we took Dan Connors, a defensive lineman at Miami, and put him at inside linebacker and in the 1970s we drafted Monte Johnson, a backup defensive tackle at Nebraska, and made him our starting inside linebacker.

Millen was huge when he first joined the Raiders, a little over 260 pounds. And he had trouble getting his weight down to 250. Over the years he refined his profile and his grasp of the game until he became one of the best run-stopping inside linebackers in the game. He wound up going to four Super Bowls, two with the Raiders, one with the 49ers and one with the Washington Redskins.

He is a sharp, well-spoken student of the game now who has captured the imagination of fans from coast to coast. I wouldn't be surprised to see him as a football analyst for television if he ever decided to leave the field.

Defensive Backs

Any Raider Dream secondary would start off with cornerback Willie Brown, who was inducted into the Hall of

Fame in 1984. He was what a true corner should be. He was big, could run, and was fearless in that he was not afraid of getting beat. With man-to-man the way we played, you had to be fearless.

Al Davis got him in a trade from Denver in 1967 because Brown appeared to be the prototype bump-and-run cornerback. He was. Willie wasn't a defensive back in college, at Grambling, but he had all the physical necessities, such as strong hands to jam receivers and play the game the way it should be played.

He is tied for the Raiders all-time lead in interceptions with 39, and that's not including his 75-yard touchdown on an interception to put a great end punctuation to our victory in Super Bowl XI.

At the other corner I would like to have Michael Haynes, who perfected the art of man coverage that Willie Brown pioneered. Haynes had the size (6-2, 195), the speed and the innate ability to mirror the moves of any receiver.

Originally a first round draft choice of the New England Patriots, Haynes was acquired in a controversial right-on-deadline trade in 1983 and immediately became a crucial factor in our march to the Super Bowl XVIII championship. The cornerback combination of Haynes and Lester Hayes has to be one of the best, if not the best, in the history of football. Hayes was a tenacious, gambling cornerback who was daring enough to paint himself on a receiver, fast enough to stay with anybody and strong enough to deliver a KO hit.

Lester's overuse of stickum not only helped him tie Brown's record of 39 interceptions, but also led to the NFL banning the use of such a substance.

Another great Raider cornerback who deserves honorable mention is Kent McCloughan, a converted college wide receiver with sprinter's speed who played defensive back in Oakland from 1965-70.

At strong safety I'll go back to the early 1970s to get a little guy who played big, George Atkinson. At 6-0, 175, George was a better size for a cornerback, which he played for a couple of years. But he was tough as nails and sometimes a little too tough, as Pittsburgh Steelers' wide receiver Lynn Swann contended.

If George played today he would be a temendous asset because he could run and cover. Because of that, he would be my strong safety. A lot of people have forgotten that George was also an outstanding punt returner and won a few games for us there.

The final guy on defense would be Jack Tatum at free safety. Tatum was a devastating hitter whose reputation made receivers leery of going over the middle. Jack was accused of making a dirty hit that paralyzed Patriots wide receiver Daryle Stingley. With all due respect and good wishes to Stingley, I disagree that Jack's hit was late. It was an unfortunate mid-air collision by two players who were going all out.

Yes, Jack was powerful, tough, vicious, aggressive, all the adjectives that would describe that style of play. And the way he played was exaggerated in history because of the Stingley incident and because Jack published a book *Call Me Assassin*. However, I know a lot of players who played outside the rules more often and more flagrantly than Tatum.

It is unfortunate that Tatum will not be recognized for what he was, one of the greatest safeties who ever played the game. Ask Ronnie Lott, everybody's All-American guy. He idolized Tatum. A lot of people were put off by Jack's mean looks. Those few who got by his physical appearance learned that Tatum was one of the smartest, best prepared safeties ever to play the game. It's unfortunate that his reputation was distorted because I believe that he played well enough to earn a place in the Hall of Fame.

I will never forget a classic head-to-head matchup between two of the hardest hitting players in pro football history, Tatum and Houston running back Earl Campbell. It was in 1979 when Tatum was playing on banged up knees. Campbell had a full head of steam when he met Tatum head-on at the two yard line. Both of them bounced backwards a little and then Campbell, obviously stunned but moving on instinct, stumbled into the end zone.

Special Teams

Ray Guy is the only punter in the history of pro football to be drafted in the first round. And we stole him there. The Raiders shocked everybody by taking Guy No. 1 out of Southern Mississippi in 1973. He was more than a great punter, he was an outstanding athlete. He was also drafted not once, but four times by Major League baseball teams. He played safety and wide receiver in practice, and as our emergency quarterback often showed that he could throw the ball farther than anybody on the team.

His incredible athletic ability was best displayed in Super Bowl XVIII when he jumped about 12 feet in the air to pull down a bad snap with a great, one-handed catch, then pounded a 50-yard punt, all in one smooth motion.

He got to a point where he was so automatic that we didn't even think about him. I can remember one case in particular, we were playing a championship game in San Diego in January of 1981 and we were on our own 30 yard line. Guy went in a tried a coffin corner kick, which means he tried to get the ball out of bounds as close to the other end zone as possible. It went out on the five. Most punters would have been thrilled to get the ball inside the 20.

His most famous punt was the one that hit the gondola that hangs high above the field in the Superdome. He did it on purpose, just showing off during a Pro Bowl. When the end of his career was near we realized how spoiled we had become with our great punter. Guy labored through his final season with back problems that rendered him only a few notches above most NFL punters.

George Blanda is an easy pick as my field goal kicker, and he's not bad to have around as a backup quarterback, either. Few people know that George also played linebacker when he first broke into pro football, but that was back in 1949 when everybody had to play both ways.

George played football longer than anybody in the history of the game, 27 years. He kicked 335 field goals, including nine of at least 50 yards. He is the Raiders all time scoring leader with 863 and he didn't even join the team until he was almost 40 years old. In his 27-year career he scored 2,002 points.

Blanda is probably the most competitive person I have ever known on or off the field. He would compete with you to see who would get through the door first. To this day he's still a competitive guy on the golf course. Here's a guy who played pro football in the 1940s, 1950s, 1960s, 1970s, 1980s. If you asked him to come kick for you tomorrow, he would be in your locker room first thing in the morning. And never mind the square-toed shoe. He'll bring his own.

fourteen

Gone North, The Seattle Seahawks

When I retired as head coach of the Raiders in 1988, I was nagged by the thought that I would become either anonymous, like when I was an assistant coach, or worse, a forgotten relic.

"You remember Tom Flores, don't you? He was a coach with the Raiders back in the 1980s. I hear he even played quarterback at one time. Can you imagine?"

I'm not one of those people who needs constant recognition or fame. But the thought of being put out to pasture and viewed as a piece of history just didn't appeal to me. I admit I was feeling a little low a week after my retirement when Barbara and I stopped at a restaurant on the way to our place in Palm Springs.

"I guess we'll just become another retired couple and disappear into the sunset, right Barb?" I said as we waited for dinner.

"Don't be so foolish, Tom," she said. "Our life's been a grand adventure so far. There haven't been many dull moments, you'll have to admit. You're just feeling a little disoriented as we head in a new direction. Believe me, we're not going to just disappear into the sunset."

As usual, Barb was right. When we were about to leave the restaurant somebody at a nearby table stood up and said "Thanks, Tom, for the great years you gave us." I was caught by surprise at first. As I nodded to acknowledge his kind words, everybody at his table stood up and began to applaud. At first I was a little embarrassed. But the next thing I know, everybody in the restaurant is standing and applauding.

Suddenly I wasn't embarrassed any more. I thought to myself, "Relax, enjoy, smell the roses. Hell, there's no game Sunday. There's no draft. Nothing. So enjoy." Instead of quickly exiting, which is what I would usually do, I took a deep breath and appreciated this spontaneous acknowledgment for a few moments. I shook the hands of a couple of people and then left.

"Barb," I said as we got into the car, "Maybe this isn't going to be so bad after all."

During my brief retirement I was able to do a few things that I had not done since I sat out the 1962 season with tuberculosis. I spent Thanksgiving with my family. I was able to plan for parties on Christmas and New Years. "So this is how the real world lives," I thought to myself.

I did stay in touch with football by working with Prime Ticket, a cable television network that covered Pac-10 Conference games. I interviewed with NBC-TV, but they told me I didn't have enough pizzaz. Big deal. What the hell does pizzaz have to do with being an expert analyst? So I

learned that the phrase "television journalism" is a contra-
diction in terms. They mean television showbiz. Pizazz is
more important than credibility.

By December a lot of coaches were on the hot seat.
I began to receive a lot of feelers, mostly indirect. A
friend of a friend of a general manager or president of a
team would just happen to ask, "By the way, if you were
to be offered a coaching job with so-and-so, would you
consider it?" I wasn't. I was still worn out from coaching
with the Raiders.

Just before Christmas, I went to a party at the home
of a close friend, John Karnish, who lived in the East Bay
Area. While I was at that party, Ken Behring dropped by for
about an hour. Karnish, Behring and I were part of a group
that had been getting together for charity golf tournaments
many years. In fact, in 1992 we had our 26th annual golf
tournament at Lake Tahoe.

So even by 1988 I obviously knew Behring for a long
time. He had not played in the tournament for a few years
because he was involved with his car collection, other chari-
ties and his new business, the Seattle Seahawks.

Behring and another long-time friend, Ken Hoffman, had purchased the Seahawks in August of 1988. I met
Hoffman in the early 1960s when I was playing for the Raiders. He was a big football fan and we both spent time at the
Athens Athletic Club in downtown Oakland. Now the two of
them owned the Seahawks, Behring 75 percent and Hoffman 25 percent.

Their team was doing great with Chuck Knox as the
head coach. In fact, if they won their final game of the season, against the Raiders, the Seahawks would have won the
AFC West Division championship for the first time in the
franchise's 13-year history. When I saw Behring I began to
congratulate him, but something else was on his mind. He
led me into a corner of the room. "Tom, if there was an open-

ing on our team, would you be interested in coming to work for the Seattle Seahawks?" he said.

I was pretty surprised. I thought Chuck Knox was an outstanding coach and they were doing real well. I also knew that Chuck had just signed a pretty big contract. I wondered what the hell Behring had in mind. But this party wasn't the place to discuss it. I told him to wait until the season was over, then we would discuss it.

The Seahawks and Raiders put on one hell of a regular season finale. Seattle quarterback Dave Krieg threw for 410 yards and four touchdowns to beat the Raiders, 43-37. But Seattle was bounced out of the playoffs on New Years Eve by the Cincinnati Bengals, 21-13.

On January 10, Behring stopped by Los Angeles on his way back east. We met in one of my favorite restaraunts in Manhattan Beach, Sausalito South. He didn't waste much time getting to the point. He's not a chatty type of guy.

"Tom, I've been thinking about your situation and our situation," he said. "What do you think about becoming the president and general manager of the Seahawks?"

At the time Mike McCormick was the president and general manager. Behring explained that he and Hoffman wanted somebody to run the team that they knew, rather than somebody they inherited in the purchase. We agreed that we would talk again after the Super Bowl.

Both Behring and Hoffman went to Super Bowl XXIII in Miami. It was between the San Francisco 49ers and the Bengals. I hosted a party in Las Vegas and we watched the game on a large screen. It was one of the best Super Bowls ever, especially if you like dramatic endings. San Francisco quarterback Joe Montana, the master of dramatic endings, pulled out a victory with a 92-yard drive that was capped by a 10-yard touchdown pass to John Taylor with 34 seconds left.

I was kind of narrating the game at the party and it was such an exciting Super Bowl that I really got into it. Montana was incredible, completing 23 of 36 passes for a Super Bowl record 357 yards. Wide receiver Jerry Rice caught 11 of those passes for another Super Bowl record of 215 yards. As an old quarterback, that was a great show to watch. I think I had enough pizazz calling that game. Anyway, I didn't care about NBC-TV any more. I was pretty sure I had a better job.

On January 30 I met with Behring and Hoffman in Palm Springs. They wanted me to run the team as the president. I asked if my decision had a bearing on what would happen to McCormick. They said they already had decided he would go no matter what. I felt a little more comfortable knowing that because I didn't want to jump somebody else's job. They told me to think about it and we would meet again on February 8.

As I thought about the opportunity for a week I told only a few people — Barbara, a couple of close friends and Al Davis. I called Al right after the meeting to get his input. He said he thought it was a great opportunity. He also talked a little about the Raiders. He had hired Mike Shanahan from the Denver Broncos as the new head coach when I retired and I don't think he felt comfortable with him.

Al Davis: *When you are together as long as Tom and I were together with the Raiders there becomes a tremendous friendship. When he left it was a bigger change than I expected. In retrospect, I think I made a mistake. I wish I had asked him to stay another year or two- . . . . That could have saved us the intermediary step. But he was obviously exhausted and rebuilding takes so much energy. It burns me up that Tom is not mentioned more often when*

they talk about the great coaches in the NFL.
Just look at his damn record, especially under
the circumstances of our move. No wonder he
was so tired. . . . He was given a great oppor-
tunity by the Seahawks. That's what I told
him. I wished him well. Except for when he
played the Raiders, of course.

In the middle of the next season Al would fire Shanahan and promote Art Shell to the head coaching job. To
those of us who grew up in the Raiders organization, that
seemed to make more sense. It's difficult for somebody from
the outside, like Shanahan, to come in and be accepted by
the Raiders.

By the time I met Behring again on February 8,
McCormick had already been fired and there was a lot of
speculation going around as to whom would be the suc-
cessor. Mike Blatt was the acting general manager and
he obviously had an eye on the job. Blatt had been an
agent who worked his way into the Seahawks adminis-
tration by helping put together the sale of the team between the Nordstroms and the Behring-Hoffman
tandem.

I agreed to take the job under one condition. I had
to be the number one person. The only people I would answer to were the owners, Behring and Hoffman. If Mike
Blatt wanted to work under me, that was fine. But I did
not intend to share my duties. That was fine with Behring, so we agreed on the terms of the contract that day.

Unfortunately, we couldn't announce it right away.
Behring was scheduled to go on a fishing trip with Chuck
Knox for ten days. While they were on the trip, Behring
would tell Chuck that I had been hired. They left February
10. Ken Hoffman also took off hunting. So I had to keep the
new job to myself for a couple of weeks. It wasn't easy be-

cause somehow the word had gotten out through the grapevine. I basically just made myself unavailable to questions.

Finally on February 21 I flew to the Bay Area to meet with Behring. We were going to fly to Seattle together and make the announcement the next day. I was met at the airport by somebody I had never seen before. It was Mike Blatt. He had waited for me in one of the Blackhawk limousines and we rode back to Behring's home together. Blackhawk is the fabulous community that Behring developed in the East Bay, near Danville. He has a home there that is so big it probably should be measured in terms of square miles instead of square feet.

On the way to Blackhawk, I get the distinct impression that Blatt has no idea I have been hired. In fact, it sounds like he still has designs on the job. I say nothing about nothing. When we got to Blackhawk, I talked to Behring for about a half hour. We ironed out the little details. It was a done deal. Then he asked me to leave the room while he talked to Blatt. Now they talk for a half hour. Suddenly Blatt comes out, shakes my hand and says he won't be going with us to Seattle. He wishes me well and leaves.

Behring had given him his choice to work under me or collect his interest in the team and move on. He chose to take his money and leave. Behring and I flew up to Seattle and announced that I was the new president and general manager of the Seahawks.

So there I was, back in football after a whole year in retirement. I didn't ride off into the sunset, after all. I rode off to Seattle.

It didn't take me long to get into a minor controversy. Soon after I was announced as the new president and general manager, I flew off to Hawaii for something that had been scheduled for almost a year.

This was the first year of Plan B free agency. That's the system that allows some players to shop for new teams, and teams to shop for some players. Each club can protect 37 players. The rest are unrestricted free agents.

I'm not a big fan of Plan B as a means to improve the team. Except for a few rare cases, there is a reason those players are available on Plan B. They couldn't fit into somebody else's plans, so why should I think they would help us build a better team?

But Plan B was new in 1989 and the media was covering it like it was something major. I came on board a little too late to get involved in that process. Chuck Knox and his coaching staff figured out which 37 players to protect. Hell, he coached them so he would know the players much better than me at that point.

In 1989 we signed eight Plan B players and none made the team. We also lost nine and the next year I think every one of them was back on Plan B again. So how major can this thing be?

Well it was major enough to cause me a lot of grief when I went to Hawaii. I recognized Plan B as something created by management council that allows us to say we do have a form of free agency in place. Technically, that's true. Realistically, I wouldn't stay awake nights trying to figure out how to rebuild my organization with Plan B players.

Aside from that, I was anxious to get to my new office when I got back from Hawaii in early March. As I flew into Seattle I realized something was very different this time than the many other trips I made into the Seattle-Tacoma Airport. I was smiling.

When I was the Raiders coach, I used to hate going to Seattle. It wasn't just because the Seahawks were a team that was always tough at home. Hell, I liked flying to other towns, like Chicago and Kansas City. But I remember several times flying into Seattle with a knot in my stomach and white knuckles. I just wouldn't let myself enjoy the place.

But this time I looked out the window and realized how beautiful Mt. Ranier is. And as we circled around SeaTac Airport to land, I didn't have a knot in my stomach.

For one thing I wasn't going to face a hostile crowd at the Kingdome, as I had on those trips with the Raiders. I remember how much I hated the noise at the Kingdome. I hated hearing all those Seahawks fans. They knew exactly when to yell so your team had a hard time communicating. They even had a gauge to measure decibles at one time, but the NFL made them take it down.

Since joining the Seahawks I have a whole new perspective on the noise at the Kingdome, which shouldn't be too surprising. Now I actually like the noise. I like flying into Seattle. I like having friends come to town so I can show them the scenary and the great places to eat, especially if they like fish.

But I wasn't hired to run a travel agency. So I should point out that Seattle is also one hell of a football town. Since day one the Seahawks fans have supported their team to the hilt. After being here a while, the devotion of the fans around Seattle reminds me a lot of the relationship the Raiders had with their fans in Oakland in the 1960s.

However, it's best not to dwell on comparisons between anything in Seattle and anything in California. I learned after being in Seattle less than a month that there is a concern about a plot to impose too many Californians on the Seahawks. Remember that the previous owners, the Nordstroms, are a big Washington-based family. Behring, Hoffman and I all are from California.

And Californians are not real popular in the Northwest, In Oregon and Washington there is a bumper sticker that tells that story.

"Don't Californicate Washington."

Fine with me. However, I was blamed for trying to make over the Seahawks with the help of a new, Raideresque design. I was ripped in the media, both newspapers and television, for changing the logo and I didn't know what the hell they were talking about. I was told that the logo on the season tickets had been changed. A shield was now imprinted on them. I asked for somebody to get me some tickets so I knew what the fuss was about.

It turns out that NFL Properties had changed its logo, which was now on a shield. But I had to go on TV and radio and defend the new design. I pointed out that it was still blue, green and silver and had a Seahawk on it. I told a couple of people in our organization that if I put a patch on the bird's eye, then they should worry. But I had no intention of changing the logo or any of the Seahawks' great traditions.

I did have some major league help when I first arrived in Seattle. Gary Wright in the public relations department knows everything and anything you would ever need to know. I don't know what I would have done without Gayle Larse. She is my secretary, the first one I ever had. Coaches didn't have secretaries with the Raiders.

My first week in Seattle I went to the copying machine and was making a bunch of copies and stacking them when Gayle walked into the room.

"Tom Flores, what are you doing?" she said. "Are you going to replace me? You are doing my job. Now you just go sit back at your desk. If you need copying done, tell me. I won't make any decisions on personnel and you leave the paper work to me, OK?"

Yes, ma'am.

Negotiating contracts, that's one of my jobs as president and general manager. I had never done that before taking the Seattle job. My first contract negotiation in 1989 was with wide receiver Steve Largent, who was going to add one more season to his incredible career.

Largent is a legend in Seattle, as well he should be. He has every pass receiving record on the books. I appreciated something else about him. He negotiated his own contract. Unlike most players, he did not have an agent. I never had an agent, either, but I think that was a function of playing and then coaching for Al Davis. If I had used an agent he might have never hired me as an assistant coach, let alone a head coach.

Largent and I went back and forth on his 1989 contract until we reached an agreement. He is a sharp guy. He doesn't need an agent. Anyway, I was happy that we made a good deal. Finally I had done something that made the media and fans in Seattle happy.

For a while, anyway.

Before I took the job as head coach in Seattle, Ken Behring showed me a whole new way to negotiate.

"How much do you think we would have to pay a new head coach?" he asked.

I said that it depended on where we got the head coach. I figured an offensive coordinator from an NFL team would cost about $350,000 in salary. A top name, like Mike Holmgren who went to the Green Bay Packers, would probably call for more than $500,000 his first season. A big name college coach would cost even more, maybe $600,000. I told Behring this.

"And Tom how about you, how much would you cost?" he asked.

Well, I knew that Chuck Knox received just about $1 million in the final year of his contract with the Seahawks. But before I could say what I thought I should get as head coach, Behring named a figure.

It was higher than the first figures I mentioned.

"That's it," I said.

And that's how we negotiated my new contract as head coach and president. Not very traditional, I suppose.

But like I said, I don't have an agent. It's worked well for me so far.

I've only been back in the saddle as a coach for a little while, but it feels great already. I missed putting together a team. I missed getting together with the coaches. I've already had a couple of minicamps and it's great to be back on the field with the players.

After being with this team since 1989 and having a hand in building it through the drafts, I feel good about the direction we are going. Seattle has had some great winning years in the past, but never a Super Bowl champion. I would like to sit here and say we are going to win a Super Bowl in my first year as coach. It's what everybody wants to hear. But I'm not a politician. I'm a coach. I know we will do well this year and I hope we make the playoffs. I expect to make the playoffs.

We're still building. The Seahawks are what I call "Not ready for prime time." We're close, however. Maybe about 5:30. But not quite prime time.

As usual the one key ingredient that must be settled is quarterback. When I took over as head coach I told all our quarterbacks that we would go into camp with a logical pecking order based on experience. But the job is open to whomever plays the best. At the time I told them the pecking order was Dave Krieg, Kelly Stouffer and Dan McGwire. Since then, Krieg went to Kansas City as a Plan B free agent. So now the pecking order is Stouffer and McGwire. We also added Plan B free agents Rusty Hilger and Stan Gelbaugh.

Nowadays you need more than one to be ready because quarterbacks just don't stay healthy for a whole season. Hopefully Stouffer will stay healthy for a change. His luck as been as though he has one of those dark rain clouds over his head. Every time we give him a chance he seems to get hurt. We haven't had a chance to really evaluate how well he can do.

The day before the draft I traded away our No. 2 and a draft pick next year to the Minnesota Vikings for defensive end Keith Millard. If he plays back to his All-Pro potential, then the Vikings get a higher pick next year. I think Keith looked great in our minicamp and I fully expect him to lift our other defensive linemen, Jacob Green, Jeff Bryant and Cortez Kennedy. I am curious to see how former linebacker Tony Woods does at defensive end.

We also traded a No. 4 pick to get running back Rueben Mayes from the New Orleans Saints. I am anxious to see if he can perform back to the level that took him to consecutive Pro Bowls.

And, of course, I am happy with with our first round draft pick, offensive lineman Ray Roberts. I expect him to step in and start very soon at tackle.

I am still looking for the right guy to be our tight end. That is a big position the way I run an offense. I was spoiled when I coached the Raiders because I had David Casper, Raymond Chester and Todd Christensen, who all made the Pro Bowl.

Change at the coaching position sometimes gets great reaction from the players. It's kind of human nature to try and make a good impression on somebody new. When the same players and same coaches work together for too many years they sometimes fall into a comfortable rut.

I'm not saying that happened in Seattle. I think our players have a great attitude. And once again I say that Chuck Knox is a great coach. But we do have different personalities. He has won a lot of games and so have I. And we did it in different ways. So it will be interesting to see how the players react this year.

I do know that we have to build an attitude here where the players know they can win a close game in the fourth quarter. That is usually the difference between the champions and the others, winning in the fourth quarter.

Often confidence is the only difference between those teams that win consistently in the final minutes those that don't. The right attitude breeds confidence.

We have the material to build toward a winning team. Now it's my job to see that we put it all together. I'm no longer the president sitting upstairs eating popcorn while the coach takes the credit and blame for what happens on the field. For the first time I am the president who is responsible for who we have on the field and the coach who is supposed to get the best out of them. So the buck stops here.

Don't be fooled if you see me standing quietly on the sidelines with my arms folded. In my case, the ice is only skin deep. Inside I'm burning up. And I love it. Yes, Barbara was right. I am a masochist. Damn, it's great to be back.

Index

Adams, Bud, 58
Air Hockey Tournament, 136
Alameda Naval base, 63
Albo, Dr. Bob, 139
Alioto, Joe, 169
All-Flores team, 213-35
Allen, Marcus, 174-77, 187-89,
   203, 217
Alzado, Lyle, 175, 176, 181,
   187-88, 226-28
American Football Conference
   (AFC), 107
      West championships, 2, 5
American Football League
   (AFL)
      All-Star game

(1966), 101-2, 104
(1963), 93, 95
beginnings, 58-59
Championship Game
   (1976), 116
   (1964), 97
   (1969), 107-9
   (1963), 93
early stability, 64
last season, 107-10
quarterback, 5
Amherst, Massachusetts, 67, 68
Anderson, George, 61-63, 67-68,
   70-71, 97-98, 140, 194
Anderson, Ken, 132
Anderson Hall, 39, 40

Anti-trust case, 171
Arrowhead Stadium, 171
Assistant coach, 7, 112-13
Athens Athletic Club, 239
Atkinson, George, 233

Badain, Al, 89
Bahr, Chris, 165, 181
Bakersfield junior college game,
    34-35
Banaszak, Pete, 120, 135
Band, 27-28
Bankston, Warren, 135
Baseball, 22
Bass, Dick, 44, 49-50
Bass, Glenn, 103
Bears (Chicago), 39, 92
Beathard, Bobby, 54
Beatty, Homer, 35
Behring, Ken, 4, 6, 7-8, 9-10,
    239-43, 247
Bennett, Barry, 140
Bias, Len, 207
Bicep injury, 97-98
Big Four pitchers, 22
Biletnikoff, Fred, 115, 116, 119,
    124-26, 135-36, 218-21
Bills (Buffalo), 9, 96, 102, 112,
    145, 149
Binns, Harvey, 58
Birdwell, Dan, 226-28
Birmingham News, 123
Blanda, George, 94-95, 235
Blatt, Mike, 242, 243
Blessing, Don, 58
Blitz, 118-19
Blue, Led, 30
Bordelon, Ken, 140
Bostic, Jeff, 185
Bosworth, Brian, 201-7
Boxing, 22-23
Bradshaw, Morris, 119, 120,
    124, 130, 138, 153
Bradshaw, Terry, 115

Branch, Cliff, 152-53, 165,
    173-74, 186, 209-11, 218-21
Brentwood, California, 14
Brodie, John, 32, 52
Broncos (Denver), 120, 154
Bronzan, Bob, 35, 36, 47
Brown, Aaron, 108-9
Brown, Jim, 188
Brown, Joe, 196
Brown, Paul, 38, 39
Brown, Willie, 135, 182, 231-32
Browning, Dave, 155
Browns (Cleveland), 38, 51, 159
Bryant, Jeff, 249
Buehler, George, 135
Buffalo, New York, 65
Bump-and-run defense, 90
Byrd, Butch, 97, 219

Cal-Berkeley game, 55-56
Call Me Assassin, 233
Campbell, Earl, 234
Campbell, Marion, 164
Canadian Football League, 3,
    52-53
Candlestick Park, 64
    free-for-all at, 70-71
Cannon, Billy, 92
Cardinals (Chicago), 58
Carnivals, 29
Cars, 38
Casper, Dave, 120, 125, 150-52,
    221-23, 249
Castro Valley, 77
Chamberlain, Wilt, 45
Chandler, Bob, 145, 165
Chargers (San Diego), 69, 93-94,
    120, 148-49, 152, 160-61
Chatfield, Chuck, 50, 53-54
Chester, Raymond, 138, 148,
    152, 173, 221-23, 249
Chiefs (Kansas City), 10, 71,
    106-7, 149-50
    AFL championship game

(1969), 108-9
  Super Bowl IV, 109, 110
Childhood, 17-23
Christensen, Todd, 92, 152, 186,
  249
Cincinnati game, 49
Clack, Jim, 185
Clark, Monte, 118
Coach, 1-11
  assistant, 7, 112-13
  college, 55-56
  head, 4, 118-26, 127-41
  as Raiders move south,
    167-80
  Seahawks, 239-50
  Super Bowl XVIII, 181-90
  Super Bowl XV, 143-66
Collarbone injury, 47-49
College coach, 55-56
College of Pacific (COP), 32,
  35-37, 39-56
  Spring Game, 59-60, 87
College years, 32-37, 39-56
Collier, Joe, 105
Colorado A&M game, 44
Colts (Baltimore), 92, 109
Colzie, Neal, 135
Concourse Plaza, 66
Conigliaro, Tony, 195
Conkright, Red, 86
Connors, Dan, 102, 108
Contract, first Raider's, 62
Corvette, 38
Courtney, Del, 194-95
Cowboys (Dallas), 6, 72
Cruising era, 28-29
Cruisin' With the Tooz, 137
Curtis, Jack, 51
Customized pads, 47-48

Dalby, Dave, 173
Daniels, Clem, 92, 99, 102, 218
Davidson, Ben, 102
Davidson, Cotton, 93, 94-96,
  104-5

Davis, Al
  coaching and, 5-8, 86-93,
    113, 118, 121-24
  intensity of, 97-102
  on moving, 64, 86
  and people, 191-201
  and plays, 4, 64, 97-102,
    113, 118, 121-24
  Plunket and, 133-34
  and Super Bowl XV, 143-46
Davis, Carol, 139-40, 193, 195
Davis, Clarence, 119, 135, 187,
  214
Davis, Mike, 156, 160
Dawson, Len, 108, 111
Dean, Fred, 161
DeBartolo, Jr., Eddie, 133
Del Rey, California, 3, 14, 16
Denton, Bob, 40, 46
Dickey, Lynn, 132
Ditka, Mike, 10, 92
Dixon, George, 80-81
Dixon, Hewritt, 100, 217
Dockery Road, 17
Doda, Carol, 136
Dolphins (Miami), 116
Douglas, Jackie, 51
Draft, 51-52, 132, 174-75
Drugs, 207-11
Duncan, Maury, 53
Durango, Mexico, 15-16, 23
Dynamite, Mexico, 15-16, 23

Eagles (Philadelphia), 161-66
Easley, Ken, 204
"East Formation," 92, 108, 109
East-West Shrine game, 51-52
Eden Valley hospital, 78-81
Elegant Farmer, 104
El Rancho Motel, 88
El Rancho Tropicana Motel,
  129-30, 177-78, 200
El Segundo, 177, 178
End Zone, 39
Erasmus Hall High, 89

Erber, Lew, 133, 197-98, 210
Erdelatz, Eddie, 59, 62, 63, 65,
    67-70, 93
Erickson, 8, 9
Ethnic pride, 22

Fairbanks, Chuck, 132
Fake handoff, 33-34, 46
Farber, Dr. Jason, 79, 82, 83, 85
Fatherhood, 76-77
Feldman, Marty, 70, 86
Finks, Jim, 52-53
Flores, Barbara Fridell (wife),
    1-2, 8, 11, 15, 40-44,
    75-77,113-14, 193, 238
Flores, Bob (brother), 3, 13,
    26-28
Flores, Jesse, 22-23
Flores, Kim (daughter), 113-15,
    177
Flores, Mark (son), 76-77, 113,
    115, 177
Flores, Nellie (mother), 16-17
Flores, Scott (son), 77, 113, 115,
    177
Flores, Tomas Cervantes
    (father), 3-4, 15-18
Fonda, Jane, 179
"The Foolish Club," 58, 59
Forty-niners (San Francisco),
    52-53, 133
Fouts, Dan, 149, 157, 160-61,
    188
Francis, Joe, 51
Frank Youell Field, 86, 93, 96,
    115
Free-for-all, at Candlestick
    Park, 70-71
Freshman Week, 39, 40
Fresno, California, 3
Fresno City College, 32-35
Fresno Community College, 57
Fresno Junior College, 46

Fridell, Barbara Ann. *See*
    Flores, Barbara Fridell
Fridell, Harriet, 77, 83
Fridell, Squire, 83
Friedan, Betty, 39
Fumble, rule change, 120
Fuqua, John "Frenchy," 115-16

Garcia, Mike, 22
Garrett, Bob, 31
Gelbaugh, Stan, 248
George, Ernie, 59
Ghost. *See* Casper, Dave
Ghost to Post play, 222-23
Giants (New York), 38-39, 65,
    157
Gillman, Sid, 90, 95, 149, 151
Giovacini, Mr., 17, 18
"Godzilla for King Kong" trade,
    222
Gold Bowl, 174
Golden Eagle Award, 180
Good Morning America, 190
Gordon, Carl, 35
Granville Elementary School,
    18
Grape Picker, 31
Grayson, Dave, 102, 108
Green, Jacob, 249
Greenwood, L.C., 225
Grimm, Russ, 185
Guy, Ray, 160, 186, 234-35

Hall, Sid, 35-36, 55
Hall, Willie, 135
Hardin, Wayne, 32
Harding Elementary School,
    21-22
Hardman, Cedric, 145, 155-56
Harney, Charley, 58
Harris, Franco, 115-16
Harris, James, 105, 113

Hawkins, Wayne, 60, 62-64, 100, 101, 107, 223-26
Hay Baler, 31
Hayden, Tom, 179
Hayes, Lester, 155-56, 173, 181, 184, 232
Haynes, Michael, 184, 232
Hazings, 39
Head coach, 4, 118-26, 127-41
    Raiders, 167-80
    Seahawks, 239-50
    Super Bowl, XVIII, 181-90
    Super Bowl XV, 143-66
Hendricks, Ted, 154-56, 160, 228-31
Herock, Ken, 92, 93
High school years, 25-31
High Sierra, 8
Hilger, Rusty, 248
Hill, J.D., 113
Hilton, Barron, 58, 59, 69, 93, 161
Hoffman, Ken, 6, 7, 239, 241-42
Holmgren, Mike, 247
Holovak, Mike, 115
Holub, E. J., 70, 71
Holyoke, Massachusetts, 67-68
"Holy Roller," 120
Home games, in Raiders early years, 64
Horizon Hotel, 8
Howe, Steve, 208
Howsam, Bob, 58
Huarte, John, 111
Hubbard, Marv, 217
Humanitarian of Year award, 180
Hunt, Lamar, 57-58, 59, 64

Ice man, 30
Idaho game, 49
"Immaculate Deception" touchdown, 120, 214

"Immaculate Reception," 115-16
Indians (Cleveland), 22
Injury
    bicep, 97-98
    collarbone, 47-49
Itinerant farmer, 3, 13-18

Jack London Square restaurant, 56
Jackson, Bo, 201-5
Jackson, Monte, 173
Jalisco, Mexico, 16
Jensen, Derrick, 157, 183, 184
Jepperson Stadium, 99
Jets (New York), 91, 98, 99, 109, 145
Johnson, Gary "Big Hands," 148, 161
Johnson, Harvey, 112
Johnson, Jimmy, 6
Johnson, Monte, 139, 185, 231
Joiner, Charlie, 160
Jones, Willie, 155, 174, 208-9

Kansas City, Kansas, 45
Kansas State game, 49
Karnish, John, 239
Keating, Tom, 102, 108, 226-28
Kelcher, Louie, 161
Kemp, Jack, 103, 105-6
Kennedy, Cortez, 249
Kerkorian, Gary, 31
Kern, Rex, 132
Keystone Kop escapade, 66
Kezar Stadium, 64
King, Kenny, 145, 152, 160, 165
Kingdome, 171
Kinlaw, Reggie, 155, 185
Klein, Gene, 161
Klosterman, Don, 52, 117-18
Knox, Shirley, 7
Knox, Chuck
    as head coach, 117, 239-40

retirement of 2, 4, 6-9, 242,
    247, 249
Korean War, 32, 34
Krieg, Dave, 10, 240, 248

La Bamba, 13-18
Ladd, Ernie, 88
Lake Tahoe, 8
Lamonica, Daryle, 103, 109,
    115, 134, 220
Lapham, Jr., Roger, 58
Largent, Steve, 247
Larschied, Jack, 40-43, 45,
    49-50, 60
Larson, Paul, 60-61
Lassiter, Ike, 102
Lawrence, Henry, 119, 124, 130,
    139, 223-26
LeBaron, Eddie, 54, 59
Lions (Detroit), 118
Livingston, Mike, 111
LoCasale, Al, 170
Lombardi Trophy, 188
Long, Howie, 174, 188, 226-28
Los Angeles Coliseum, 33, 146
Los Angeles Valley Junior
    College game, 33-34, 46
Lott, Ronnie, 233
Lucky, Dr., 59
Lugo's Pizzeria, 53
Lytle, Rob, 154

McCloughan, Kent, 102, 232
McCormick, Mike, 240, 241, 242
McCrea, Dr., 77, 82
McGah, Ed W., 58
McGwire, Dan, 10, 248
Mackey, John, 92
McKinny, Odis, 179
Madden, John
    as coach, 5, 10, 115, 117-18,
        121-23, 215
    college years, 54
    on sidelines, 128, 133-34
Maguire, Paul, 107

Maier, Cornel, 146, 169-70
Malavasi, Ray, 118
Man coverage, 232
Mangiero, Dino, 149
Manhatten Beach, California,
    180
Mann, Errol, 121
Manning, Archie, 132, 188
Manoukian, Don, 60, 63-64
Marquette game, 49
Marriage, 68
Marshall, Jim, 187, 225
Martin, Rod, 155, 156, 165,
    228-31
Martinez, Manuel, 20, 26
Marvin, Mickey, 182
Mattioli, Rudy, 33
Matuszak, John, 136-38, 154-55,
    162, 198-201
May, Mark, 185
Mayes, Rueben, 249
Mays, Willie, 65-66
Melendy's, 130, 136
Memorial Coliseum, 55
Mercer, Mike, 95
Merger, NFL with AFL, 100-1
Mexican heritage, 3-4, 22-23
Meyers, Jack "Moose," 35, 51-55
Mile High Stadium, 119, 171
Millard, Keith, 249
Millen, Matt, 146, 156, 182,
    185, 228-31
Mischak, Bob, 92
Mistake by the Lake, The, 159
Modesto, California, 18
Montalban, Ricardo, 180
Montana, Joe, 176, 215, 240-41
Montgomery, Bill, 132
Moore, Myrel, 154
Moorish, Bill, 169
Moses, Haven, 113
Music, 27-28, 3

Namath, Joe, 109, 196
National Football League, 6

draft, 51-52
head coach in, 1
merger agreement with
AFL, 100-1, 107
Naval Acadamy, 32, 59
Nelson, Bob, 156, 185
Nelson, Darrin, 175
Newsome, Ozzie, 160
Nicksovich, John, 46, 47
NosOtros, 180

O'Steen, Dwayne, 156
Oakland Tribune, 83
Oakland Coliseum, 146
Oilers (Houston), 69, 92, 94,
143, 145, 152, 158
*One Flew Over the Cuckoo's
Nest*, 40
Orange Crush, Denver's, 154
Original Raider, 61
Ortmayer, Steve, 183
Osborne, Robert, 58
Otto, Jim, 61, 63, 88, 98, 100-1,
173, 223-26
Owen, Tom, 133
Owens, Burgess, 145, 156, 157

Paclers (Green Bay), 6, 104
Palm Springs, California, 6-8
Palomar Hotel, 62
Pancho Villa, 3, 16
Papac, Nick, 29, 7
Parilli, Babe, 60, 62-63
Passodelis, Nick, 33
Pastorini, Dan, 10, 132, 143,
146-50, 158
Patriots (Boston), 67, 86
Patriots (New England), 132-33
Phillips, Bum, 144, 158-59
Pickel, Bill, 188
Pitts, Henry, 123, 124
Pittsburgh vs USC, 33
Plan B free agency, 244
Play-action pass, 33-34, 46, 50
Player rep, 104

Playoff game, 157-59
Plunkett, Jim
college years, 131-35
injuries, 172-73, 206, 214
as quarterback 10, 131-33,
180-81, 186
running option, 133-35
Super Bowl XV, 143,
147-48, 150, 160-61,
165-66
The Jim Plunkett Story, 128-29
Polo Grounds, 65-66
Porterville Junior College, 32
Powell, Art, 91-92, 96-97, 101,
103, 218-21
Powell, Charlie, 71, 218
President
Raiders, 8
Seahawks, 8-10, 240-50
Prime Ticket, 238
Prlain, Dr. George, 83
Pro scouts, 51-52
Prothro, Tommy, 51
Pruitt, Greg, 175

Quonset Hut, 40
Radio receivers, on
quarterbacks, 38
Raiders (Oakland/Los Angeles),
2, 4, 115
AFL championship game
(1969), 108-9
as head coach, 4-6, 10,
127-41
moving south, 167-72
1976 season, 116-17
1964 season, 96-100
1961 season, 69-74
1960 season, 62-68
1966 season, 101-3
1963 season, 85-96
as quarterback for, 29
in Super Bowl II, 103-4
Rams (Los Angeles), 6, 7, 9, 52,
117-18, 134, 177

Ramsey, Derrick, 134, 152
Rauch, John, 101-6, 110, 112, 117
Reagan, President Ronald, 189
Receivers coach, 115-18
Redskins (Washington), 54-55, 149, 180, 181-88
Red Star fireworks, 77
Retirement, 4-5, 8, 237-39
Reynolds, Jim, 45
Rice, Jerry, 219, 241
Riggins, John, 182, 185
Riggs, Gerald, 175
Road trips, in Raiders early years, 64-65
Roberson, Bo, 91-92
Roberts, Ray, 249
Robinson, John, 177
Rock and Roll, 38
Rogers, Don, 207
Rookie night, 136-37
Roosevelt High, 57
Ross, George, 83
Rowe, Dave, 135
Royal Hawaiian Hotel, 194
Rozelle, Pete, 100, 164, 169, 188
Rutigliano, Sam, 159
Rutter, Roland, 40

Saban, Lou, 113
Saints (New Orleans), 140
Sanders, Red, 50
San Francisco Examiner, 196
Sanger, California, 3, 16, 19, 25-31
Sanger Ice House, 30, 31
Sanger Union High Apaches, 25-31
San Joaquin Memorial game, 29-30
San Joaquin Valley, 14
San Jose, California, 18
San Jose State, 35
    game, 47, 49

Santa Cruz, California, 60
Santa Rosa, California, 88
Sausalito South restaurant, 240
Schramm, Tex, 169
Scouting players, 113
Sea of Hands" touchdown, 214
Seahawks (Seattle), 2, 5, 6, 8, 9, 11, 121, 204-5
    as head coach and president, 239-50
Seasonal jobs, 31
Semi-pro football, 53-54
Senors (Oakland), 60
Shanahan, Mike, 241
Sharecroppers, 17-18
Shaw, Dennis, 113
Shaw, John, 6
Shea Stadium, 98, 99
Shell, Art, 5, 117, 151, 173, 187, 223-26, 241
Shoulder surgery, 54
Siani, Mike, 115, 136, 220
Simpson, O.J., 112, 188
Sipe, Brian, 159-60
Slaughter, Clair, 30
Smith, Bubba, 222
Sneakers, 39
Soda, Y.C. "Chet," 58
Spoilers (Bakersfield), 53-54, 62
Sportscaster, 112
Sportswriter, 83, 86
Spring Game, 59-60, 87
Squirek, Jack, 186, 187
Stabler, Ken "Snake"
    in playoff, 115
    as quarterback 6, 134-35, 140-41, 214-16
    rough year, 119-25, 129-30
    traded 10, 143-44, 158
Stampeders (Calgary), 52-53, 117
Stanford, 31-32, 37, 51-52
Stanky, Eddie, 90
Starlight Foundation, 178-79

Steelers (Pittsburgh), 6, 115, 116, 152-53, 185
Stingley, Darryl, 233
Stirling, Scotty, 95, 102
Stockton, California, 36
Stoical demeanor, 15
Store owners, 19
Stouffer, Kelly, 10, 248
Stram, Hank, 106, 108, 110, 111
Suisun, California, 14
Sullivan, Billy, 58
Summer jobs, 30-31
Sumner, Charlie, 154, 185, 186
Super Bowl, 5, 11
    Championship (1980), 10
    Championship (1983), 10
    Championship (1976), 10
    Championship (1967), 103-4
    XVIII, 181-90, 203, 217, 226, 232, 234, 240-41
    XV, 161-66, 182, 188, 189
    IV, 109, 110
    XI, 185, 187, 203, 215, 220, 225, 230, 232
    XVI, 175
Svihus, Bob, 108-9
Swann, Lynn, 233

Taft Junior High, 21-22, 27
Tatum, Jack, 115-16, 145, 230, 233-34
Taylor, Chuck, 31-32, 51
Taylor, John, 240
Television, 38
Texans (Dallas), 70-72
Theismann, Joe, 132, 180, 184, 186, 187
Thomas, Emmitt, 109
Thomas, Skip, 135
Thunderbird, 38
Tillman, Rusty, 8
Titans (New York), 64, 66
Tooz. *See* John Matuszak
Townsend, Greg, 188

Training camp, 60, 88, 129-31, 135-39
Transitor radios, 38
Trey-O, Bob, 187, 203
Tuberculosis, 3-4, 78-83
Tucson, Arizona, 53
Tulsa game, 47
Twombly, Wells, 196-97

UCLA game, 50
University of Kansas game, 45-47
University of Miami Hurricanes, 8, 9
Upshaw, Gene, 130, 151, 173, 182, 223-26

Valens, Richie, 13
Valley, Wayne, 58, 80, 86, 101
Van Eeghen, Mark, 159, 187, 217
Vella, John, 119, 223-26
Vermeil, Dick, 163
Vikings (Minnesota), 109, 116-17
Villapiano, Phil, 145, 228-31
Vintage restaurants, 7

Walsh, Bill, 118
Washington, Joe, 180
Washington State game, 47
Wells, Warren, 109
White, Mike, 55-56
Whittington, Arthur, 119
Wild card playoff berths, 156-58
Wilkinson, Bud, 35
Williams, Ike, 22-23
Williams, Roy, 56
Wilson, Lionel, 146, 169-70
Wilson, Marc, 136, 145, 158, 172-73, 180-81
Wilson, Ralph, 58, 112
Wilson Grammar School, 19, 22
Winter, Max, 58, 59

Wismer, Harry, 58, 64, 66
Wolf, Ron, 113, 133, 155
Wooden, John, 90
Woods, Tony, 249
Woolfson family, 58, 59
Wright, Gary, 7, 246
Wright, Louis, 156

Year of Quarterback, 131-32
Zemen, Bob, 136, 202
Zorn, Jim, 121